DANVILLE PUBLIC LIBRARY

W9-AAW-995

WITHDRAWN

WEST'S LAW SCHOOL
ADVISORY BOARD

JESSE H. CHOPER
Professor of Law,
University of California, Berkeley

DAVID P. CURRIE
Professor of Law, University of Chicago

YALE KAMISAR
Professor of Law, University of Michigan

MARY KAY KANE
Dean and Professor of Law, University of California,
Hastings College of the Law

WAYNE R. LaFAVE
Professor of Law, University of Illinois

ARTHUR R. MILLER
Professor of Law, Harvard University

GRANT S. NELSON
Professor of Law, University of California, Los Angeles

JAMES J. WHITE
Professor of Law, University of Michigan

CHARLES ALAN WRIGHT
Charles Alan Wright Chair in Federal Courts
The University of Texas

INTERNATIONAL TRADE AND INVESTMENT

IN A NUTSHELL

Second Edition

By

RALPH H. FOLSOM
University Professor of Law
University of San Diego

MICHAEL WALLACE GORDON
Chesterfield Smith Professor of Law
University of Florida

JOHN A. SPANOGLE
William Wallace Kirkpatrick Professor of Law
The George Washington University

WEST
GROUP

ST. PAUL, MINN.
2000

Nutshell Series, In a Nutshell, the Nutshell Logo and the West Group symbol are registered trademarks used herein under license.

COPYRIGHT © 1996 WEST PUBLISHING CO.
COPYRIGHT © 2000 By WEST GROUP
                              610 Opperman Drive
                              P.O. Box 64526
                              St. Paul, MN 55164-0526
                              1-800-328-9352

All rights reserved
Printed in the United States of America

ISBN 0-314-24094-2

TEXT IS PRINTED ON 10% POST
CONSUMER RECYCLED PAPER

341.753
FoL
cop 1

We dedicate this book to those who teach international business in all of its various forms, and especially to the many faculty who have so thoughtfully helped us over the years to improve as teaching materials the successive editions of our problem-oriented Coursebook and Nutshells.

*

III

PUBLIC LIBRARY
DANVILLE, ILLINOIS

PREFACE

This Nutshell has roots in the fourth edition of the *International Business Transactions in a Nutshell* by the same authors. The fourth edition, published in 1992, included 548 pages, stretching the concept of a Nutshell beyond expected boundaries. With the conclusion of the North American Free Trade Agreement (NAFTA) and the new World Trade Organization (WTO) negotiations, the fifth edition would have challenged Webster's Unabridged Dictionary for volume. The sensible course suggested by West Publishing Co. was to divide the material into two Nutshells. Together, these Nutshells cover all significant areas of international business, from selling a few goods across borders to major foreign direct investments abroad, plus the role of nations in regulating trade, both unilaterally and by participation in multilateral agreements. The result was the 1996 publication of the fifth edition of the authors' *International Business Transactions in a Nutshell*, and the introduction of the initial edition of *International Trade and Investment in a Nutshell*. The sixth edition of the *IBT Nutshell* is being published concurrently with this second edition of the *ITI Nutshell*.

International Business Transactions in a Nutshell focuses principally on international commercial transactions, letters of credit, currency issues, transfers of technology, market and transition economies, and litigation and arbitration issues, including state immunity and act of state. *International Trade and Investment in a Nutshell* focuses on controls on imports and exports, foreign investment, expropriation and risk insurance, business immigration and extraterritorial antitrust issues, plus such multilateral trade associations as the European Union, WTO, NAFTA, and other regional integration.

The allocation of chapters between the two Nutshells required some value judgments, as did the decisions on what to include in each chapter. These judgments will be familiar to those who have read or adopted our *International Business Transactions: a Problem-Oriented Coursebook*, originally published in 1986 and followed with a Second Edition in 1991, a third Edition in 1995 and a Fourth Edition in 1999.

Our primary objective has been to produce a Nutshell which law and business students, and professionals who are not specialists in international trade and investment, will find helpful. We also hope to contribute to the general body of knowledge about the vast and intensely controversial field of international business law.

This Nutshell has been a collaborative effort. Each of us, however, has been primarily responsible for certain areas. Professor Folsom has been primarily responsible for the materials on the European Union, NAFTA and other regional organizations outside Europe and North America, plus extraterritorial antitrust laws. Professor Gordon has been primarily responsible for the materials on the regulation of exports and foreign investment. Professor Spanogle has been primarily responsible for the materials on the regulation of imports, and the GATT and the World Trade Organization, which are treated in their own chapter for the first time.

We have been aided by colleagues at our own law schools and others both in this country and abroad, by student research assistants and by persons in practice. We welcome continued suggestions for the next edition.

RALPH H. FOLSOM
MICHAEL W. GORDON
JOHN A. SPANOGLE

November, 1999

*

OUTLINE

IX

*

RESEARCH REFERENCES

Use Westlaw® for Researching the Law of International Trade and Investment

Access Westlaw, the computer-assisted legal research service of West Group, to search a broad array of legal resources, including case law, statutes, practice guides, current developments and various other types of information. Consult the online Westlaw Directory to determine databases specific to your needs.

Searching on Westlaw

With Westlaw, you can use the Natural Language search method, which allows you to simply describe your issue in plain English. For example, to retrieve federal cases discussing the dumping of steel products, access the Federal International Law–Cases database (FINT-CS) and type the following Natural Language description: dumping steel products

You can also use the Terms and Connectors search method, which allows you to enter a query consisting of key terms from your issue and connectors specifying the relationship between those terms. For example, to search for either dumping or anti-dumping in the same sentence as steel, type the following Terms and Connectors query: dumping anti-dumping /s steel

Use KeyCite® to Check Your Research

KeyCite is the citation research service available exclusively on Westlaw. Use KeyCite to see if your cases or statutes are good law and to retrieve cases, legislation or articles that cite your cases and statutes.

For more information regarding searching on Westlaw, call the West Group Reference Attorneys at 1–800–REF–ATTY (1–800–733–2889).

TABLE OF CASES

References are to Pages

TABLE OF CASES

INTERNATIONAL TRADE AND INVESTMENT

IN A NUTSHELL

Second Edition

*

INTRODUCTION

FROM BROCKTON AND BUR-BANK TO BRASILIA AND BOMBAY

Representing a Boston client who (1) manufactures goods, for example children's clothing and knapsacks, for sale to numerous retail store buyers in the United States, for example in Brockton and Burbank, and who (2) purchases the parts for such products from United States sellers, for example in Salem and San Francisco, usually does not involve the application of United States trade law governing imports and exports. But our Boston client is an "international" company—it sells and buys where it can obtain the best price. That means it sells to and buys from parties in foreign nations as well as in the United States. Consequently, United States trade law affecting *exports* is applicable when our Boston client sells the goods abroad, for example to buyers in Brasilia and Bombay. United States trade law affecting *imports* is applicable when our Boston client purchases parts for the manufacture of its products from Singapore or Sao Paulo.

In each case, importing or exporting, our client must be familiar with the characteristics of competition on an international scale. The client assumes different risks and becomes subject to different laws. Those laws are not only the United States laws affecting imports and exports, but the laws affecting imports and exports of the foreign nations in which our client does business. The foreign laws may include rules which appear to exist solely to protect domestic industries. There may be high tariffs, or quotas, or a vast array of nontariff barriers affecting our client's exports. But that also may be how the foreign buyer or seller views the laws of the United States. The United States is not exempt from creating nontariff barriers. The Boston client's importers (buyers) in Brasilia or Bombay may be charged with dumping the Boston sourced goods on the local market, or benefitting from United States subsidies. The Boston client may not believe it is acting unfairly in selling to buyers in Brasilia or Bombay, but it has become subject to protective legislation in these foreign nations.

Just as it may be the target in one case, our client may shoot the arrows in another. If the Boston client is unable to sell to its old buyers in Brockton or Burbank, because Singapore or Sao Paulo sellers are not only selling parts to our client, but also finished products in competition directly to the Brockton or Burbank buyers, the United States trade laws may help our client. This is not because our client is an international trader, but because it is a *domestic* entity which is part of an industry injured or threatened with injury by the foreign goods. The same laws might help a United States company which has never engaged and has no intention of engaging in international trade.

Assume that in the small town of Bartow, Florida, a company employs about thirty people and for decades has manufactured a variety of textile products for sale solely in Florida from material produced in North Carolina. It makes children's clothing and knapsacks, just as does the Boston entity described above. But unlike our Boston client, the Bartow company does not sell abroad. It does not even sell in Georgia! Its owners and employees work hard in meeting the demand for its products in Florida. It pays fair, but not excessive wages. Management is very cost conscious, but believes the company can compete with anything produced by companies subject to the same rules of minimum wages, pollution controls, workshop safety, social security, etc.

Two problems have arisen in the past few months, however, which have involuntarily thrust this small town enterprise into being a participant in international business. A large Florida department store chain which had bought its clothing for years from the Bartow entity informed the company that it was dropping its line of products and replacing it with nearly identical products manufactured by parties in Singapore and Sao Paulo. These are the same foreign sellers that the Boston client has claimed are causing it harm. The foreign made clothing costs the Florida retail chain 40 percent less than they had been paying the Bartow manufacturer. The second concern arose when the company was asked by a local tourist attraction to bid on the manufacture of 1,000 children's knapsacks in the form of dolphins. The company wanted the job and cut its profit to a narrower margin than it normally accepted. When it presented the design and the bid to the buyer it was told the same knapsacks could be had for half the price in Singapore or Sao Paulo.

Why is it possible that the prices could be so low? Both the Boston and the Bartow companies are clearly being injured by these imports. Further inquiry may disclose similar injury to the United States children's clothing and knapsack industries as a whole, rather than to just these two domestic companies. Perhaps the products were being subsidized by the foreign governments. That may allow the Boston or Bartow company to request that the United States government commence an investigation under United States trade laws which may end in the conclusion that subsidies were present and there was material injury, or a threat of such injury, consequently calling for the imposition of countervailing tariff duties.

Or the foreign companies may be dumping (in contrast to the foreign governments providing subsidies) the products on the United States market. If they are doing so, meaning selling their products for "less than fair value", i.e., the price for which they are sold in the foreign domestic market where they are manufactured, the United States government may begin an investigation. If it is concluded that dumping was present and there was material injury, or a threat of such injury, there may be an imposition of antidumping duties. If the source of the foreign goods were Shanghai, where there may be an inadequate market economy cost analysis, it may be very difficult to establish the presence of subsidies, or sales at less than fair value to establish dumping. If China is defined as a nonmarket economy, another section of the United States trade laws may allow the Boston or Bartow companies to challenge the Shanghai products without proof of dumping or subsidies, essentially because they come from a nation with a political system we do not regard with favor. This action, called a "market disruption" or Section 406 action, has been used infrequently in the past for foreign policy reasons. It will diminish in use even more as nonmarket nations move along the path towards market economies with democratic governments.

If the foreign goods are from the vast majority of market economy nations, and if they cause or threaten *serious* as opposed to *material* injury to the United States industry, the Boston or Bartow company may make use of the United States safeguard or Section 201 "escape clause" action provision to limit their entry. But how the United States government responds to a domestic company's claim of injury from foreign competition may be based more on political relations with the foreign nation than an accurate interpretation of the United States law. The Boston or Bartow company may correctly feel more a pawn in international politics than a player in international business. For example, the United States may not wish to irritate the government of Singapore if it is helping the United States open more air routes in Asia to United States carriers, or to irritate the government of Brazil if the two nations are close to a settlement of a longstanding dispute over intellectual property protection, or to irritate the government of China if there are sensitive negotiations over the use of prison labor or freeing a political dissident.

The Bartow company never intended to engage in international trade. It has not. It still sells nothing abroad. But it is fearful that soon it will sell nothing in Florida as well. Its officials and lawyers must learn about international business law if the company is to survive, or even if it is not to survive, to provide its former employees with United States trade adjustment assistance made available to companies which lose out to foreign competition.

Although there are significant variations in the trade laws of different nations, for most nations there are some accepted norms. Most trading nations are members of the World Trade Organization (WTO), the successor to the General Agreement on Tariffs and Trade (GATT). Since its formation at the end of World War II, the GATT has grown in membership, in reducing tariffs, and in successfully abolishing many nontariff trade barriers. The rules noted above of various nations which allow countervailing duty, dumping and safeguard (escape clause) actions all have some of their roots in the GATT. The GATT's successor, the WTO, will also help limit restrictions on foreign investment, and thus affect our Boston client when it considers a direct foreign investment abroad.

It should appear from the above that trade law has many variations. Our client, whether it is the Boston or Bartow entity, is likely to be more interested in stopping the foreign competition than in how it is stopped. It may make little difference whether the action chosen is against foreign subsidies, dumping, surges of imports, market disruption, or any other actionable activity under any part of the trade laws. It is the end result the client wishes to achieve, a reduction or elimination of the allegedly "unfair" foreign competition. The path to that result will be the recommended course of action suggested by the client's counsel. Thus counsel must know about the full array of choices available under the United States trade laws.

The choice may differ depending on the nature of the foreign nation's economic and political characterization. **Developed** nations do use barriers to imports and offer subsidies to exports. They tend to be fewer in number and often are more sophisticated than barriers or subsidies in developing nations. **Developing** nations may use a greater variety of trade barriers, and justify them because they are developing economically. Trade organizations such as the World Trade Organization may grant developing nations special rights to impose barriers against imports, or assist exports. **Nonmarket economy** nations (NMEs) by definition lack market economy characteristics and may substantially subsidize industry. The United States does not allow countervailing duty actions to be brought against imports from a nonmarket economy nation, because the subsidies of those nations are not bounties or grants within the meaning and purpose of the countervailing duty law, because of the nature of nonmarket economy nations, and because Congress has provided for dealing with such nations under other trade law provisions. The identity of the foreign country as developed or developing, and as market or nonmarket, is thus important to the application of the appropriate trade law provisions.

There are fewer nonmarket economies today than a decade ago, and many nonmarket economies are in a stage of transition to market economies. Thus there may be a question regarding the nature of the foreign economy. It may be both a developing and a nonmarket economy. It may be an advanced developing country (ADC) or newly industrializing country (NIC), but still be a nonmarket economy. It may be a nonmarket economy trying to become a market economy, but having difficulty overcoming decades of state central planning and government involvement in the production and distribution of goods. Or it may be a nonmarket economy which prefers to remain a nonmarket economy, but which finds it necessary to do business with market economies and opens the door to market economy characteristics only enough to achieve specific goals.

Most of the above comments have involved restrictions on imports. United States restrictions on imports would help our Boston client in so far as it is a seller of its products within the United States to buyers in Brockton or Burbank, but might hurt that client if the imports of components for its production from Singapore or Sao Paulo are restricted and cause it to buy higher priced domestic components in the United States from Salem or San Francisco. Some reference has been made to controls on exports. To the extent that such controls exist in the United States, and limit our Boston client from exporting to buyers in Brasilia or Bombay, our client would be harmed. If export controls are imposed by the governments in Singapore or Sao Paulo on the components our client needs, it may have to buy them at higher prices from Salem or San Francisco.

Export controls usually are not imposed for the same reasons as import controls, with the exception that some nations, mainly developing countries, may tax both imports and exports as a revenue raising device. But the United States, and many other nations, usually limit exports for such reasons as national security, foreign policy goals, or scarcity of certain domestic resources. Most nations encourage exports, often providing incentives, and often engaging in assistance which may constitute unfair trade such as subsidies. Because export controls often are intended to serve political goals, the executive may be given considerable discretion in imposing export limitations to certain nations. In the United States, conflict between the Congress, which believes it has authority over all aspects of foreign commerce, and the President, who believes the executive has control over all aspects of foreign policy, has led to frequent conflict and inability to enact new export laws.

Our Boston client may be prohibited from exporting some or all of its products to all nations, or may be prohibited from exporting anything to specific nations. Export controls are thus designed to limit certain goods to any nation, or limit any goods to certain nations, or certain goods to certain nations. To assure compliance, exports may have to have a license. The export rules in the United States long divided licenses for the most part between *general* and *validated* licenses. General licenses did not require an application to and approval by the government, only furnishing certain information upon export which was useful for compiling trade statistics. Validated licenses required an application to and permission from the Department of Commerce, often with the scrutiny of and sometimes inordinate delay of approval by, the Department of Defense. This complex matrix of general and validated licenses may be replaced by a scheme intended to be more exporter-friendly. The end of the Cold War, the movement of many nonmarket economy nations towards democracy and market economics, and the realization by many developing nations that joining the developed world was more promising than leading the third world, has encouraged the United States to adopt a simpler export control scheme.

As we have noted, governments participate in regulating the transfer of goods across borders—imports and exports. Our Boston client may have decided that the maze of laws and regulations in those areas where it has sold its products, such as Brasilia and Bombay, or perhaps Beijing, is so extensive that the only way to penetrate that market is to establish a direct foreign investment. It might also choose to transfer technology to a domestic manufacturer in one or more of those areas, but it may feel that to control the technology, and to maximize profits, direct foreign investment is the best alternative.

If our seller in Boston decides to manufacture its products not in its aging factory in Boston, but a few miles away in Brockton, it faces few problems in either licensing a Brockton enterprise to make the products, or creating its own branch or subsidiary in Brockton. Brockton has no registry for filing and approving technology contracts which local businesses enter into with "foreign" businesses, whether the foreign business is from Boston, Burbank or a truly foreign location in another country. The Massachusetts corporation law which governs the creation of a corporation in Boston, is the same law which governs one formed in Brockton. If the decision of the Boston client is to manufacture its products in Burbank, technology is easily transferred either to a separate unrelated California firm, or to a branch or California subsidiary of the Massachusetts company.

Like Brockton as a city and Massachusetts as a state, neither Burbank nor California have rules which require the registration of the "foreign" technology. Creating a branch factory in Burbank will require little more than renting factory space, setting up machinery and starting production. If a California subsidiary is preferred, the California corporation law will present few surprises to the Boston lawyer. California corporation law is generally considered more protective of shareholders than such laws as Delaware, or state laws based on the Revised Model Business Corporation Act, but the differences between Massachusetts and California corporation law are for the most part quite minor. But what if the Massachusetts company would like to manufacture the products in Brasilia or Bombay, either by a local licensee or at a branch or subsidiary owned by the Boston client? The legal problems surrounding licensing and foreign investment are considerably more complex than those affecting the transfer of goods across borders under the traditional documentary sale.

If licensing abroad proves to be successful, or if the Boston company believes it could profit more or make better products by owning the factory in Brasilia or Bombay, it may decide to open a branch or establish a wholly owned subsidiary. Neither would create any difficulty if undertaken in Brockton or Burbank. But establishing, operating and withdrawing from a foreign direct investment abroad may be very different. If a foreign branch is desired, the local laws may in writing or by policy disallow the branch and require a subsidiary. The branch would, under United States conflict of laws principles, be subject to the law of the state of incorporation, i.e., Massachusetts, while the subsidiary, being a Brazilian or Indian creation, would be subject to the laws of those nations, respectively.

Another factor would enter the decision. What would be the tax consequences of a branch versus a subsidiary? If a branch, would Brazilian or Indian corporate income taxes be imposed on the profits of the branch only, or levied against the licensor's entire worldwide corporate operations? Accepting the fact that a subsidiary would probably be required by the host nation, the Boston company would be establishing an entity under a corporation or company law quite different than that in Boston. Brazilian law is civil law based, and the Boston lawyer would have to learn some foreign corporation law to understand the choices to be made in the formation and operation of the Brazilian subsidiary. A proposed subsidiary in Bombay will be governed by Indian company law, which although rooted in English company law, contains significant differences from the Massachusetts corporation law. If the subsidiary is to be established in Beijing, it will quickly be apparent that nonmarket economies do not always have privately owned corporations with the ownership reflected by shares of stock. The corporate entity may be more a contractual creation resulting from negotiations with the government, than an entity created by way of drafting articles of incorporation and issuing shares of stock under an enabling corporation law.

The subsidiary in Brasilia is likely to be wholly owned by the Boston company. But in Bombay and Beijing, and in many other developing and nonmarket economies, a joint venture with host nation equity may be required. For the Beijing subsidiary, the Boston company may be limited to owning a maximum of 49 percent of the equity, meaning the PRC government or a state-owned enterprise will own the controlling 51 percent. Were the subsidiary in a developing nation without nonmarket economy characteristics, such as that in Bombay, but which mandated joint ventures, the 51 percent majority equity might be owned by host nation private investors. If the 51 percent local ownership is broadly held by many shareholders, the concentrated 49 percent held by the Boston company might suggest retention of control. But the law may mandate that the percentage of nationals on the governing board be at least the same as the percentage of local equity ownership. Thus the Boston company would have to accept both local majority ownership and control, or seek a way to retain a disproportionate amount of control to equity, such as a management contract.

Joint ventures were a prevalent form of foreign direct investment for two decades in the 1970s and 1980s, but there were many ways in which the foreign investor could seek an exemption and retain total ownership and control. They could agree to locate in an economically depressed area, or establish research and development facilities along with the manufacturing process, or export a substantial percentage of the production. In the 1990s joint ventures have been more voluntary than mandatory, as nations diminish barriers to foreign investment as well as to foreign trade. With the many possible restrictions to investing present in foreign nations, an investment in Brockton or Burbank may look pretty good.

Our Boston company has entered the world of international trade and investment, and has learned quickly of the complexities of dealing with Brasilia or Bombay or Beijing, rather than Brockton or Burbank, in selling, transferring technology or manufacturing its products. And it has learned of the complexities of dealing with Singapore or Sao Paulo or Shanghai, rather than Salem or San Francisco, in purchasing components for manufacturing its products. It might decide not to deal with developing nations (Brazil or India) or nonmarket economies (PRC), but to sell to, or license or establish a direct foreign investment in only those nations which are more developed and which are market economies. It may choose Brussels.

In selling goods to a Brussels buyer it will not confront import licenses; it will receive a strong, convertible currency; and it will not be asked to accept countertrade. But it may have to deal in another language and, depending on the nature of the product, it may confront European Union tariff and nontariff barriers absent in domestic United States sales. If the Boston company licenses a Brussels firm to make its products, it will have its intellectual property protected, but with some variations from the form of protection received in the United States. If it creates a subsidiary in Belgium it will not have to adopt a joint venture. But it will face civil law tradition corporate concepts and possibly some workers' rights not present in the United States. The company will have to learn something about dealing in an economically integrated market, in this case the European Union. The similarities to dealing in Brockton or Burbank are as prevalent in Europe as the disparities in dealing with Brasilia or Bombay or Beijing. That is partly why a very large part of United States trade and investment abroad is with developed, market economy nations.

What follows in the chapters ahead is an introduction to the laws and policies, the organizations and entities, and the people that are involved in some of the activities that are intended to be included in the term "international trade and investment". This Nutshell will cover government imposed restrictions on imports and exports; the GATT and the World Trade Organization (WTO); commencing, insuring, operating and withdrawing foreign investment; expropriation; the international movement of business persons; and economic integration with an emphasis on the European Union and the North American Free Trade Agreement. The author's International Business Transactions in a Nutshell complements this Nutshell. The former covers such issues as the negotiation of business transactions, the documentary sale and use of letters of credit, currency issues, technology transfers, transactions in developing and nonmarket economies, dispute settlement, and the use of the defenses of foreign state immunity and the act of state doctrine in commercial transactions. The two Nutshells are intended to provide a broad introduction to the people and institutions who practice international business transactions, and the government and multilateral organizations which both encourage and restrict trade and investment.

CHAPTER ONE

WORLD TRADE AND MULTINATIONAL ENTERPRISES

The United States is one of a few central players in the world in international trade. It has engaged in foreign trade from the moment of its independence over two centuries ago. One of the reasons independence from England was sought was England's imposition of severe restrictions on trade between the colonies and foreign nations. In less than two centuries from achieving independence, the United States became the leading trading power in the world. For over a decade after World War II, the United States was in the envious and economically advantageous position of being the major center of production of finished goods for export. But with extraordinary economic growth in Japan and Europe in the 1960s and 1970s, by the 1980s the United States no longer dominated world trade. It had to compete for sales abroad, and also in the domestic market within the United States. Traditional surpluses in the balance of trade with most nations in some cases began to be reversed. The United States had to deal with increasingly large trade deficits with Japan.

Although the United States shares economic power with Japan and the European Union, the United States is the only nation which is a power in both the economic and political spheres. Europe's harmony is economic in form. When it treads on political sensitivities, such as monetary union, the harmony is replaced with a dissonance threatening even the economic success. No single European nation has the political authority of the United States, and the political power of the former U.S.S.R. vanished with its disintegration. Japan has not sought world political power, content with limiting its political role to assuring its continued economic success. China's political power, aspirational and real, exceeds Japan's, and China's economic progress may one day cause it to join the United States as a second major economic and political force.

The status of United States international trade in the 1990s has caused trade to be a topic of common conversation, much because of perceived threats to jobs for the American worker, and the quality of life of the American people. The trade surplus of earlier decades has become a trade deficit of disturbing proportions. This has generated annual Congressional proposals of an increasingly restrictive nature, drawing comparisons with the depression inducing Smoot–Hawley law of 1930. United States exports have continued to grow, but imports have grown more rapidly. Even the steady fall of the dollar since 1986 has not reversed the deficit. The importance of trade should be apparent. But the huge capacity of the United States to consume foreign products is out of balance with its ability to find reciprocal consumption for its products abroad. That is due to many reasons, problems of quality, real and perceived, problems of barriers to trade imposed by every nation, and problems of government leadership. Those who view the United States from abroad continually point to excessive consumption and inadequate savings, and to the budget deficit, as the principal reasons for the deteriorating United States trade position. Washington hears the complaints, but makes few corrections. It is easier to blame other nations. After all, the United States still generates a formidable share of world trade and will continue to do so.

Even individual states have remarkable trade statistics. California alone generates over $20 billion of United States world trade, making its "gross state product" greater than the gross national products of all but some seven nations of the world. In the last few years, however, the per capita standard of living of several other nations has reached and arguably exceeded that in the United States. The periodic issuance of impressive aggregate trade figures from Washington tends to mask an ebbing and equalizing status and role in the world community. Status as an economic power is gained slowly when the nation's energy is directed towards the production and distribution of goods and services, but is lost quickly when that energy is directed more to consumption than production, more to producing self-serving statistics than a tangible surplus.

PATTERNS OF WORLD TRADE

Trade traditionally has been measured by the exchange of tangible goods, both raw materials and finished products. The prominence of oil as a trading commodity, and the economic power exerted in the 1970s by the Organization of Petroleum Exporting Countries (OPEC), resulted in a considerable shift of wealth caused by remarkable changes in the price of a single commodity. But the power of OPEC diminished due to an oversupply of oil and conflict both within the oil industry and within OPEC. That conflict quickly moderated that shift of wealth. Petroleum remains an important commodity, however, and it played a critical role in the decision of the United States to commence the "Gulf War". Extractable raw materials remain the principal source of wealth for many nations. Nations which produce many natural and agricultural resources, from tin to bananas, attempt to create cartels which will give them the moment of economic glory that was once OPEC's.

In recent years attention on items of trade and therefore value has shifted from an exclusive focus on tangibles and technology, to an area of trade far more difficult to define. That area is trade in such services as advertising, banking, insurance, accounting, consulting, entertainment, tourism and the vast area of computer services. United States trade in these "invisibles" may exceed $150 billion annually. Trade in tangibles is marred by an increasing

deficit, but trade in services is marked by an increasing surplus. Many other nations are eager to
develop their own services, and to protect them
from encroachment from the developed nations.
The negotiations in the Uruguay Round on trade in
services was an especially difficult part of the overall trade talks. The industrialized nations, led by
the United States, for the most part successfully
negotiated lowering trade barriers to services, over
the objections of such important developing nations
as India and Brazil. These nations fear dominance
in ownership of services by the industrialized nations. The final agreement reflects many restrictions and reservations by developing nations determined to establish their own service sectors. The
ability of the new WTO to regulate trade in services
will be critical to keeping such service oriented
nations as the United States a part of this important multilateral trade regulating organization.

Viewing the constantly changing world trade patterns as they have developed to the end of the
1990s, the dominance of the United States which
was prevalent two decades ago has both diminished
substantially and is unlikely to reoccur in the next
few decades. It is attributable to the increasing
prominence of Japan in manufacturing products
which meet current consumer demands, to the entry of China in the world trade arena, to the cooperation of the European nations within the European
Union, and to the movement through successive
stages of development of many developing nations,
especially the "Four Dragons" or "Four Tigers" of

Asia—Hong Kong, Korea, Singapore and Taiwan. Increased "world market share" is the goal of every nation, and nations joust over international trade issues. They more closely regulate foreign investment coming into the country, and create new trade incentives to stimulate greater exports to (and foreign investment within) other countries.

The spectacular success of Japan as an exporter combined with a creativity to block imports (Japanese intestines are shorter than Americans' and therefore American beef ought not be admitted because it cannot be properly digested) has led to a sequence of protests and threats of sanctions by the United States and by the European Union. However Japan may be accused of being an unfair trader and of using a host of nontariff trade barriers (NTBs) to keep foreign goods and investment out of Japan, the United States often fails to consider that trade imbalances may be as much caused by domestic failures as by foreign intransigence.

Japan is not alone in using nontariff barriers. They have arisen to protect domestic industry as the earlier protection by high tariffs has diminished. Every nation has developed its own methods of keeping imports at bay. The French have provoked a stream of protest by requiring that documentation for imported goods be written in French. Moreover, the French reaped criticism, and some plaudits for originality, by requiring for a brief time that all imported video recorders (principally from Japan) enter into France through only one, tiny French customs port. France established a "consultative commission for international trade" charged to watch for "abnormal" and excessive imports and unfair export practices of other countries. Meaning, of course, an agency for domestic business to complain to when affected by exports, regardless of the efficiency in production of the domestic business.

Other nations have responded in various ways to the impact of imports. Restricted by their agreements to specific tariff levels as members of the WTO, they have carried nontariff barriers to a new height of originality. These barriers may assume the form of health or safety standards, packing or labelling requirements, and many other rules which may in theory seem justified, but in practice are structured or interpreted so as to eliminate or reduce imports and benefit domestic industries. Those who must be retained to deal with these nontariff barriers, as well as subsidies, dumping or rules of origin, have become the major beneficiaries of our complex trade laws. They alone know how to work through the maze of details in lengthy definitions included in trade laws and multilateral agreements. Foreign targets of a United States dumping charge must expend enormous resources on responding to such charges, thus making these actions themselves become another form of nontariff barrier.

Goods which are sold in one nation are not necessarily either goods produced domestically by locally owned manufacturers, or goods produced abroad by foreign owned manufacturers. They may be goods produced *domestically* by *foreign* owned manufacturers. Investing abroad is an alternative to exporting the goods abroad. Foreign investment shares some benefits of trade. The foreign manufacturer receives the profit from the manufacture abroad, but the host nation of the foreign investment creates jobs. Raw materials or parts may be sent by the foreign manufacturer, to create what is little more than an assembly plant in the host nation, or raw materials and parts may be purchased in the host nation, adding to the benefits of permitting investment owned by foreign entities.

The United States is the major source of foreign investment, representing nearly half of world totals, more than $150 billion. More than 40 percent of all foreign investment is placed within Germany, Japan, the United Kingdom and the United States. While it is the investment within developing nations which receives the headlines of expropriation and mandatory joint ventures, the purchasing power and stability remains in the industrialized market economies. Although total foreign investment in any one developing nation might seem insignificant standing before the figures of aggregate world foreign investment, the sum of investments in such nations as Brazil, India, Indonesia, Malaysia, Mexico, Nigeria and Venezuela is considerable and important to trade and development.

While trying to hold imports to reasonable levels, every nation wants to be a major exporter. It is, after all, exports that provide the means to pay for imports. The urge to export leads to another scheme of laws. They are usually laws of encouragement in contrast to the laws of discouragement which typify the import rules. They may be fashioned in the way of granting tax benefits, offering export financing or insurance, overlooking trade restraint elements of permitted export cartels, or tying permitted imports to the level of exports. The United States, in enacting the 1982 Export Trading Company (ETC) Act, followed the practice of such nations as Japan in assisting exporters. The ETC Act was designed to permit small and medium United States firms to gain information about foreign trade opportunities and techniques and to have easier access to financing for export activity.

The ETC Act defines an export trading company as one "which does business under the laws of the United States or any State, which is exclusively engaged in activities related to international trade, and which is organized and operated principally for purposes of exporting goods or services produced in the United States by providing one or more trade services". Major features of the Act attempt to reduce antitrust liability of exporters from the United States, and to limit or at least to make more clear the extraterritorial application of United States antitrust laws. On the state level in the United States, more than a dozen states have increased efforts to provide export financing assistance by establishing state "Export Banks." Curiously, state promotional activities may be subsidized by the federal government in the form of tax exempt backing, yet pursue state goals which are contrary to federal policy.

Every nation which engages in international business transactions develops a legal framework defining its role. That framework will consist of its own domestic trade laws, including its acceptance of international laws regulating international transactions, and its participation in international organizations which also establish rules. The United States has developed by legislative and executive action an extensive set of domestic rules governing trade and investment. It has also been a major participant in many international organizations which influence or govern trade, licensing and investment. The World Trade Organization, successor to the GATT, is by far the most important such organization. The United Nations has played a disappointingly minor role in trade, although more recently UNCITRAL, the United Nations Commission on International Trade Law, has become an important forum for the harmonization of rules affecting trade, such as the Convention on International Sale of Goods (CISG).

Regional economic integration has also increased trade among small groups of nations. The European Union and the NAFTA are the two most important areas which have reduced barriers to internal trade, although sometimes at the expense of increasing barriers to external trade. But however important participation in bilateral or multilateral trade agreements or organizations may be, the will of a single participant to abide by freer trade rules will be expressed in its domestic trade laws and policies.

UNITED STATES TRADE LAWS

Rules and sources of law for United States international trade and investment are mostly found in a sequence of specific trade acts which make up the basic framework for import and export trade. To these, however, must be added numerous provisions of other laws which are directed to specific trade issues. For example, the Foreign Corrupt Practices Act does not stand alone as a separate trade law, but consists of amendments to the securities laws. United States trade case law tends to be limited. Trade rules have evolved in legislative chambers and multilateral organizations rather than in the courts. There is really no common law of trade; the decisions which do exist are almost exclusively interpretations of the statutory rules.

In some areas of the law a single law governs most activity. That is true of corporation law. Each state has a corporation law which is periodically updated and sometimes totally replaced by a new law, such as the adoption of the Model Business Corporation Act, or the subsequent Revised version. That format makes a search for the applicable law relatively easy. For international business transactions, however, there is no easy single source. New trade laws do two things. They create some new trade rules and thus have some permanency standing alone. But they also modify earlier trade laws. Thus a search requires checking several trade laws, although certain subjects tend to be identified with a single trade law. For example, the Tariff Act of 1930 is where the tariff schedules are located; the Trade Act of 1974 is where rules governing trade with less favored nations, i.e., those not benefitting from MFN status, and more than most favored nations, i.e., those benefitting from the generalized system of preferences (GSP) program, are located; and the Trade Agreements Act of 1979 is where the rules governing government procurement and standards are located. Trade is thus governed principally by a matrix of separate trade laws from the Tariff Act of 1930 to the Uruguay Round Implementation Act of 1994.

The first of the principal laws regulating current imports to the United States is the Tariff Act of 1930. This is the famous Smoot–Hawley Tariff Act, which raised tariff walls to substantial heights and worsened the world depression of the early 1930s. The severe tariffs of Smoot–Hawley have since been largely diminished for those nations which benefit from most favored nation (MFN) status, but remain for those less favored. One reason the 1930 Act remains in force is that it is the location of the hundreds of pages of tariffs—the tariff schedules. In addition to tariffs, the 1930 Act includes the organization and functions of the International Trade Commission. It controls some of the actions which the Commission may take, including of considerable importance, what are commonly referred to as Section 337 actions challenging unfair practices in import trade. There are extensive provisions for the promotion of foreign trade, and also the major pro-

PUBLIC LIBRARY
DANVILLE, ILLINOIS

vision protecting American trademark goods from the entry of counterfeit products, Section 526. And finally, the Tariff Act of 1930 includes the United States rules governing countervailing and anti-dumping duties.

Although other trade acts were enacted subsequent to the 1930 Act, the next which includes provisions important to current trade is the Trade Act of 1974. This Act includes executive negotiating authority for agreements with other countries, the creation of the office of the United States Trade Representative and provisions governing the interrelationship of Congress and the President with regard to trade actions. Furthermore, it includes important provisions regulating relief from injury caused by import competition, particularly Section 201 actions, known as "escape clause" actions. Part of the relief from injury includes adjustment assistance for workers, firms and communities. Another title of this 1974 act addresses the enforcement of United States rights under trade agreements, which are reflected in Section 301 actions. A separate title of the Act governs trade relations with countries not currently receiving nondiscriminatory treatment, meaning essentially nonmarket economies. These provisions are becoming less useful as many nonmarket economies have attempted to shed such status for participation in the world market economy. These provisions include the little used but potentially important Section 406, allowing "market disruption" actions. Finally, the Act includes the generalized system of preferences (GSP) scheme, which gives to certain developing nations tariff status even better than most favored nations receive.

The Trade Agreements Act of 1979 is the third of our important trade acts. This Act was passed principally to implement several of the codes negotiated in the Tokyo Round of the GATT, concluded after negotiations in the mid–1970s. Thus, it has sections dealing with government procurement and technical barriers to trade (standards). Changes to the rules governing countervailing and antidumping duties, and to customs valuation, both part of then newly adopted GATT codes, were implemented by this Act, but as amendments to the Tariff Act of 1930 rather than enduring provisions identified with this 1979 Act.

The fourth important act is the Trade and Tariff Act of 1984. In addition to making amendments to the earlier acts, this Act extended negotiating authority and provided for the development of a trade agreement with Israel.

The fifth act is the Omnibus Trade and Competitiveness Act of 1988. This Act authorized the President to enter into the ongoing Uruguay Round of GATT negotiations. It also implemented the Harmonized Tariff Schedule (HTS) of the United States. Special attention was devoted in this Act to amending Section 301 of the 1974 Trade Act. It is the source of the notorious "Super 301" and "Special 301" procedures whereby the United States targets nations with which it has major trade or intellectual property disputes.

When the United States became a signatory to the North American Free Trade Agreement in 1993, Congress soon thereafter enacted the North American Free Trade Implementation Act, which made NAFTA part of U.S. trade law. Similarly, when the United States became a signatory to the Agreement Establishing the World Trade Organization in 1994, and its associated agreements and understandings, Congress enacted the Uruguay Round Agreements Act, which made the WTO a part of U.S. trade law.

To understand the United States regulation of imports, one must thus turn to several trade acts and agreements. To understand the regulations of exports as opposed to imports, the path is somewhat clearer and less cluttered.

There is no similarly extensive sequence of laws regulating United States exports. A nation tends to encourage its exports, rather than limit them. Limitations are imposed principally for reasons of national security or shortage of certain raw materials. There is one major U.S. export law which is especially important to those engaging in international business transactions. This is the Export Administration Act of 1979 (EAA). This Act makes a number of Congressional policy statements indicating an intent to restrict export controls only to the extent necessary. It outlines the licensing procedure for exports, requiring a validated license only in a limited number of specific export situations. It includes the concept of "foreign availability", that export controls should not be placed on goods which are readily available from other sources. It is within this EAA that Congress has placed the foreign anti-boycott provisions, which prohibit United States persons from taking part in boycotts against countries friendly to the United States. The provisions in this Act, as in the case of several trade laws, are followed up by extensive administrative regulations. Finally, this Act includes very severe penalties for violating United States export controls, including loss of all export rights.

These are not the only laws which govern United States trade. There are many other acts which regulate trade, some of which appear as amendments to other laws. For example, the Foreign Corrupt Practices Act, intended to reduce the making of improper payments to government officials abroad, is a relatively brief act which modifies the securities laws. The Foreign Sovereign Immunities Act is of substantial importance in litigation involving foreign nations. The Caribbean Basin Economic Recovery Act extends special duty free import rights to goods from that developing area. The Buy American Act of 1933 grants government procurement preferences to U.S. manufacturers and service providers.

All of these laws provide the basic domestic law framework governing United States international business. When combined with United States obligations in international organizations and agreements such as the WTO, the International Monetary Fund, the World Bank, etc., one begins to understand the complexity and diversity of United States international trade law.

FOREIGN INVESTMENT LAW

The GATT was not created to regulate foreign investment among its member nations. But the WTO includes such regulation in the form of Trade Related Aspects of Investment Measures, or TRIMs. It is a major accomplishment: the United Nations was never able to reach beyond the rhetoric of the North–South debate in its determination, through the Centre for Transnational Corporations, to govern only conduct of multinational corporations, without any responsibility of host nations regarding the treatment of such international corporations. Even with the investment provisions of the WTO in place, individual nations will continue to have considerable latitude in controlling MNEs, unilaterally, by means of bilateral investment treaties (BITs) or through free trade areas such as the NAFTA.

United States investment abroad is extensive. It exists in developed and developing nations, as well as in market and nonmarket economies. Foreigners reciprocate. Investment in the United States is increasing. Foreign investment originates from virtually all nations with which the United States has normal commercial relations.

As the first Secretary of the Treasury, Alexander Hamilton, observed in a Congressional report, "Rather than be judged a rival it (foreign investment in the United States) ought to be considered as a most valuable auxiliary; conducing to put in motion a greater quantity of productive labor and a greater proportion of useful enterprise than could exist without it." Foreign investment helped to finance the Louisiana Purchase. At the close of the Civil War, foreign investment (mostly in bank deposits and real estate holdings) exceeded $7 billion, with $1.3 billion of that amount being placed in the United States as direct investment.

Direct investment is usually calculated to be that amount which involves a sufficient ownership interest in an enterprise or asset to provide a significant degree of control, although the concept of "control" is itself amorphous. U.S. government standards label an investment as direct when 25 percent of voting stock is controlled by a foreign person. Some parts of the executive, such as the Department of Commerce, as well as the U.S. Congress, suggest that even a 10 percent figure provides sufficient control to merit calling the foreign investment direct. Foreign investment may be called "indirect" or "portfolio" investment when it does not involve outright ownership of real or personal property, or is an ownership interest of less than 25 percent in other forms of legal enterprises.

Foreign investment touches broad sectors of the U.S. economy. Well over 1,500 domestic companies are currently foreign controlled, with foreign acquisition of domestic companies occurring at a rate in excess of 200 per year. For example, an investment tally has revealed foreign acquisition activity in U.S.

companies which produce aluminum windows, chemicals, construction equipment, electronics, pharmaceuticals, photographic materials, steel and steel bearings, and televisions. Significant acquisition activity has been reported in service/marketing enterprises such as banking, brokerage, coffee processing, food distribution, hotel and resort developments, garden seed sales, music recording, securities investment and wine making.

Reported acquisition activity may not reflect certain other purchases that foreign investors make within the United States. For example, the United States Department of Agriculture has noted that foreign investors have an ownership investment of five percent or more in 5.6 million acres of farmland located in 49 of the 50 states—approximately one-half of one percent of all farmland in the United States.

The relatively open United States attitude toward foreign investment has been challenged by an assumption that loosely controlled foreign investment should be feared. The prospect of foreign controlled oil companies bidding successfully in the United States for offshore oil leases and then shipping the oil to countries other than the United States, all in disregard of the country's policy of independence from foreign produced oil, is a scenario possible in a country where there is not very extensive or accurate knowledge about the nature and scope of foreign investment activity. That is the case of the United States.

Congressional response has had to begin with simple information gathering in an environment where the executive branch of government has opted deliberately for no policy regarding private investment, where treaties of friendship, commerce and navigation commit the United States to nonrestrictive treatment of foreign investment, and where the privacy of personal and corporate information, coupled with the widespread use of nominee shareholders, are considerable barriers to information access.

A 1973 Senate inquiry, with assistance from various parts of the executive branch, revealed that there was no existing, comprehensive scheme for identifying and regulating foreign investment, although several existing laws did provide for regulation in certain industries and in limited subject matter areas. For example, the Federal Communications Act prohibits issuance of a federal communication license to non-citizens. The Atomic Energy Act bars non-citizens from holding a license for atomic energy operation, utilization or production facilities. Unless authorized by the Comptroller of the Currency, foreigners cannot serve as bank directors. Foreigners cannot obtain insurance or guarantees from the Overseas Private Investment Corporation, obtain war risk aircraft insurance, or obtain special government agricultural loans for natural disaster or for family farms. The Federal Communications Act prohibits merger approval of telegraph carriers that would lead to foreign control of more than 20 percent of company stock. The Communications

Satellite Corporation cannot be more than 20 percent owned or controlled by foreign interests. Foreigners generally cannot hold more than a 25 percent ownership interest in an air carrier, or in vessels engaged in coastal or fresh water shipping. Subject to waiver or other approval, foreigners may not acquire or charter vessels during national emergency and may not acquire control of a domestic bank or form a new bank.

Other statutory restrictions also affect foreign investment in oil pipelines and mineral leases, in leases for developing geothermal resources, in ownership of federal land, in commercial fishing in offshore areas, in customs brokerage firms, in underwater salvage, in Edge Act Corporations, and in defense work. No person may act as an agent for a foreign principal before filing appropriate registration information with the Attorney General of the United States. In addition to federal restrictions on foreign investors, many of the States impose additional restrictions.

In response to the need to have current information about foreign investment in the United States, Congress enacted the Foreign Investment Study Act of 1974. The Act authorized and directed the Secretaries of Commerce and Treasury to study and to report to the Congress about foreign direct and foreign portfolio investments in the United States. In April of 1976, the Secretary of Commerce reported to Congress as required by the Foreign Investment Study Act of 1974. Noting that the report was the first comprehensive attempt since 1959 to survey foreign direct investment in the United States, the Secretary recommended that Congress authorize periodic, mandatory benchmark investment surveys with increased emphasis given to labor effects of foreign direct investment, to the impact such investment has upon localities in the United States and upon local investment incentive, and to the extent to which land is directly and indirectly foreign owned.

In response, Congress enacted the International Investment Survey Act of 1976 in order "to provide clear and unambiguous authority" for the President to collect information about international investment and to provide analyses of such information to the Congress, to executive agencies, and to the general public. The Act authorized the President to conduct, at least every five years, a comprehensive benchmark survey of United States direct investment abroad and of foreign direct investment in the United States. The President is authorized also to conduct a benchmark survey of foreign portfolio investment in the United States at least once every five years and to conduct a similar survey of United States portfolio investment abroad within five years from the date of enactment of the Act. Within the Executive Branch, the Council on International Economic Policy is charged to review the results of studies and of surveys conducted pursuant to the Act and to report annually to the Committee on International Relations of the House of Representatives and to appropriate committees of the Senate about any investment trends or developments which may have national policy implications and which, in the Council's opinion, warrant a review by Congress. Congress further enacted the Foreign Direct Investment and International Financial Data Improvement Act of 1990 to report on foreign owned firms' participation in the United States. The initial report was completed in September, 1991, and confirms a rapid growth of foreign investment (portfolio and direct) in the United States.

Concern about foreign investment has resurfaced annually, increasing in intensity as foreign investors found bargains in the U.S. as the dollar fell in the second half of the 1980s. The President has typically threatened to veto any new form of regulation of foreign investment in the United States. But the Exon–Florio provisions amending the Defense Production Act of 1950 were adopted in the 1988 Omnibus Trade and Competitiveness Act. These provisions give the President the authority to block mergers and acquisitions by foreigners of U.S. companies in the interest of "national security." This authority has been exercised sparingly, but it was used to keep a People's Republic of China company from buying a U.S. firm specializing in aircraft parts and technology.

THE MULTINATIONAL ENTERPRISE (MNE)

One important and controversial business form for engaging in international trade may be called the multinational enterprise (MNE). The most visible MNEs are the largest multinational corporations engaged in "durational" business over decades in every sector of the globe. The MNE may be one of several less structured business forms, such as partnerships and joint ventures, used in "transactional" business of short duration in only a few places in the world. A transaction may be an international business transaction whether the principal players come from private enterprise, from national or local government, or from a combination of both private enterprise and government.

The MNE has aroused concern and prompted new regulatory attempts by governments, acting singly and in concert. Although history may not yet identify the MNE as having been a primary catalyst in pressing diverse and proud countries into a measure of sustained global order, the utility and proper role of the MNE have engendered vigorous debate involving much unclear data.

At the core, there is no agreement about the amount of enterprise autonomy needed for satisfactory MNE activity, about the proper impact of such activity on the industrial development of all countries, and about the permissible economic and social disquiet which should be tolerated along the way. In the debate, certain things are clear. Over 200 MNEs each have annual sales exceeding $1 billion (U.S.), and have more currency reserves at their disposal than do most governments of the world. Each of the top ten MNEs enjoys annual revenues larger than the yearly gross national product of two-thirds of the countries in the world, with a ranking of the

100 largest concentrations of global economic wealth revealing that individual MNEs comprise nearly 40 percent of that group. The remaining entities are countries, which only a few decades past could have laid unchallenged claim to being the world's fundamental economic and political units.

The catalog of concerns about MNE behavior includes complaints that little is known about the organizational structure and policy formation procedures of the MNE, with annual reports revealing scant information. The cost of acquiring vital information about secretive MNEs is prohibitively high, and coordinated information gathering by several countries is currently difficult. MNEs are sometimes insensitive to the host country's need for cultural cohesion, frequently because the enterprise philosophy is different from philosophical underpinnings of the host country's society, and the insensitivity impinges upon the developmental policies of the host. MNE planning often fails to include adequate consideration for the host country's capacity to absorb total consequences of MNE activity. MNEs may waste the environment by using high polluting means of production and rigorous resource extraction processes.

MNE financial practices concerning credit, retail prices, transfer pricing, industrial property and valuation of imports and of liabilities owed abroad often hurt the host country's balance of payments posture and taxation efforts. The MNEs currently enjoy freedom from control by any single legal jurisdiction, especially that of the host country, through the use of choice of forum clauses in contracts, use of tax haven countries, and subjection to extraterritorial application of one country's legal rules (often those of the parent enterprise's home country) at the expense of otherwise governing legal rules of the host country. The MNE has undue strength in labor negotiations worldwide because of easy relocation to a less expensive labor environment in another country and because of the capacity to freeze indefinitely numbers of available jobs by freezing investment levels. MNE practice tends to avoid upgrading the quality of local labor while total resources available to the MNE permit displacement of local entrepreneurship, including that of other MNEs in an internationally inefficient way. MNE practices restrict the development and dissemination of technology.

MNEs intrude upon the sovereignty of a host country by becoming directly involved in local political processes, by paying bribes (but are they extorted?), by serving as an intelligence gathering conduit for the government of another country (usually that where the parent MNE has a home base), and by cooperating with another country in the operation of certain politically inspired trade policies directed at the host country. The more forebearing the host country may be in its international agreements with other countries the less latitude the host has in dealing easily with problems raised by activities of the MNE. In short, the charge is that the MNE is uncontrolled and arrogant.

Supporters of the MNE point out that internationalization of the country economies in the world permits a matching of efficiently supplied capital and technology with large economic problems. The MNE can take greater investment risks because enterprise flexibility and diversification permit dislocation effects in one market to be absorbed by other, unaffected markets. Stringent regulation of the MNE encourages an attitude toward taking high, short-term profits instead of a more measured, longer-term return on investment. Individual host regulation of MNEs has been inefficient. Bargaining resources available to the MNE serve to encourage a grouping of small, host country economies. The success of MNE activity has in no small part been due to its relevance to the developmental aspirations of appropriate interest groups in host countries. The host country people's interests have not been set forth with long-term clarity.

Unpersuaded by arguments for maximal MNE latitude, many countries have responded with laws regulating foreign investment. The laws are designed to prevent industries perceived as vital (e.g., banking, communications, defense suppliers, natural resource extraction, transportation) from being vulnerable to control or information access by foreigners. The laws are designed also to monitor foreign investment activity, to determine the conditions under which investment may he made, and to regulate the product and technology flows that such investment produces.

International organizations have considered ways to lessen the widespread discomfort felt about present MNE activity. For example, within the United Nations the Commission on Transnational Corporations assigned priority to drafting a code of conduct for the MNE. After years of effort, the project failed. The Commission, through its Secretariat (Centre), did make some improvement in host countries access to information about dealing with MNEs, by providing the countries with world wide data about specific companies, by providing consultants and by conducting training sessions for host country representatives.

The U.N. Economic and Social Council and the General Assembly have considered an international agreement to meet the problem of illicit MNE payments given to decision makers in host countries. Considered, but gone no further. The U.N. Conference on Trade and Development (UNCTAD) has debated vigorously a code of conduct for the transfer of technology. As is the case of so much of the efforts of the UN towards multinational enterprises and their relationships with and treatment by host nations, the proposed Transfer of Technology Code died in discussion. The U.N. General Assembly did adopt a code on restrictive business practices in 1980, another UNCTAD product. But it has been given little attention by governments, many of whom view it as an obstacle to trade and irrelevant to the 1990s. It is a sad record for those with great expectations for the UN.

Since 1976 the approximately 24 industrialized member countries within the Organization for Economic Cooperation and Development (OECD) have published a Code of Conduct for Multinationals which sets forth voluntary guidelines for appropriate enterprise behavior. With interpretative assistance of the OECD Investment Committee, MNEs operating within OECD member countries are being encouraged to speed compliance with Code provisions dealing with disclosure of enterprise information, employment and industrial relations, and taxation and transfer pricing. Representatives from the member countries of the International Institute for the Unification of Private Law (UNIDROIT) worked on an international trade law code regarding the formation and interpretation of contracts, especially leasing agreements. The European Union favors regulating MNE activity on a sector basis, such as in areas of company law, taxation, and employment policy.

International regulation of MNEs shows every prospect of increasing, in part due to the role illicit MNE payments play in generating public demand for closer MNE regulation. Often such payments are a fact of international commercial life, whether they are characterized as "advertising expenses", "commissions", or more simply as "grease" or "bribes". Business enterprises from the United States are constrained by the 1977 Foreign Corrupt Practices Act, which makes it criminally unlawful for any "domestic concern ... to make use of the mails ... or any means ... of interstate commerce

corruptly in furtherance of ... the giving of anything of value to ... any foreign official ... or any
foreign political party for purposes of ... influenc-
ing ... or inducing [action] ... to ... assist ... in
obtaining or retaining business." 15 U.S.C.A.
§ 78dd–2. Amendments to the Act in 1988 removed
the controversial basis for liability when the MNE
had "reason to know" that some of their payments
through intermediaries would end up in the hands
of foreign officials.

FORMS OF THE MNE

A typical MNE may do business internationally
through several business forms. For example, a
MNE may have a wholly owned subsidiary company
in one country, a parent company branch in another country, a licensee (franchisee) in still another
country, and may do business through participation
in a joint venture in yet another country. The joint
venture business form is favored in many developing countries, with 49 percent equity participation
by the MNE investor and 51 percent equity participation by the national government, a state enterprise or a private party. The use of the joint venture
as a *mandatory* form is however decreasing as a
result of international agreements such as the WTO
and NAFTA, and especially the change in attitude
in developing and nonmarket economy nations towards the foreign investor. One federal court has
described these options as follows:

Choice among the various modes of entering a
market—licensing arrangement, joint venture,

minority, majority, or wholly-owned subsidiary—
has significant implications for the control exercised by the parent. The decision of marketing-
oriented firms to choose wholly-owned subsidiaries means that they can exercise more control
over their foreign operation in subtle indirect
ways as well as directly.... The expanding multinational corporation generally traverses a number of stages. At first it exports its goods to
markets abroad. Next, it establishes sales organizations abroad. Then, it may license the use of its
patents, and ultimately it may establish foreign
manufacturing facilities.... The use of the wholly-owned subsidiary form reflects the desire for
unambiguous control over sales and marketing to
ensure uniform quality and promotion of the
products sold. Bulova Watch Co., Inc. v. K. Hatto-
ri & Co., Ltd., 508 F.Supp. 1322 (E.D.N.Y.1981).

THE ROLE OF CORPORATE
COUNSEL TO A MNE

The role of corporate counsel (house counsel) to a
MNE is not different professionally from that of any
other brand of lawyer in relation to a client. Unlike
many other lawyers, however, counsel is also in a
team member relationship with MNE management
personnel. Counsel has an employment obligation to
support the MNE management structure. Counsel's
corporate legal function may he viewed as one vehicle through which headquarters control, in both its
constraint and freedom aspects, is exercised over

affiliated, sub-parts of the MNE. The access to information and exclusive knowledge of information possessed by counsel are visible and substantial parts of the power dimension of MNE global management. For example, counsel's working relationship with foreign assisting counsel in each country where a sub-part of the MNE operates, and that assisting counsel's working relationship with the principal, MNE sub-part (line) management person within each country, play a substantial role in MNE headquarters control and financial success.

If the principal line management person within each country is willing to explore legal aspects of new business ideas with the assisting counsel in that country, and if assisting counsel has a close reporting and consultative relationship with MNE headquarters counsel, chances increase for the "preventive" side of legal practice to help in shaping management decisions and to reduce large, unanticipated (surgical) legal costs at a later time. The success of counsel's communication with management may generate an ad hoc assignment to a line management function in connection with particular MNE business transactions.

Such closeness can also raise ethical considerations which intersect with counsel's professional responsibilities as a lawyer. For example, in the early 1970s, currency control measures in Chile prevented (blocked) MNE revenues earned in Chile from being remitted to a foreign location. Moreover, the rate of monetary inflation within Chile was such that revenues left there were subject to sub-

stantial devaluation. There is an acute ethical problem for counsel, as a lawyer, who considers the idea
that funds within Chile might be carried secretly at
night over the mountains into neighboring Argentina, and then exchanged for non-Chilean currency
and remitted from Argentina for deposit in a jurisdiction where inflation is not severe.

Corporate line managers are charged with providing needed revenues. Corporate counsel are engaged
principally in minimizing legal "overhead", costs of
the corporation. Corporate presidents often enjoy
talking more about revenues than about overhead
costs, including possible legal overhead costs. Many
current presidents of corporations in the United
States are lawyers and have served as corporate
counsel in that same corporation before being appointed president. Corporate presidents, vice presidents and other line managers are sensitive to this
history when dealing with corporate counsel. They
are mindful also of the fact that they (unless already a lawyer) are ineligible to become a corporate
counsel. Sensitivity becomes acute when, without
permanently changing status as a staff person, corporate counsel is asked to assume a line management role in helping to shape the economic contours
of a MNE's international business transaction or in
negotiating a transaction and in securing subsequent, corporate approvals.

Counsel's usual tasks cover a predictable spec-
trum. The transnational movement of people may
raise questions about visas and other entry permits,
work permits, the drafting of employment agree-

ments, employee non-discrimination, and legal considerations bearing upon employment termination in circumstances where employees have simultaneous connections with several countries. Movement of goods and of services often raises concern about tax, antitrust, "corporate veil", and governmental permit problems, as well as liability questions incident to worldwide advertising. Transfers of information raise questions about patent/trademark/service mark/trade name/applied art as well as about legal aspects of corporate confidentiality. The movement of money stimulates thought about illegal corporate payments; the legal significance of intra-corporate loans; currency restrictions regarding remittances, repatriations and permissible forms of currency; taxes; undercapitalization; and information reporting requirements. Each MNE transaction is touched potentially by the possible extraterritoriality of United States laws, and by the laws of other countries, as well as by conflicts of law considerations.

Requests by line management to put recurring types of company agreements into "standard form" contracts must be squared with the reality of enforcing those contracts in several different national legal systems, with divergent views about the sanctity of contracts made by a corporate body. Counsel may assist in securing approvals from governmental regulatory bodies or persons charged with overseeing MNE activity, and often must testify on the MNE's behalf before people who need not listen at all or who may only care to listen in an abbreviated way. The activities of a MNE, and of each of its subsidiary companies, must be documented adequately by corporate minutes of directors' and shareholders' meetings, evidencing due consideration given to corporate resolutions—all in accord with applicable local law. Outside counsel are engaged commonly to do certain kinds of nonlitigious work, such as ensuring that the MNE has adequate trademark protection throughout the world.

Although a MNE may handle its litigation interests by using only in-house counsel, corporate counsel coordinate and frequently shape the MNE's litigation interests in colloquy with outside counsel, retained to handle the mechanics of litigation in appropriate countries. Colloquy is made easier to the extent that corporate counsel has an understanding of other countries' legal systems and the varying roles played by legally trained persons in those countries. Corporate counsel plays a primary role in engaging outside counsel for a particular litigation or type of litigation, in ensuring that outside counsel enjoys the confidence of appropriate persons in line management and understands the MNE's decision making processes, and thereafter, in using letters, memoranda, telex, and telephone to coordinate the overall direction of the litigation from the MNE's headquarters.

A HYPOTHETICAL DAY FOR MNE CORPORATE COUNSEL

By way of hypothetical illustration, a typical office day for corporate counsel to a MNE might include work on problems such as: Senegal has served notice that a MNE's revenues worldwide will be taxed unitarily irrespective of the MNE's tax posture in other countries; the MNE's use of its trade name in Western Canada is impeded by a "prior use" problem in Saskatoon; a Uruguayan appeals court has held that the MNE's trade name is generic and thus not subject to legal protection in Uruguay; a line management employee of the MNE's Austrian subsidiary company needs an "L" visa to spend some time at the MNE's headquarters offices in the United States; new advertising from the MNE's advertising department has possible legal implications if placed in newspapers throughout Europe; reports of resale price maintenance agreements being made by certain companies in Transylvania and Neverland need to be checked in light of antitrust implications under United States law and Article 82 implications within the European Union.

Moreover, the MNE's products stolen in Hamburg must be traced through INTERPOL; ways must be explored to get blocked currencies from New Country to the MNE's headquarters in the United States; testimony needs to be prepared for presentation to an environmental control authority in Germany; a presentation must be made to the transportation commissioner of the Province of Ontario to secure permits to increase haulage capacity of the MNE's subsidiary company in Canada; charges of employee discrimination in the Far Islands need to be answered; sale-leaseback agreements need to be negotiated in Sydney; a company needs to be formed for trade name protection in the Unusual Islands; an expropriation in Libya requires attention; the Philippine and Saudi Arabian governments want to increase their equity participation in all existing MNE's joint ventures in each country; certain inquiries by the United States Federal Trade Commission need to he answered; someone from the American Bar Association wants counsel to serve on an international trade committee; all standard form contracts used by the MNE and its subsidiary companies are due for another review; line management people are interested in hearing ideas about ways to avoid legal problems in connection with their proposals for new company activity.

If problems are not to be in the same posture when the MNE's corporate counsel arrives at the office the following day, effective assisting counsel in various countries must be available to help with advancing the MNE's legal interests.

CHAPTER TWO

THE WORLD TRADE ORGANIZATION (WTO)

The need to balance the protection of local industries from harm by foreign competitors and the encouragement of trade across national borders is a recurrent theme in the law of international business transactions. There has been a shift in recent years toward freer international trade because of diminished restrictions on imported goods. However, trade problems associated with the movement of goods across national borders still arise because of restrictive trade devices which impede or distort trade.

Common devices include tariff barriers (e.g., import duties and export duties) as well as certain nontariff trade barriers (NTBs) such as import quotas, import licensing procedures, safety, environmental and other minimum manufacturing standards, import testing requirements, complex customs procedures (including valuation), government procurement policies, and government subsidies or countervailing measures. For example, during a part of 1982, France required that all video recorders entering France had to do so through a small customs post at Poitiers and carry documentation written in French. Product distribution practices have been an effective NTB in Japan. The Japanese have banned from importation a food preservative which is essential to preserve the edibility of certain agricultural products from abroad.

Efforts by countries to limit disruptive trade practices are commonly found in bilateral treaties of friendship, commerce and navigation (FCN), which open the territory of each signatory nation to imports arriving from the other signatory nation. Such bilateral FCN treaty clauses are usually linked to other preferential trade agreements. In a bilateral arrangement, such linkage will most often be through a reciprocal "most favored nation" (MFN) clause. In a MFN clause, both parties agree not to extend to any other nation trade arrangements which are more favorable than available under the bilateral treaty, unless the more favorable trade arrangements are immediately *also* available to the signatory of the bilateral treaty.

In various parts of the world, two or more countries have joined in customs unions or free trade areas in order to facilitate trade between those countries and to acquire increased bargaining power in trade discussions with countries which already enjoy a strong trade position. (See Chapter 10, page 388, below, for a more extended discussion.)

The General Agreement on Tariffs and Trade (GATT), now replaced by the new World Trade Organization (WTO), was an international arrangement with over one hundred countries as Contracting States which regularly held multilateral trade negotiations (MTN) seeking ways of making international trade more open. These periodic negotiations cumulatively reduced tariff barriers by an average of up to eighty percent below those existing three decades before. After the most recent multilateral negotiations, the Uruguay Round, average tariff rates of developed countries on dutiable manufactured imports were cut from 6.3 percent to 3.9 percent. Tariff reductions are one of the success stories of GATT. But not all nations participated in the GATT or are members of its replacement, the WTO. For example, both Russia and China are seeking membership in the WTO, but are not yet Members. Late in 1999, China and the United States finally reached agreement on WTO membership terms and conditions for the PRC. Nontariff trade barriers (NTBs) are also addressed in the WTO Covered Agreements, which include agreements designed to lessen or to eliminate NTBs such as complex customs valuation procedures, import licensing systems, product standards, subsidies and countervailing duties, and dumping practices.

An international investor may be concerned primarily about the amount of tariff costs in the United States or in a host country, or in knowing what prohibitions or delays may interfere with the taking of goods into or out of a country. A recognition that the lawyer helping to shape an international business transaction may be interested equally in trade barrier trends, associated with the WTO and United

States participation in it, makes necessary some familiarity with overall, framework mechanisms of international trade in goods.

THE GENERAL AGREEMENT ON TARIFFS AND TRADE: HISTORY AND PROVISIONS

Participants in the Bretton Woods meetings in 1944 recognized a post-War need to reduce trade obstacles in order to foster freer trade. They envisioned the creation of an International Trade Organization (ITO) to achieve the desired result. Fifty-three countries met in Havana in 1948 to complete drafting the Charter of an ITO that would be the international organizational umbrella underneath which negotiations could occur periodically to deal with tariff reductions. A framework for such negotiations had already been staked out in Geneva in 1947, in a document entitled the General Agreement on Tariffs and Trade (GATT). Twenty-three nations participated in that first GATT session, India, Chile, Cuba and Brazil representing the developing world. China participated; Japan and West Germany did not. Stringent trading rules were adopted only where there were no special interests of major participants to alter them. The developing nations objected to many of the strict rules, arguing for special treatment justified on development needs, but they achieved few successes in drafting GATT.

The ITO Charter was never ratified. The United States Congress in the late 1940s was unwilling to join more new international organizations, thus U.S. ratification of the ITO Charter could not be secured. Nonetheless, and moving by way of the President's power to make executive agreements, the United States did join twenty-one other countries, as Contracting Parties, in signing a Protocol of Provisional Application of the General Agreement on Tariffs and Trade (61 Stat.Pts. 5, 6) (popularly called the "GATT Agreement").

From 1947 to 1986, GATT was concerned primarily with international trade of goods. The central features of GATT, as reflected by the Articles of the Agreement, include Article I, which makes a general commitment to the long standing practice of most favored nation treatment (MFN) by requiring each Contracting Party to accord unconditional MFN status to all other Contracting Parties. Thus, any privilege granted by any Contracting Party to any product imported from any other country must also be "immediately and unconditionally" granted to any "like product" imported from any Contracting Parties.

Although addressed to national treatment regarding internal taxation and regulation, GATT Article III incorporates the practice of according national treatment to imported goods by providing, with enumerated exceptions, that the products of one Contracting State, when imported into any other Contracting State, shall receive most favored nation (MFN) treatment. In this context, MFN treatment requires that the products of the exporting GATT Contracting State be treated no less favorably than domestic products of the importing Contracting State under its laws and regulations concerning sale, internal resale, purchase, transportation and use.

In addition to requiring MFN treatment, GATT prohibits any use of certain kinds of quantitative restrictions. Although GATT does permit "duties, taxes or other charges", Article XI prohibits the use of other "prohibitions or restrictions" on imports from Contracting Parties. It specifically prohibits the use of "quotas, import or export licenses or other measures" to restrict imports from a Contracting Party. Article XIII requires non-discrimination in quantitative trade restrictions, by barring an importing Contracting State from applying any prohibition or restriction to the products of another Contracting State, "unless the importation of the like product of *all* third countries ... is similarly prohibited or restricted." (emphasis added).

While GATT does permit nondiscriminatory "duties, taxes and other charges," the powers of a Contracting Party are limited even as to these devices. First, GATT Article X requires that notice be given of any new or changed national regulations which affect international trade, by requiring the prompt publication by any Contracting Party of those "laws, regulations, judicial decisions and administrative rulings of general application" which pertain to the classification or the valuation of products for customs purposes, or to rates of duty, taxes or other charges, or to requirements, restrictions or prohibitions on imports or exports or on the transfer of payments therefor, or affecting their sale, distribution, transportation, insurance, warehousing, inspection, exhibitions, processing, mixing or other use....

Second, the Contracting Parties commit themselves, under GATT Article XXVIII to a continuing series of MTN ("from time to time") to seek further reductions in tariff levels and other barriers to international trade. Such negotiations are to be "on a reciprocal and mutually advantageous basis." GATT negotiated tariff rates (called "concessions" or "bindings"), which are listed in the "tariff Schedules", are deposited with GATT by each participating country. These concessions must be granted to imports from any Contracting Party, both because of the GATT required MFN treatment, and also because Article II specifically requires use of the negotiated rates.

Framers of GATT were well aware that a commitment to freer trade could cause serious, adverse economic consequences from time to time within part or all of a country's domestic economy, particularly its labor sector. The GATT contains at least seven safety valves (in nine clauses of the Agreement) to permit a country, in appropriate circumstances, to respond to domestic pressures while remaining a participant in GATT. Two safety valves deal with antidumping duties and countervailing subsidies.

"Dumping" occurs when the products of one country are introduced into the commerce of another country at less than the fair value of the products, at least as measured by the normal sale price in the domestic market of the exporting company. Article VI recognizes that dumping must be prevented, if it causes or threatens material injury to an established industry in the importing Contracting State or materially retards the establishment of a domestic industry in it. Article VI permits a country to impose an antidumping duty under appropriate circumstances when dumping has caused such harm.

A "subsidy" or "bounty" may be bestowed by the exporting Contracting State on goods produced within its territory. Article VI also recognizes that such subsidies must be prevented, if they cause or threaten material injury to an established industry of the importing Contracting State or materially retard the establishment of a domestic industry in it. The Article authorizes a country to impose a countervailing duty as a special duty levied for the purpose of offsetting any bounty or subsidy bestowed, directly or indirectly, by a Contracting State on merchandise produced and exported from it. However, the countervailing duty must not be levied in an amount greater than the estimated bounty or subsidy granted.

THE GATT MULTINATIONAL TRADE NEGOTIATIONS (ROUNDS)

Under the auspices of GATT Article XXVIII, the Contracting Parties committed themselves to hold periodic multinational trade negotiations (MTN or "Rounds"). They have held eight such Rounds to date, but the Millennium Round failed to start as scheduled late in 1999. An array of diverging interests, and street protests in Seattle led by labor and environmental groups, caused the delay.

While the first five Rounds concentrated on item by item tariff reductions, the "Kennedy Round" (1964–1967) was noted for its achievement of across-the-board tariff reductions. In 1961, GATT began to consider how to approach the increasing trade disparity with the developing world. In 1964, GATT adopted Part IV, which introduced a principle of "diminished expectations of reciprocity". Reciprocity remained a goal, but developed nations would not expect concessions from developing nations which were inconsistent with developmental needs. For the developing nations, nonreciprocity meant freedom to protect domestic markets from import competition. Import substitution was a major focus of developmental theory in the 1960s, and developing nations saw keeping their markets closed as a way to save these domestic industries. Although they also sought preferential treatment of their exports, that was a demand which would remain unsatisfied for another decade.

The "Tokyo Round" (1973–1979) engendered agreements about several areas of nontariff barrier (NTB) trade restraints. Nearly a dozen major agreements on nontariff barrier issues were produced in the Tokyo Round. In the early 1970s, national and regional generalized preference schemes developed to favor the exports of developing nations. The foreign debt payment problems of the developing nations suggest that they need to generate revenue to pay these debts, and that developmental theory must shift from import substitution to export promotion.

In 1986, the "Uruguay Round" of multilateral trade negotiations began at a Special Session of the GATT Contracting States. This Uruguay Round included separate negotiations on trade in goods and on trade in services, with separate groups of negotiators dealing with each topic. Subtopics for negotiation by subgroups included nontariff barriers, agriculture, subsidies and countervailing duties, intellectual property rights and counterfeit goods, safeguards, tropical products, textiles, investment policies, and dispute resolution. The negotiating sessions were extraordinarily complex, but were able to achieve a successful conclusion at the end of 1993.

Because protectionist barriers to international trade in services were stifling, the United States and several other countries insisted that there should be a General Agreement on Trade in Services (GATS) within GATT. In the United States, trade in services accounts for two-thirds of the

Nation's GNP; services provide work for nearly two-thirds of the work force. Services account for almost one-third of U.S. trade abroad.

The 1947 GATT Agreement and its subsequent multinational negotiating rounds were quite successful in reducing tariff duty levels on trade in goods. This was its original purpose, and the mechanism was well-adapted to accomplishing that purpose. However, its effectiveness was also limited to trade in goods, and primarily to reduction of tariffs in such trade. It was not designed to affect trade in services, trade-related intellectual property rights or trade-related investment measures. As tariff duty rates declined, the trade-distorting effects of these other issues became relatively more important.

Even within "trade in goods," the 1947 GATT had limitations. It included a Protocol of Provisional Application which allowed numerous grandfathered exceptions to Members' obligations under the GATT Agreement. The Protocol exempted from GATT disciplines the national laws of Member States which were already enacted and in force at the time of adoption of the Protocol. Further, the 1947 GATT did not have an institutional charter, and was not intended to become an international organization on trade. It did later develop institutional structures and acquired quasi-organizational status, but there was always a lack of a recognized organizational structure. This lack was most often perceived in the inability of GATT to resolve disputes which were brought to it. Dispute settlement procedures were dependent upon the acquiescence of the individual Member States.

THE WORLD TRADE ORGANIZATION (WTO) AND GATT 1994

The WTO is the product of the Uruguay Round of GATT negotiations, which was successfully completed in 1994. The Uruguay Round produced a package of agreements, the Agreement Establishing the World Trade Organization and its Annexes, which include the General Agreement on Tariffs and Trade 1994 (GATT 1994) and a series of Multilateral Trade Agreements (the Covered Agreements), and a series of Plurilateral Trade Agreements. See 33 Int. Legal Mat. 1130 (1994).

GATT 1947 and GATT 1994 are two distinct agreements. GATT 1994 incorporates the provisions of GATT 1947, except for the Protocol of Provisional Application, which is expressly excluded. Thus, the problems created by exempting the existing national laws at the time of the adoption of the Protocol will now be avoided by this exclusion in the Covered Agreements. Otherwise, in cases involving a conflict between GATT 1947 and GATT 1994, GATT 1947 controls. The WTO will be guided by the decisions, procedures and customary practices under GATT.

Annexed to the WTO Agreement are several Multilateral Trade Agreements. As to trade in goods, they include Agreements on Agriculture, Textiles, Antidumping, Subsidies and Countervailing Measures, Safeguards, Technical Barriers to Trade, Sanitary and Phytosanitary Measures, Pre-shipment Inspection, Rules of Origin, and Import License Procedures. In addition to trade in goods, they include a General Agreement on Trade in Services and Agreements on Trade–Related Aspects of Intellectual Property Rights and Trade–Related Investment Measures. Affecting all of these agreements is the Understanding on Rules and Procedures Governing the Settlement of Disputes. All of the Multilateral Trade Agreements are binding on all Members of the World Trade Organization.

In addition to the Multilateral Trade Agreements, there are also Plurilateral Trade Agreements which are also annexed to the WTO Agreement. These agreements, however, are not binding on all WTO Members, and Members can choose to adhere to them or not. They include Agreements on Government Procurement, Trade in Civil Aircraft, International Dairy and an Arrangement Regarding Bovine Meat. States which do not join the plurilateral trade agreements do not receive reciprocal benefits under them.

The duties of the World Trade Organization are to facilitate the implementation, administer the operations and further the objectives of all these agreements. Its duties also include the resolution of disputes under the agreements, reviews of trade policy and cooperation with the International Monetary Fund (IMF) and the World Bank. To achieve these goals, the WTO Agreement does provide a charter for the new organization, but provides for only a minimalist institution, with institutional and procedural capabilities, but with no substantive competence being given to the organization itself. Thus, there is a unified administration of pre-existing and new obligations under all agreements concerning trade in goods, including the Uruguay Round Agreements. In addition, the administration of the new obligations on trade in services and intellectual property are brought under the same roof.

On the other hand, both the International Monetary Fund (IMF) and the World Bank have executive powers for their institutions, which the WTO does not have. The WTO as an institution has no power to bring actions on its own initiative. Under the provisions of the WTO Agreement, only the Members of WTO can initiate actions under the Dispute Settlement Understanding. Enforcement of WTO obligations is primarily through permitting Members to retaliate or cross retaliate against other members, rather than by execution of WTO institutional orders. However, the WTO has an internationally recognized organizational structure, which is a step forward from the status of GATT as an organization.

WTO DECISION–MAKING

The World Trade Organization is structured in three tiers. One tier is the Ministerial Conference, which meets biennially and is composed of representatives of all WTO Members. Each Member has an equal voting weight, which is unlike the representation in the IMF and World Bank where there is weighted voting, and financially powerful states have more power over the decision-making process. The Ministerial Conference is responsible for all WTO functions, and is able to make any decisions necessary. It has the power to authorize new multilateral negotiations and to adopt the results of such negotiations. The Ministerial Conference, by a three-fourths vote, is authorized to grant waivers of obligations to Members in exceptional circumstances. It also has the power to adopt interpretations of Covered Agreements. When the Ministerial Conference is in recess, its functions are performed by the General Council.

The second tier is the General Council which has executive authority over the day to day operations and functions of the WTO. It is composed of representatives of all WTO Members, and each member has an equal voting weight. It meets whenever it is appropriate. The General Council also has the power to adopt interpretations of Covered Agreements.

The third tier comprises the councils, bodies and committees which are accountable to the Ministerial Conference or General Council. Ministerial Conference committees include Committees on Trade and Development, Balance of Payment Restrictions, Budget, Finance and Administration. General Council bodies include the Dispute Settlement Body, the Trade Policy Review Body, and Councils for Trade in Goods, Trade in Services and Trade–Related Intellectual Property Rights. The Councils are all created by the WTO Agreement and are open to representatives of all Member States. The Councils also have the authority to create subordinate organizations. Other committees, such as the Committee on Subsidies and Countervailing Measures are created by specific individual agreements.

Of the General Council bodies, the two which are likely to be most important are the Dispute Settlement Body (DSB) and the Trade Policy Review Body (TPRB). The DSB is a special meeting of the General Council, and therefore includes all WTO Members. It has responsibility for resolution of disputes under all the Covered Agreements, and will be discussed in more detail below, under Dispute Resolution.

The purpose of the Trade Policy Review–Mechanism (TPRM) is to improve adherence to the WTO agreements and obligations, and to obtain greater transparency. Individual Members of WTO each prepare a "Country Report" on their trade policies and perceived adherence to the WTO Covered Agreements. The WTO Secretariat also prepares a report on each Member, but from the perspective of the Secretariat. The Trade Policy Review Body (TPRB) then reviews the trade policies of each Member based on these two reports. At the end of the review, the TPRB issues its own report concerning the adherence of the Member's trade policy to the WTO Covered Agreements. The TPRB has no enforcement capability, but the report is sent to the next meeting of the WTO Ministerial Conference. It is then up to the Ministerial Conference to evaluate the trade practices and policies of the Member.

The process of decision-making in the WTO Ministerial Conference and General Council relies upon "consensus" as the norm, just as it did for decision-making under GATT 1947. "Consensus", in this context means that no Member formally objects to a proposed decision. Thus, consensus is not obtained if any one Member formally objects, and has often been very difficult to obtain, which proved to be a weakness in the operation of GATT. However, there are many exceptions to the consensus formula under WTO, and some new concepts (such as "inverted consensus", discussed below) which are designed to ease the process of decision-making under WTO.

Article IX(1) of the WTO Agreement first provides that "the practice of decision-making by consensus" followed under GATT shall be continued. The next sentence of that provision, however, states that "where a decision cannot be arrived at by consensus, the matter at issue shall be decided by voting", except where otherwise provided. The ultimate resolution of the conflict between these two sentences is not completely clear.

There are a number of exceptions to the requirement for consensus that are expressly created under the WTO Agreement. One such exception is decisions by the Dispute Settlement Body, which has its own rules (see below). Another set of exceptions concerns decisions on waivers, interpretations and amendments of the Covered Agreements. Waivers of obligations may be granted and amendments adopted to Covered Agreements only by the Ministerial Conference. Amendments of Multilateral Trade Agreements usually require a consensus, but where a decision on a proposed amendment cannot obtain consensus, the decision on that amendment is to be made in certain circumstances by a two-thirds majority vote. In "exceptional circumstances", the Ministerial Conference is authorized to grant waivers of obligations under a Covered Agreement by a three-fourths vote. Another exception to the consensus requirement allows procedural rules in both the Ministerial Conference and the General Council to be decided by a majority vote of the Members, unless otherwise provided.

However, in addition to these express exceptions, Article IX (1) seems to indicate that where a decision would normally be made by consensus, but consensus cannot be obtained, the matter will then be decided "by voting." Whether this provision destroys the basic consensus requirement whenever there is an impasse is not yet clear. It is possible that any issue which fails to obtain a consensus, but has majority support, can be determined "by voting", as long as there is no other express provision. It is also not completely clear what procedure is to be used to satisfy the "by voting" standard. It is also possible, however, that this provision is only to be applied to decisions which the Ministerial Conference must make to assure the continuance of a workable WTO system. An illustration of such a decision could be the continuation, modification or termination of the dispute settlement procedure.

WTO AGREEMENTS AND U.S. LAW

The WTO Covered Agreements concern not only trade in goods, but also trade in services (GATS), and trade-related aspects of intellectual property (TRIPS). The basic concepts that GATT applied to trade in goods (described above) are now applied to these areas through GATS and TRIPS. In the WTO Covered Agreements, the basic concepts of GATT 1947 and its associated agreements are elaborated and clarified. In addition, there is an attempt to transform all protectionist measures relating to agriculture (such as import bans and quotas, etc.) into only tariff barriers, which can then be lowered in subsequent MTN Rounds (a process known as "tariffication"). WTO also contains some superficial provisions on trade-related investment measures (TRIMS). Some of the WTO provisions, particularly those concerning trade in goods, will be discussed in more detail below, in relation to United States trade law.

As of 2000, there were 136 Member States of the World Trade Organization. This does not include Russia or the other formerly Soviet nations or the People's Republic of China, although both Russia and China are seeking membership. The United States enacted legislation to implement WTO and the Covered Agreements on December 3, 1994, but did not ratify them as a treaty. The implementing legislation was submitted to Congress under the "fast track" procedures of 19 U.S.C.A. § 2112, which required that the agreement and its implementing legislation be considered as a whole by Congress, and which also prohibits Congressional amendments to the implementing legislation. The Congressional authority for "fast track" procedures also required that the President give ninety days notice of his intention to enter into such an agreement. This "fast track" legislation expired on October 3, 1994, and has not yet been renewed.

Neither GATT 1947 nor the WTO Agreement, GATT 1994 and the other Covered Agreements have been ratified as treaties, and therefore comprise international obligations of the United States only to the extent that they are incorporated in United States' implementing legislation. GATT 1947 was not considered controlling by the courts of the United States, and these courts have always held themselves bound to the U.S. legislation actually enacted. See, e.g., Suramerica de Aleaciones Laminadas, CA v. United States, 966 F.2d 660 (Fed. Cir.1992). The WTO Covered Agreements will be considered to have a non-self-executed status, and therefore are likely to be regarded in the same manner as GATT 1947.

DISPUTE SETTLEMENT UNDER WTO

WTO provides a unified system for settling international trade disputes through the Dispute Settlement Understanding (DSU) and using the Dispute

Settlement Body (DSB). The DSB is a special assembly of the WTO General Council, and includes
all WTO Members. There are five stages in the
resolution of disputes under WTO: 1) Consultation;
2) Panel establishment, investigation and report; 3)
Appellate review of the panel report; 4) Adoption of
the panel and appellate decision; and 5) Implementation of the decision adopted. There is also a parallel process for binding arbitration, if both parties
agree to submit this dispute to arbitration, rather
than to a DSB panel. In addition, during the implementation phase (5), the party subject to an adverse
decision may seek arbitration as a matter of right.

Although the DSU offers a unified dispute resolution system that is applicable across all sectors and
all WTO Covered Agreements, there are many specialized rules for disputes which arise under them.
Such specialized rules appear in the Agreements on
Textiles, Antidumping, Subsidies and Countervailing Measures, Technical Barriers to Trade, Sanitary
and Phytosanitary Measures, Customs Valuation,
General Agreement on Trade in Services, Financial
Services and Air Transport Services. The special
provisions in these individual Covered Agreements
govern, where applicable, and prevail in any conflict
with the general provisions of the DSU.

Under WTO, unlike under GATT 1947, the DSU
practically assures that panels will be established
upon request by a Member. Further, under WTO,
unlike under GATT 1947, the DSU virtually en-
sures the adoption of unmodified panel and appellate body decisions. It accomplishes this by requir-

ing the DSB to adopt panel reports and appellate body decisions automatically and without amendment unless they are rejected by a consensus of all Members. This "inverted consensus" requires that all Members of the DSB, including the Member who prevailed in the dispute, decide to reject the dispute resolution decision; and that no Member formally favor that decision. Such an outcome seems unlikely. This inverted consensus requirement is imposed on both the adoption of panel reports or appellate body decisions and also on the decision to establish a panel.

The potential resolutions of a dispute under DSU range from a "mutually satisfactory solution" agreed to by the parties under the first, or consultation phase, to authorized retaliation under the last, or implementation, phase. The preferred solution is always any resolution that is mutually satisfactory to the parties. After a panel decision, there are three types of remedies available to the prevailing party, if a mutually satisfactory solution cannot be obtained. One is for the respondent to bring the measure found to violate a Covered Agreement into conformity with the Agreement. A second is for the prevailing Member to receive compensation from the respondent which both parties agree is sufficient to compensate for any injury caused by the measure found to violate a Covered Agreement. Finally, if no such agreement can be reached, a prevailing party can be authorized to suspend some of its concessions under the Covered Agreements to the respondent. These suspended concessions, called "retaliation," can be authorized within the same trade sector and agreement; or, if that will not create sufficient compensation, can be authorized across trade sectors and agreements.

Phase 1: Consultation. Any WTO Member who believes that the Measures of another Member are not in conformity with the Covered Agreements may call for consultations on those measures. The respondent has ten days to reply to the call for consultations and must agree to enter into consultation within 30 days. If the respondent does not enter into consultations within the 30 day period, the party seeking consultations can immediately request the establishment of a panel under DSU, which puts the dispute into Phase 2.

Once consultations begin, the parties have 60 days to achieve a settlement. The goal is to seek a positive solution to the dispute, and the preferred resolution is to reach whatever solution is mutually satisfactory to the parties. If such a settlement cannot be obtained after 60 days of consultations, the party seeking consultations may request the establishment of a panel under DSU, which moves the dispute into Phase 2.

Third parties with an interest in the subject-matter of the consultations may seek to be included in them. If such inclusion is rejected, they may seek their own consultations with the other Member. Alternatives to consultations may be provided through the use of conciliation, mediation or good offices, where all parties agree to use the alternative

process. Any party can terminate the use of conciliation, mediation or good offices and then seek the
establishment of a panel under DSU, which will
move the dispute into Phase 2.

*Phase 2: Panel establishment, investigation and
report.* If consultations between the parties fail, the
party seeking the consultations (the complainant)
may request the DSB to establish a panel to investigate, report and resolve the dispute. The DSB must
establish such a panel upon request, unless the DSB
expressly decides by consensus not to establish the
panel. Since an "inverted consensus" is required to
reject the establishment of the panel and the complainant Member must be part of that consensus, it
is very likely that a panel will be established.
Roughly 100 panels were established in the first five
years of operation of the DSU.

The WTO Secretariat is to maintain a list of well-
qualified persons who are available to serve as
panelists. The panels are usually composed of three
individuals from that list who are not citizens of
either party. If the parties agree, a panel can be
composed of five such individuals. The parties can
also agree to appoint citizens of a party to a panel.
Panelists may be either nongovernmental individuals or governmental officials, but they are to be
selected so as to ensure their independence. Thus,
there is a bias towards independent individuals who
are not citizens of any party. If a citizen of a party
is appointed, his government may not instruct that
citizen how to vote, for the panelist must be independent. By the same reasoning, a governmental

official of a non-party Member who is subject to instructions from his government would not seem to fit the profile of an independent panelist.

The WTO Secretariat proposes nominations of the panelists. Parties may not normally oppose the nominations, except for "compelling reasons." The parties are given twenty days to agree on the panelists and the composition of the panel. If such agreement is not forthcoming, the WTO Director–General is authorized to appoint the panelists, in consultation with other persons in the Secretariat.

The "cases" brought to DSB panels can involve either violations of Covered Agreements or nonviolation nullification and impairment of benefits under the Covered Agreements. A prima facie case of nullification impairment arises when one Member infringes upon the "obligations assumed under a Covered Agreement." Such infringement creates a presumption against the infringing Member, but the presumption can be rebutted by a showing that the complaining Member has suffered no adverse effect from the infringement.

The panels receive pleadings and rebuttals and hear oral arguments. Panels can also engage in fact development from sources outside those presented by the parties. Thus, the procedure has aspects familiar to civil law courts. A panel can, on its own initiative, request information from any body, including experts selected by the panel. It can also obtain confidential information in some circumstances from an administrative body which is part of the government of a Member, without any prior consent from that Member. Finally, a panel can establish its own group of experts to provide reports to it on factual or scientific issues.

A panel is obligated to produce two written reports—an interim and a final report. A panel is supposed to submit a final written report to the DSB within six months of its establishment. The report will contain its findings of fact, findings of law, decision and the rationale for its decision. Before the final report is issued, the panel is supposed to provide an interim report to the parties. The purpose of this interim report is to apprise the parties of the panel's current analysis of the issues and to permit the parties to comment on that analysis. The final report of the panel need not change any of the findings or conclusions in its interim report unless it is persuaded to do so by a party's comments. However, if it is not so persuaded, it is obligated to explain in its final report why it is not so persuaded.

The decisions in panel reports are final as to issues of fact. The decisions in panel reports are not necessarily final as to issues of law. Panel decisions on issues of law are subject to review by the Appellate Body, which is Phase 3, and explained below. Any party can appeal a panel report, and as is explained below it is expected that appeals will usually be taken.

Phase 3: Appellate review of the panel report. Appellate review of panel reports is available at the request of any party, unless the DSB rejects that request by an "inverted consensus." There is no threshold requirement for an appellant to present a substantial substantive legal issue. Thus, most panel decisions are appealed as a matter of course. However, the Appellate Body can only review the panel reports on questions of law or legal interpretation.

The Appellate Body is a new institution in the international trade organization and its process. GATT 1947 had nothing comparable to it. The Appellate Body is composed of seven members (or judges) who are appointed by the DSB to four year terms. Each judge may be reappointed, but only once, to a second four year term. Each judge is to be a recognized authority on international trade law and the Covered Agreements. The review of any panel decision is performed by three judges out of the seven. The parties do not, however, have any influence on which judges are selected to review a particular panel report. There is a schedule, created by the Appellate Body itself, for the rotation for sitting of each of the judges. Thus, a party might try to appear before a favored judge by timing the start of the dispute settlement process to arrive at the Appellate Body at the right moment on the rotation schedule, but even this limited approach has difficulties.

The Appellate Body receives written submissions from the parties and has 60, or in some cases 90, days in which to render its decision. The Appellate Body review is limited to issues of law and legal interpretation. The panel decision may be upheld, modified, or reversed by the Appellate Body decision. Appellate Body decisions will be anonymous, and ex parte communications are not permitted, which will make judge-shopping by parties more than usually difficult.

Phase 4: Adoption of the panel or Appellate Body decision. Appellate Body determinations are submitted to the DSB. Panel decisions which are not appealed are also submitted to the DSB. Once either type of decision is submitted to the DSB, the DSB must automatically adopt them without modification or amendment at its next meeting unless the decision is rejected by all Members of the DSB through the form of "inverted consensus" discussed previously.

An alternative to Phases 2 through 4 is arbitration, if both parties agree. The arbitration must be binding on the parties, and there is no appeal from the arbitral tribunal's decision to the DSB Appellate Body.

Phase 5: Implementation of the decision adopted. Once a panel or Appellate Body decision is adopted by the DSB, implementation is a three-step process. In the first step, the Member found to have a measure which violates its WTO obligations has "a reasonable time" (usually 15 months) to bring those measures into conformity with the WTO obligations. That remedy is the preferred one, and this form of implementation is the principal goal of the

WTO implementation system. To date, most disputes have resulted in compliance in this manner.

If the violating measures are not brought into conformity within a reasonable time, the parties proceed to the second step. In that second step, the parties negotiate to reach an agreement upon a form of "compensation" which will be granted by the party in violation to the injured party. Such "compensation" will usually comprise trade concessions by the violating party to the injured party, which are over and above those already available under the WTO and Covered Agreements. The nature, scope, amount and duration of these additional concessions is at the negotiating parties' discretion, but each side must agree that the final compensation package is fair and is properly related to the injury caused by the violating measures.

If the parties cannot agree on an appropriate amount of compensation within twenty days, the complainant may proceed to the third step. In the third step, the party injured by the violating measures (complainant) seeks authority from the DSB to retaliate against the party whose measures violated its WTO obligations (the respondent). Thus, complainant seeks authority to suspend some of complainant's own WTO obligations in regard to the respondent. The retaliation, thus proposed may be within the same sector and agreement as the violating measure. "Sector" is sometimes broadly defined, as all trade in goods, and sometimes narrowly defined, as in individual services in the Services Sectoral Classification List. "Agreement" is also broadly defined. All the agreements listed in Annex IA to the WTO Agreement are considered to be a single "agreement." If retaliation within the sector and agreement of the violating measure is considered insufficient compensation, the complainant may seek suspension of its obligations across sectors and agreements.

Within 30 days of the complainant's presentation of the request to retaliate, the DSB must grant the request, unless the request is rejected by all the members through an "inverted consensus." However, the respondent may object to the level or scope of the retaliation. Upon such an objection, the issues raised by the objection will be examined by either the Appellate Body or by an arbitrator. The respondent has a right, even if arbitration was not used in Phases 2 through 4, to have an arbitrator review in Phase 5 the appropriateness of the complainant's proposed level and scope of retaliation. The arbitrator will also examine whether the proper procedures and criteria to establish retaliation have been followed. The Phase 5 arbitration is final and binding and the arbitrator's decision is probably not subject to DSB review.

The amount of a U.S. retaliation permitted after the WTO "Bananas" and "Beef Hormones" decisions were not implemented by the EU was contested. The arbitration tribunals for these issues were the original WTO panels, which did not allow the almost $700 million in retaliatory tariffs proposed by the U.S. At the date of publication of this book, the U.S. has levied authorized retaliatory tariffs amounting to about $300 million against European goods because of the EU failure to implement these two WTO decisions. Some notable United States "losses" in WTO dispute settlement concern Japanese film distribution practices (a panel decision the U.S. did *not* appeal), internationally discriminatory U.S. gasoline production requirements, the U.S. shrimp import ban to conserve endangered sea turtles, and U.S. "DISC" corporation export tax shelters.

In antidumping and subsidy cases, the DSB can authorize the imposition of antidumping and countervailing measures.

Both "compensation" in the second step and "retaliation" in the third step of implementation provide only for indirect enforcement of DSB decisions. There is no mechanism for direct enforcement by the WTO of its decisions through WTO orders to suspend trade obligations. Some commentators believe that retaliation will be an effective implementation device; other commentators believe that it will be used rarely. The device was available under GATT 1947, but was actually used only once, in the U.S. Dairy Quotas case.

The division represented by these conflicting commentators represents two different approaches to the nature of both international law and international trade law. One approach seeks a rule-oriented use of the "rule of law"; the other approach seeks a power-oriented use of diplomacy. The United States and less developed countries have traditionally sought to develop a rule-oriented approach to international trade disputes. The European Union and Japan have traditionally sought to use GATT primarily as a forum for diplomatic negotiations, although the EU has begun to file more formal complaints.

A Member which feels its rights under WTO have been violated does not need to take the dispute to the DSB. Even if it does so, and obtains a DSB decision that there is a violation of WTO obligations and authority to retaliate, that authority can be used in two different ways. One use would be to view it as a court order in a domestic judicial proceeding, but one which allows the complainant to use self-help in executing the court order. A second use would be to view it as a device to get the respondent's attention and persuade it to finally engage in serious negotiations because the complainant has exhausted all necessary procedures and now does have a "big stick."

The proponents of the first view believe that DSB decisions will terminate the dispute and allow the parties to put the dispute behind them quickly and proceed to develop their trade relationships further. The quick resolution is believed to be more advantageous than the risk that the "legal approach" will deepen hostility between Members. The proponents of the second view believe that diplomatic use of DSB decisions will provide a more complex, but a more effective, resolution of disputes as the parties use persuasion to negotiate a mutually satisfactory solution to their dispute. This negotiated resolution is believed to be more advantageous than the risks created by the extra delays and frictions which arise in resolving the dispute by negotiation. At this point, it is not possible to predict which of these approaches will actually dominate the use of DSB decisions and authority.

These different views created part of the conflict at the December 1999 Seattle WTO meeting (which failed to launch the Millennium Round). If the DSB is a court, its proceedings should be open and "transparent." However, if it is just another form of government-to-government diplomacy, that has always been held in secret.

IMPORT QUOTAS AND LICENSES UNDER THE WTO

Quantity restrictions, such as numerical quotas on the importation of an item or upon a type of item, continue to exist , despite GATT Article XI which calls for their elimination. Import quotas may be "global" limitations (applying to items originating from anywhere in the world), "bilateral" limitations (applying to items originating from a particular country) and "discretionary" limitations. Quantitative limitations may have arisen from a Treaty of Friendship, Commerce and Navigation or from a narrow international agreement, such as agreements on trade in textiles and textile products. Discretionary limitations, when coupled with a requirement that importation of items must be licensed in advance by local authorities, provide an effective vehicle for gathering statistical data and for raising local revenues. "Tariff-rate quotas" admit a specified quantity of goods at a preferential rate of duty. Once imports reach that quantity, tariffs are normally increased.

The WTO has significantly reduced the number of trade quotas. The Agreement on Textiles will ultimately eliminate the quotas long maintained under the Multi–Fibre Arrangement. Voluntary export restraints (quotas) are severely limited by the Safeguards Agreement. In addition, the WTO removes trade quotas by pressuring for "tariffication," or replacing them with tariffs—sometimes even at extraordinarily high tariff rates. Tariffication is the approach adopted in the WTO Agricultural Agreement. It is expected that high tariff rates will be reduced in subsequent negotiating Rounds. Import licensing schemes are also being phased out under WTO agreements.

GATT/WTO NONTARIFF TRADE BARRIER CODES

There are numerous nontariff trade barriers applicable to imports. Many of these barriers arise out of safety and health regulations. Others concern the environment, consumer protection, product standards and government procurement. Many of the relevant rules were created for legitimate consumer and public protection reasons. They were often created without extensive consideration of their international impact as potential nontariff trade barriers. Nevertheless, the practical impact of legislation of this type is to ban the importation of nonconforming products. Thus, unlike tariffs which can always be paid, and unlike quotas which permit a certain amount of goods to enter the market, nontariff trade barriers have the potential to totally exclude foreign exports.

Multilateral GATT negotiations since the end of World War II have led to a significant decline in world tariff levels, particularly on trade with developed nations. As steadily as tariff barriers have disappeared, nontariff trade barriers (NTBs) have emerged. Health and safety regulations, environmental laws, rules regulating products standards, procurement legislation and customs procedures are often said to present NTB problems. Negotiations over nontariff trade barriers dominated the Tokyo Round of the GATT negotiations during the late 1970s. A number of NTB "codes" (sometimes called "side agreements") emerged from the Tokyo Round. These concerned subsidies, dumping, government procurement, technical barriers (products standards), customs valuation and import licensing. In addition, specific agreements regarding trade in bovine meats, dairy products and civil aircraft were also reached. The United States accepted all of these NTB codes and agreements except the one on dairy products. Most of the necessary implementation of these agreements was accomplished in the Trade Agreements Act of 1979.

Additional GATT codes were agreed upon under the Uruguay Round ending in late 1993. They revisit all of the NTB areas covered by the Tokyo Round Codes and create new codes for sanitary and phyto-sanitary measures (SPS), trade-related investment measures (TRIMs), preshipment inspection, rules of origin, escape clause safeguards and trade-related intellectual property rights (TRIPs). The United States Congress approved and implemented these Codes in December of 1994 under the Uruguay Round Agreements Act.

One problem with nontariff trade barriers is that they are so numerous. Intergovernmental negotia-tion intended to reduce their trade restricting im-pact is both tedious and difficult. There are continu-ing attempts through the World Trade Organization to come to grips with additional specific NTB prob-lems. Furthermore, various trade agreements of the United States have been undertaken in this field. For example, the Canadian–United States Free Trade Area Agreement and the NAFTA built upon the existing GATT agreements to further reduce NTB problems between the United States, Canada and Mexico.

In the *EU Beef Hormones* case, the EU banned imports of growth-enhancing hormone-treated beef from the U.S. and Canada as a health hazard. The Appellate Body ruled that, since the ban was more strict than international standards, the EU needed scientific evidence to back it up. However, the EU had failed to undertake a scientific risk assessment, and the EU's scientific reports did not provide any rational basis to uphold the ban. In fact, the pri-mary EU study had found no evidence of harm to humans from the growth-enhancing-hormones. The Appellate Body ruled that the ban violated the EU's SPS obligations and required the EU to produce scientific evidence to justify the ban within a reasonable time, or to revoke the ban. Arbitrators later determined that 15 months was a reasonable time, but the EU has failed to produce such evidence and the U.S. has retaliated.

THE URUGUAY ROUND AGREEMENT ON AGRICULTURE

Agricultural issues played a central role in the Uruguay Round GATT negotiations. More than any other issue, they delayed completion of the Round from 1990 to 1993. The agreement reached in December of 1993 is a trade liberalizing, market-oriented effort. Each country has made a number of commitments on market access, reduced domestic agricultural support levels and export subsidies. The United States Congress approved of these commitments in December of 1994 by adopting the Uruguay Round Agreements Act.

Broadly speaking nontariff barriers (NTBs) to international agricultural trade are replaced by tariffs that provide substantially the same level of protection. This is known as "tariffication." It applies to virtually all NTBs, including variable levies, import bans, voluntary export restraints and import quotas. Tariffication applies specifically to U.S. agricultural quotas adopted under Section 22 of the Agricultural Adjustment Act. All agricultural tariffs, including those converted from NTBs, are to be reduced by 36 and 24 percent by developed and developing countries, respectively, over 6 and 10 year periods. Certain minimum access tariff quotas apply when imports amount to less than 3 to 5 percent of domestic consumption. An escape clause exists for tariffed imports at low prices or upon a surge of importation depending upon the existing degree of import penetration.

Regarding domestic support for agriculture, some programs with minimal impact on trade are exempt from change. These programs are known as "green box policies." They include governmental support for agricultural research, disease control, infrastructure and food security. Green box policies are also exempt from GATT/WTO challenge or countervailing duties for 9 years. Direct payments to producers that are not linked to production are also generally exempt. This will include income support, adjustment assistance, and environmental and regional assistance payments. Furthermore, direct payments to support crop reductions and *de minimis* payments are exempted in most cases.

After removing all of the exempted domestic agricultural support programs, the agreement on agriculture arrives at a calculation known as the Total Aggregate Measurement of Support (Total AMS). This measure is the basis for agricultural support reductions under the agreement. Developed nations must reduce their Total AMS by 20 percent over 6 years, developing nations by 13.3 percent over 10 years. United States reductions undertaken in 1985 and 1990 suggest that little or no U.S. action will be required to meet this obligation.

Agricultural export subsidies of developed nations must be reduced by 36 percent below 1986–1990 levels over 6 years and the quantity of subsidized agricultural exports by 21 percent. Developing nations must meet corresponding 24 and 14 percent reductions over 10 years.

All conforming tariffications, reductions in domestic support for agriculture and export subsidy alterations are essentially exempt from challenge for 9 years within the GATT/WTO on grounds such as serious prejudice in export markets or nullification and impairment of agreement benefits. However, countervailing duties may be levied against all unlawfully subsidized exports of agricultural goods except for subsidies derived from so-called national "green box policies" (discussed above).

WTO PUBLIC PROCUREMENT CODE

Where public procurement is involved, and the taxpayer's money is at issue, virtually every nation has some form of legislation or tradition that favors buying from domestic suppliers. The Tokyo Round GATT Procurement Code was not particularly successful at opening up government purchasing. Only Austria, Canada, the twelve European Union states, Finland, Hong Kong, Israel, Japan, Norway, Singapore, Sweden, Switzerland and the United States adhered to that Procurement Code. This was also partly the result of the 1979 Code's many exceptions. For example, the Code did not apply to contracts below its threshold amount of $150,000 SDR (about $171,000 since 1988), service contracts, and procurement by entities on each country's reserve list (including most national defense items). Because procurement in the European Union and Japan is often decentralized, many contracts fell below the SDR threshold and were therefore GATT exempt. By dividing up procurement into smaller contracts national preferences were retained. United States government procurement tends to be more centralized and thus more likely to be covered by the GATT Code. This pattern may help explain why Congress restrictively amended the Buy American Act in 1988.

Chapter 13 of the North American Free Trade Area Agreement opened government procurement to U.S., Canadian and Mexican suppliers on contracts as small as $25,000. However, the goods supplied must have at least 50 percent North American content. These special procurement rules effectively created an exception to the GATT Procurement Code which otherwise applied. The thresholds are $50,000 for goods and services provided to federal agencies and $250,000 for government-owned enterprises (notably PEMEX and CFE). These regulations are particularly important because Mexico, unlike Canada, has not traditionally joined in GATT procurement codes.

The Uruguay Round Procurement Code took effect in 1996 and replaced the 1979 Tokyo Round GATT Procurement Code. The Uruguay Round

Code expanded the coverage of the prior GATT Code to include procurement of services, construction, government-owned utilities, and some state and local (subcentral) contracts. The U.S. and the European Union applied the new Code's provisions on government-owned utilities and subcentral contracts as early as April 15, 1994.

Various improvements to the procedural rules surrounding procurement practices and dispute settlement under the Uruguay Round Code attempt to reduce tensions in this difficult area. For example, an elaborate system for bid protests is established. Bidders who believe the 1979 Code's procedural rules have been abused will be able to lodge, litigate and appeal their protests. The Uruguay Round Procurement Code became part of U.S. law in December of 1994 under the Uruguay Round Agreements Act. The United States has made, with few exceptions, all procurement by executive agencies subject to the Federal Acquisition Regulations under the Code's coverage (i.e., to suspend application of the normal Buy American preferences to such procurement).

CHAPTER THREE
RESTRICTIONS ON IMPORTS

An importable item must "pass customs". Usually, the passage through customs and physical entry into a country occur simultaneously. An exception occurs when goods enter certain locations, within a country, which are classified as "free trade zones" (called in the United States "foreign trade zones"), discussed below. When goods arrive at the United States border, the consignee (or an agent, such as a customs broker) files both "entry" and "entry summary" forms which are used to determine the classification and valuation of the imported goods. At the same time, a deposit of the amount of estimated customs duties is made with customs officials. A procedure for immediate release of imported goods is available, as is the use of consolidated periodic statements for all entries made during a billing period.

THE ORIGINS OF UNITED STATES TARIFFS

Article I, Section 8, of the United States Constitution authorizes Congress to levy uniform tariffs on imports. Tariff legislation must originate in the House of Representatives. Although tariffs were primarily viewed as revenue-raising measures at the founding of the nation, it was not long before tariffs became used for openly protectionist purposes. The Tariff Act of 1816 initiated this change in outlook. During much of the Nineteenth Century, the United States legislated heavy protective tariffs. These were justified as necessary to protect the country's infant industries and to force the South to engage in more trade with the North (not with Europe). Exceptions were made to the high level of tariffs for selected United States imports. These typically flowed from conditional most-favored-nation reciprocity treaties. The first of these treaties involved Canada (1854) and Hawaii (1875).

As the United States moved into the 20th Century, additional tariffs in excess of the already high level of protection were authorized. "Countervailing duty" tariffs were created in 1890 to combat export subsidies of European nations, particularly Germany. After 1916, additional duties could also be assessed if "dumping practices" were involved. Early American dumping legislation was largely a reaction to marketplace competition from foreign cartels. Throughout all of these years the constitutionality of protective tariffs was never clearly resolved. In 1928, however, the United States Supreme Court firmly ruled that the enactment of protective tariffs was constitutional. This decision, followed by the crash of the stock market in 1929, led to the enactment of the Smoot–Hawley Tariff Act of 1930. This Act set some of the highest rates of tariff duties in the history of the United States. It represents the last piece of tariff legislation that Congress passed without international negotiations. These tariffs remain part of the United States law and are generally referred to as "Column 2 tariffs" under the Harmonized Tariff Schedule (HTS).

Since 1930, changes in the levels of tariffs applicable to goods entering the United States have chiefly been achieved through international trade agreements negotiated by the President and affirmed by Congress. During the 1930s and 40s, the Smoot–Hawley tariffs generally applied unless altered through bilateral trade agreements. The Reciprocal Trade Agreements Act of 1934 gives the President the authority to enter into such agreements, and under various extensions this authority remains in effect today. An early agreement of this type was the Canadian Reciprocal Trade Agreement of 1935.

UNITED STATES TARIFF RATES

United States tariffs generally take one of three forms. The most common is an ad valorem rate. Such tariffs are assessed in proportion to the value of the article. Tariffs may also be assessed at specific rates or compound rates. Specific rates may be measured by the pound or other weight. A compound rate is a mixture of an ad valorem and specific rate tariff. Tariff rate quotas involve limitations on imports at a specific tariff up to a certain amount. Imports in excess of that amount are not prohibited, but are subject to a higher rate of tariff.

Thus tariff rate quotas tend to restrict imports that are in excess of the specified quota for the lower tariff level.

These are three sets of United States tariff rates: Column 1 General, Column 1 Special and Column 2. Column 1 General tariff rates, known as most favored-nation (MFN) tariffs, are the lower and most likely to be applicable. Column 2 tariff rates, originating in the Smoot–Hawley Tariff Act of 1930, are the higher and least likely to be applicable. In addition, there are a variety of selective Column 1 Special, usually duty free entry programs to which the U.S. subscribes. These include the Generalized System of Tariff Preferences of the United States (GSP), the Caribbean Basin Initiative, the Andean Trade Preference Act and Section 9802.00.80 of the HTS. The Israeli and the North American Free Trade Agreement (NAFTA), generally provide for duty free access.

COLUMN 1 TARIFFS AND THE GATT

The Trade Agreements Extension Act of 1945 authorized the President to conduct multilateral negotiations in the trade field. It was out of this authority that the General Agreement on Tariffs and Trade (GATT) was negotiated. The GATT became effective on January 1, 1948 and was implemented in the United States by executive order. Indeed, despite its wide-ranging impact on United States tariff levels since 1948, the GATT has never been ratified by the United States Congress. Nevertheless, it is the source of the principal tariffs assessed today on imports into the United States. These duties, known as most-favored-nation (MFN) tariffs or "Column 1 tariffs," have been dramatically reduced over the years through successive rounds of GATT trade negotiations. They are unconditional MFN tariffs, meaning that reciprocity is not required in order for them to apply. Multilateral GATT tariff agreements have predominated over bilateral negotiations since 1948.

The term "most-favored-nation" is misleading in its suggestion of special tariff arrangements. It is more appropriate to think of MFN tariffs as the normal level of U.S. tariffs, to which there are exceptions resulting in the application of higher or lower tariffs. At this point, the average MFN tariff applied to manufactured imports into the United States is approximately 3.5 percent.

FOREIGN TRADE ZONES

"Free trade zones" are located throughout the U.S., many of them located near airports. While imported goods remain in the zones, they are not subject to U.S. tariffs. The imported goods are subject to U.S. tariffs when they leave the zones, but only if they are then brought into the U.S. If they are exported from the free trade zone to another country, they will never be subjected to U.S. tariffs. Thus, such zones serve as distribution centers, encourage assembly of certain manufactured items for export, provide local employment, and may lessen overall tariffs which must be paid before an assembled item crosses the zone for routine importation into the country. In the U.S., zones are supervised by the Foreign Trade Zones Board (located within the Commerce Department) and by the Customs Service.

CUSTOMS CLASSIFICATION

The classification problem may be illustrated as follows: Are parts of a wooden picture frame, imported piece by piece in separate packages for later assembly within a country, to be assessed duties prescribed for wood picture frames or for strips of wood moulding? Is "wood picture frame" even an appropriate nomenclature, or should what is commonly known to be a wood picture frame have a tariff nomenclature of "art object" or "forest product" or simply "personal belonging"?

For decades, most of the countries in the world, except the United States and Canada, classified imports according to the Brussels Tariff Nomenclature (BTN), which identifies items along a progression from raw materials to finished products. The United States had its own system of classification set out in the Tariff Schedule of the United States (TSUS). However, beginning in 1982, the United States initiated steps to convert the TSUS into a Harmonized Commodity Description and Coding System (HS) of classification, in common with the classification system used by most other countries and developed by the Customs Cooperation Council in Brussels. The United States adopted the Harmonized System as the Harmonized Tariff Schedule (HTSUS) for classification of all imports by enactment of the Omnibus Trade and Competitiveness Act of 1988, with an effective date of Jan. 1, 1989. Approximately forty other nations have adopted HS and use it for U.S. exports.

If the importer and the United States customs officials disagree about the proper classification of an imported item, the United States Court of International Trade (CIT) has exclusive jurisdiction to resolve their dispute. In cases decided under TSUS, the CIT has followed its own logic, without reference to decisions of other courts, because the approach of the U.S. statute (TSUS) was so unique. In the cases decided so far under HTSUS, the CIT has continued this tradition in its decisions under the new classification system, rather than viewing the decisions of foreign courts as to the interpretation of HS as persuasive.

CUSTOMS VALUATION AND RULES OF ORIGIN

Even though an imported item may be classified and have a known rate of duty, expressed as a percentage of the item's value, difficulty may still arise in getting the importer and customs authorities to agree upon the item's value. For decades, United States customs valuation of an imported item was gauged by the American Selling Price (ASP) of the item—i.e., the usual wholesale price at which the same item manufactured in the United States was offered for sale.

However, Article VII of GATT requires that "value for customs purposes ... should not be based on the value of merchandise of national origin or on arbitrary or fictitious values." The 1979 Tokyo Round produced the Customs Valuation Code, which established the details of an approach which was quite different from ASP. The GATT approach was incorporated into the U.S. Trade Agreements Act of 1979. United States customs valuation is now calculated by the "transaction value" of the imported item and, if that cannot be determined, by certain fall-back methods which are, in descending order of eligibility for use, the transaction value of identical merchandise, the transaction value of similar merchandise, the resale price of the merchandise with allowances for certain factors or the cost of producing the imported item. "Transaction value" is "the price actually paid or payable for the merchandise when sold for exportation to the United States" plus "certain amounts reflecting packing costs, commissions paid by buyer, any assist, royalty or license fee paid by buyer, and any resale, disposal, or use proceeds that accrue to seller." This approach to valuation forms the core of the new Agreement on Implementation of Article VII of GATT 1994.

When a country's tariff schedules provide that duties on an imported item may vary depending upon the country from which the item comes, certain "rules of origin" may come into play. Two common situations raising questions of origin are the circumstance that a product is shipped to the United States from Country "X" but has been manufactured in fact in Country "Y" and the circumstance where a product is shipped to the United States from Country "X", in which the product was made, but certain component parts of the product have originated in Country "Y".

The "Rule of Origin" is provided in 19 U.S.C.A. § 2518(4)(B) that "An article is a product of a country ... only if ... it is wholly the growth, product, or manufacture of that country ..., or ... in the case of an article which consists in whole or in part of materials from another country ... it has been substantially transformed into a new and different article of commerce with a name, character, or use distinct from that of the article or articles from which it was so transformed." Under the new Agreement on Rules of Origin, there will be an effort to harmonize the rules of origin on a world-wide basis, under the auspices of the WTO. A committee of experts is charged with creating rules which are "objective, understandable, and predictable." They are likely to differ from the current U.S. rules.

The Rule of Origin is relevant in determining the rate at which customs duty is charged (MFN rate or not). It is also relevant in the context of 19 U.S.C.A. § 2511(a) and (b), which empower the President to waive the application of any law regarding United States Government procurement with respect to eligible products of any foreign country if application of the law would result in that country's products receiving less favorable treatment than is accorded to products from the United States.

GENERALIZED PREFERENCES FOR DEVELOPING NATIONS

The Generalized System of Preferences (GSP), 19 U.S.C.A. §§ 2461–2465, recognizes that economic development of the third world requires the assistance of industrialized nations, and grants preferences to products of developing countries without demanding reciprocity. In addition to obtaining MFN tariff rates, developing countries can ship goods duty free into U.S. and other major industrial markets under GSP. These special arrangements for developing countries are permitted by the provisions of GATT, and have been implemented by the U.S., the EU, Japan and other major industrialized nations, although they differ in structure and approach.

Under the U.S. GSP, goods are admitted duty free if both the product *and* its country of origin meet the statutory requirements. The designation of developing countries as eligible for the GSP benefits has always been politicized to some extent—e.g., by declaring all communist states to be ineligible, and by declaring all but three OPEC member states to be ineligible. In addition, under 1984 amendments, the President must evaluate whether a country recognizes "internationally recognized

worker's rights" and adequately protects intellectual property rights before that country can be designated as a GSP beneficiary. Also, the GSP beneficiary designation should not be given to nations which
give more preferential treatment to imports from
other developed nations than to U.S. products, assist terrorists, expropriate U.S. owned investments,
or refuse to cooperate in drug enforcement or recognize international arbitration awards.

The GSP rule of origin requires that the product
be shipped directly from the beneficiary developing
country to the U.S. Where the goods are locally
produced from local resources, there is no further
problem. However, where the goods exported by the
beneficiary country are produced from materials
imported into the developing country, further analysis is necessary. In such cases, the present GSP
rule of origin requires that at least 35 percent of the
value of an item be added within a developing
country for the item to be considered as "originating" in that developing country. Thus, Toyotas
manufactured in Japan, but shipped to the U.S.
through a GSP beneficiary country, would not qualify for GSP duty free treatment. But Toyotas manufactured in the GSP beneficiary country from parts
manufactured in Japan could so qualify, if the value
of the parts aggregated only 60% of the value of the
final product. In addition, the Federal Circuit Court
of Appeals has ruled that the processing of goods in
the GSP country must create two substantial trans-
formations in the identity of the goods for GSP

treatment to be available. See Torrington Co. v. United States, 764 F.2d 1563 (Fed.Cir.1985).

Products of particular GSP beneficiary countries can be added or removed to the list of GSP qualified goods by petition by interested persons. The petitions, and the resultant certification or de-certification, are determined by the U.S. Trade Representative, with the advice of the ITC. The criterion used is "import sensitivity," which means that American industry or labor must actively seek protection from this foreign competition. The tendency of the decisions has been not to displace American interests, and to regard the GSP benefits as a "gift" to developing countries.

A separate principle is known as "graduation" from the GSP list. While the principle can be applied to an entire country, the current use has been to "graduate" specific products from specific countries from the GSP list to the MFN list. The 1984 amendments required the President to complete a general review of all GSP products to determine whether they were "sufficiently competitive" to graduate. Graduation has had its greatest impact on so-called "newly industrialized countries." In 1989, South Korea, Taiwan, Hong Kong and Singapore were graduated entirely from the GSP list. At the same time, Bahrain, Brunei, Nauru and Bermuda were dropped from the list because their per capita GNP exceeded the statutory limit. In 1995, the Bahamas and Israel were similarly dropped, and in 1997 Malaysia was entirely graduated.

CARIBBEAN BASIN AND ANDEAN TRADE PREFERENCES

The European Union has had for many years a policy which grants substantial duty free entry into its market for goods originating in Mediterranean Basin countries. The United States has duplicated this approach for the Carribean Basin. This is accomplished through the Carribean Basin Economic Recovery Act of 1983. (19 U.S.C.A. § 2701). For these purposes, the Carribean Basin is broadly defined to include nearly all of the islands in that Sea, and a significant number of Central and South American nations bordering the Carribean. So defined, there are 28 nations which could qualify for purposes of the United States Caribbean Basin Initiative. As with the GSP program, the Carribean Basin Initiative (CBI) involves presidential determinations to confer beneficiary status upon any of these eligible countries. However, unlike the GSP, there are no presidential determinations as to which specific products of these countries shall be allowed into the United States on a duty free basis. All Carribean products except those excluded by statute are eligible. Moreover, there are no "competitive need" or annual per capita income limits under the CBI. Lastly, unlike the GSP program which must be renewed periodically, the Caribbean Basin Initiative is a permanent part of the U.S. tariff system.

The Andean Trade Preference Act (ATPA) of 1991 (19 U.S.C.A. § 2703(f)) authorizes the President to grant duty free treatment to imports of eligible articles from Columbia, Peru, Bolivia and Ecuador. Venezuela is not included as a beneficiary under this Act. The Andean Trade Preference Act is patterned after the Carribean Basin Economic Recovery Act of 1983. Goods that ordinarily enter duty free into the United States from Caribbean Basin nations will also enter duty free from these four Andean countries. The same exceptions and exclusions discussed above in connection with the Carribean Basin Initiative generally apply. However, while the CBI is a permanent part of United States Customs law, the ATPA is only authorized initially for a period of ten years. Furthermore, the guaranteed access levels for Caribbean Basin textile products, separate cumulation for antidumping and countervailing duty investigations, and the waiver of the Buy American Act for procurement purposes are not authorized by the ATPA. Broadly speaking, the passage of the ATPA represents assistance to these nations economically, in return for their help in containing narcotics.

GOODS INCORPORATING UNITED STATES COMPONENTS

Section 9802.00.80 of the Harmonized Tariff Schedule of the United States (formerly Section 807.00 of the Tariff Schedule of the United States) is an unusual "duty free" provision. This section allows for the duty free importation of United States fabricated components that were exported ready for assembly abroad. If qualified, goods assembled abroad containing U.S. components are subject only to a duty upon the value added through foreign assembly operations. In order for this to be the case, Section 9802.00.80 requires that the components be fabricated and a product of the United States, that they be exported in a condition ready for assembly without further fabrication, that they not lose their physical identity by change in form, shape or otherwise, and that they not be advanced in value or improved in condition abroad except by being assembled and except by operations incidental to the assembly process such as cleaning, lubricating and painting.

If all of the Section 9802.00.80 criteria are met, the tariff that will be assessed upon the imported assembled product will be limited to a duty upon the full value of that product less the cost or value of U.S. made components that have been incorporated into it. Those who seek to take advantage of Section 9802.00.80 must provide the United States Customs Service with a Foreign Assembler's Declaration and Certification. This is known as Form 3317. The assembly plant operator certifies that the requirements of Section 9802.00.80 are met, and the importer declares that this certification is correct. Billions of dollars of ordinarily tariffed value have been excluded as a result of this Customs law provision. Motor vehicles, semiconductors, office machines, textiles and apparel, and furniture are good examples of the kinds of products assembled abroad with fabricated U.S. components so as to meet the requirements of Section9802.00.80. Historically, many of these products were assembled in Japan, Germany or Canada. In more recent times, the assembly operations (maquiladoras) to which Section 9802.00.80 frequently applies have more commonly been found in the developing world.

DUTY FREE ACCESS TO THE UNITED STATES

The end-game so far as exporters and importers to the United States are concerned is unlimited duty free access. Except for raw materials and Canadian, Israeli or Mexican free trade articles, few exports will ordinarily qualify for such treatment. However, products of developing Andean or Caribbean nations may achieve this goal. This is possible because of United States adherence to the generalized system of tariff preferences (GSP) program approved by the GATT (19 U.S.C.A. § 2461), the Caribbean Basin Economic Recovery Act (1983) (19 U.S.C.A. § 2701), the Andean Trade Preference Act of 1991, and tariff concessions on the assembly of U.S. components abroad (e.g. maquiladoras, see HTS § 9802.00.80).

There are, of course, exceptions and controls (quotas, NTBs) that may apply under these duty free programs. Nevertheless, the United States market is so lucrative that careful study of these external trade rules is warranted. Such studies can realize unusually advantageous trade situations. For example, many developing nations have duty free rights of entry into the European Union under the Lomé Conventions, the Union's Mediterranean Basin Policy or the EU version of the GSP program. The goods of some of these nations may also qualify for duty free access to the United States market. A producer strategically located in such a nation (e.g., Jamaica) can have the best of both worlds, duty free access to the European Union and the United States.

U.S. IMPORT QUOTAS

The United States has employed import quotas for many years. Tariff-rate quotas have been applied to dairy products, olives, tuna fish, anchovies, brooms, and sugar, syrups and molasses. Quite a few absolute quotas originate under Section 22 of the Agricultural Adjustment Act. These quotas are undertaken when necessary to United States farm price supports or similar agricultural programs. They have been used on animal feeds, dairy products, chocolate, cotton, peanuts, and selected syrups and sugars. Some U.S. agricultural quotas are being converted into tariffs under the WTO Agreement on Agriculture. Some quotas imposed by the U.S. are sanctions for unfair trade practices, as against tungsten from China. Other quotas originate in international commodity agreements, and important restraints on textile imports are achieved as a result of the international Multi–Fiber Arrangement, which is to be phased out under the WTO Textiles Agreement.

The Agricultural Act of 1949 requires the President to impose global import quotas on Upland Cotton whenever the Secretary of Agriculture determines that its average price exceeds certain statutory limits. Whenever this is the case, unlike the ordinary restrictive import quota, the importation of Upland Cotton is duty free. Like the Meat Import Act, this provision tends to be countercyclical to market forces for cotton in the United States.

Lastly, the United States sometimes imposes import restraints for national security or foreign policy reasons. Many of these restraints originate from Section 232 of the Trade Expansion Act of 1962. This provision authorizes the President to "adjust imports" whenever necessary to the national security of the country. Trade embargoes are sometimes imposed on all the goods from politically incorrect nations (e.g., Cuba). Product-specific import bans also exist for selected goods, e.g., narcotic drugs and books urging insurrection against the United States. The importation of "immoral" goods is generally prohibited, even for private use, and the obscenity of such items is decided by reviewing the community standards at the port of entry. Generally, as well, goods produced with forced or convict labor are excluded from the United States. This ban has of late been applied to certain goods from the People's Republic of China.

If a quota system is created, a fundamental subsidiary issue is: How will the quotas be allocated? The U.S. Customs Service generally administers quotas on a first-come, first-served basis. This approach creates a race to enter goods into the United States. The President is authorized to sell import licenses at public auctions. One advantage of an auction system is its revenue raising potential. The U.S. Tariff Act of 1930 also provides that to the extent practicable and consistent with efficient and fair administration, the President is to insure against inequitable sharing of imports by a relatively small number of the larger importers. In fact, allocating quotas among U.S. importers rarely happens. Instead, in the past, quotas usually have seen part of a "voluntary restraint" or orderly market agreement between the U.S. and one or more foreign governments, and represent adherence by those governments to U.S. initiatives. The negotiations have typically concentrated on obtaining foreign government agreement to limitations on exportation of their products into the U.S. market, and have not pursued limitations on who might use the resulting allocations. Thus, instead of an auction system, the U.S. has usually used a Presidentially managed system of import allocations, especially in regard to agricultural import quotas.

UNITED STATES PARTICIPATION IN TRADE NEGOTIATIONS–THE UNITED STATES TRADE REPRESENTATIVE

Removing trade barriers is usually done on a reciprocal basis, and requires lengthy bargaining and negotiations between the sovereign states. Congress is not adapted to carry on such negotiations, so it routinely delegates limited authority to the President to negotiate agreements reducing existing import restrictions when the President finds that such restrictions, either of the United States or of a foreign country, are unduly burdensome. Some recent efforts to reduce trade restrictions have been multilateral efforts (e.g., the WTO and the North American Free Trade Agreement). In these situations, Congress has given quite broad authority to the President, or his representative, to reduce or eliminate United States tariffs on a reciprocal basis.

The President's, or his representative's, power to negotiate for international trade advantage within the framework of multilateral, or even bilateral, negotiations, has been summarized in a 1975 letter by the (then) Acting Assistant Secretary of State for Congressional Relations, Mr. Kempton Jenkins, to a Congressional committee (which is reprinted in 69 *Am.J.Int'l Law* 651–52 (1975)):

The Trade Act of 1974, [19 U.S.C.A. § 2101 et seq.] which became law on January 3, 1975, provides the President with substantial new authority in the area of trade negotiations. He may, under certain circumstances, enter into trade agreements, and, as a result thereof, decrease existing tariffs or harmonize, reduce or eliminate nontariff barriers to and other distortions of trade. This authority may be exercised through both multilateral and bilateral trade agreements. Agreements regarding nontariff barriers are subject to congressional approval.... Finally, Title IV of the Trade Act contains a number of limitations on the President's authority to make commercial agreements with nonmarket economy countries, including provisions relating to congressional approval or disapproval of such agreements.

Section 1102 of the Omnibus Trade and Competitiveness Act of 1988 (P.L. 100–418) extended, until June 1, 1993, the President's authority under the Trade Act of 1974 (19 U.S.C.A. § 2112(b)) to "enter into trade agreements with foreign countries ... providing for the reduction or elimination of [NTBs]; or the prohibition of, or limitations on the imposition of, such barrier or other distortion." (This authority was later extended to October 3, 1994, but has not been extended further.) In response to Section 1104 of the Trade Agreements Act of 1979 (P.L. 96–39), the President reviewed the structure of the international trade functions of the Executive Branch. Although this did not lead to the establishment of a new Department of International Trade and Investment, it did lead to an enhancement of the Office of the Special Representative for Trade Negotiations, which has since been renamed the United States Trade Representative (USTR). The powers of the USTR were expanded and its authority given a legislative foundation. (The office had been established by an Executive Order in 1963.)

As established under 19 U.S.C.A. § 2171, the USTR is appointed by the President, with the advice and consent of the Senate. The Office of the

USTR has been the principal vehicle through which trade negotiations have been conducted over the past several years on behalf of the United States. Among other things, the USTR has had continuing responsibility in connection with implementation and development of the Codes produced by the 1979 MTN, and authorized by section 2 of the Trade Agreements Act of 1979 (to an extent not in conflict with existing United States statutes). The USTR is the contact point for persons who desire an investigation of instances of noncompliance with any trade agreement. It is charged (by the Trade Act of 1979) to provide, upon receipt of written request from any person, information about "the nature and extent of a specific trade policy or practice of a foreign government or instrumentality with respect to particular merchandise, to the extent that such information is available." (Other parts of the Executive Branch and several regulatory agencies have responsibilities in connection with aspects of international trade. They include the Departments of Agriculture, Commerce, Defense, Labor, State and Treasury, and government bodies such as A.I.D., C.A.B., C.I.A., F.A.A., F.P.C., F.T.C., Foreign Agricultural Service, Foreign Claims Settlement Commission, and the International Trade Commission.)

The international setting in which the USTR functions is that provided by the WTO and NAFTA and, to a lesser extent by the International Monetary Fund (IMF).

PUBLIC PROCUREMENT

In federal nations like the United States, these rules can extend to state and local purchasing requirements. The principal United States statute affecting imports in connection with government procurement is the Buy American Act of 1933. This Act requires the government to buy American unless the acquisition is for use outside the U.S., there are insufficient quantities of satisfactory quality available in the U.S., or domestic purchases would be inconsistent with the public interest or result in unreasonable costs.

As currently applied, the United States Buy American Act requires federal agencies to treat a domestic bid as unreasonable or inconsistent with the public interest only if it exceeds a foreign bid by more than six percent (customs duties included) or ten percent (customs duties and specific costs excluded). Exceptions to this general approach exist for reasons of national interest, certain designated small business purchases, domestic suppliers operating in areas of substantial unemployment and demonstrated national security needs. Bids by small businesses and companies located in labor surplus areas are generally protected by a 12 percent margin of preference. Bids from U.S. companies are considered foreign rather than domestic when the materials used in the products concerned are below 50 percent American in origin. These rules apply to civil purchasing by the United States government, but are suspended for purchasing subject to the WTO Procurement Code.

The Department of Defense has its own Buy American rules. Generally speaking, a 50 percent price preference (customs duties excluded) or a 6 or 12 percent preference (customs duties included) whichever is more protective to domestic suppliers is applied. However, intergovernmental "Memoranda of Understanding" (MOU) on defense procurement provide important exceptions to the standard Department of Defense procurement rules. Additional procurement preferences are established by the Small Business Act of 1953. Under this Act, federal agencies may set aside certain procurement exclusively for small U.S. businesses. In practice, the federal government normally sets aside about 30 percent of its procurement needs in this fashion. Special set-aside rules apply to benefit socially and economically disadvantaged minority-owned businesses. These preferences are excepted from U.S. adherence to the WTO Procurement Code.

A number of federal statutes also contain specific Buy American requirements. These include various GSA, NASA and TVA appropriations bills, the AMTRAK Improvement Act of 1978, the Public Works Employment Act of 1977, various highway and transport acts, the Clean Water Act of 1977, and the Rural Electrification Acts of 1936 and 1938. Many of these statutes involve federal funding of state and local procurement. All are generally excepted from the WTO Procurement Code as applied by the United States.

The Buy American Act generally conformed to the GATT Procurement Code negotiated during the Tokyo Round. However, Congress has expressed its displeasure with the degree to which that Code opened up sales opportunities for United States firms abroad. It therefore amended the Buy American Act in 1988 to deny the benefits of the GATT Procurement Code when foreign governments are not in good standing under it. United States government procurement contracts are also denied to suppliers from countries whose governments "maintain ... a significant and persistent pattern of practice or discrimination against U.S. products or services which results in identifiable harm to U.S. businesses." Presidential waivers of these statutory denials may occur in the public interest, to avoid single supply situations or to assure sufficient bidders to provide supplies of requisite quality and competitive prices.

The European Union was one of the first to be identified as a persistent procurement discriminator by the USTR. This identification concerns longstanding heavy electrical and telecommunications disputes that were partly settled by negotiation with the EU in 1993. The remaining disputes led to U.S. trade sanctions and Union retaliation. This did not occur with Greece, Spain and Portugal (where the EU procurement rules do not apply), and with Germany which broke ranks and negotiated a pathbreaking bilateral settlement with the U.S. In 1993, also, Japan was identified as a persistent procurement discriminator in the construction, architectural and engineering areas.

In addition to the Buy American Act, state and local purchasing requirements may inhibit import competition in the procurement field. For example, California once had a law which made it mandatory to purchase American products. This law was declared unconstitutional as an encroachment upon the federal power to conduct foreign affairs. A Massachusetts ban on contracting with companies with investments in Myanmar (Burma) was likewise stuck down. State statutes which have copied the federal Buy American Act, on the other hand, and incorporated public interest and unreasonable cost exceptions to procurement preferences, have generally withstood constitutional challenge. For example, a Pennsylvania statute requires state and local agencies to ensure that contractors do not provide products containing foreign steel.

A practice known as "unbalanced bidding" has arisen in connection with the Buy American Act. Unbalanced bidding involves the use of United States labor and parts by foreigners in sufficient degree so as to overcome the bidding preferences established by law for U.S. suppliers. This occurs because the United States value added is *not* included in the calculations of the margin of preference for the U.S. firms. Thus foreign bids minus the value of work done in the U.S. are multiplied by the 6, 12 or 50 percent Buy American Act preference. If the U.S. bids are above the foreign bids but within the margin of preference, the U.S. company gets the contract. If the U.S. bids are higher than the foreign bids plus the margin of preference, the foreigners get the contract.

PRODUCT STANDARDS

Under United States law, state and federal agencies may create standards which specify the characteristics of a product, such as levels of quality, safety, performance or dimensions, or its packaging and labelling. However, these "standards-related activities" must not create "unnecessary obstacles to U.S. foreign trade," and must be demonstrably related to "a legitimate domestic objective" such as protection of health and safety, security, environmental or consumer interests. Sometimes there is a conflict between federal and state standards. For example, federal law licensing endangered species' articles preempted California's absolute ban on trade in such goods. The Office of the USTR is charged with responsibility for implementation of the GATT Standards Code within the United States.

The Secretary of Commerce maintains a "standards information center" (National Bureau of Standards, National Center for Standards and Certification Information), in part to "serve as the central national collection facility for information relating to standards, certification systems, and standards-related activities, whether such standards, systems or activities are public or private, domestic or foreign, or international, regional, national, or local [and to] make available to the public at ... reasonable fee ... copies of information required to be collected."

United States standards have been attacked in international tribunals as violating international obligations. Sometimes the standards have been upheld, sometimes not. For example, a binational arbitration panel established under Chapter 18 of the Canada—U.S. FTA issued a decision upholding a United States law setting a minimum size on lobsters sold in interstate commerce. The panel found that, since the law applied to both domestic and foreign lobsters, it was not a disguised trade restriction.

On the other hand, in August of 1991, a GATT panel found that United States import restrictions designed to protect dolphin from tuna fishers did violate the GATT. The panel ruled that GATT did not permit any import restrictions based on extraterritorial environmental concerns, whether they were considered disguised trade restrictions or not. This decision suggested difficulty with a number of United States laws which concern health, safety and environmental conditions in exporting nations. A 1994 decision by a second GATT panel recognized the legitimacy of environmental regulations, but ruled against the tuna boycott by the U.S. because of its focus on production methods and the unilateral imposition of standards by the U.S. In 1997, Congress enacted legislation that replaced the domestic restrictions on imported tuna with international restrictions stated in the Declaration of Panama. This Declaration, with internationally accepted standards, may finally place U.S. tuna legislation in conformity with its WTO obligations.

In 1998, the WTO Appellate Body ruled against a U.S. ban on shrimp imports from nations that fail to use turtle exclusion devices comparable to those required under U.S. law. The Appellate Body found the U.S. ban undermined the multilateral trading system because the security and predictability of the system would be compromised if other Members adopted similar measures. The unilateral use of extraterritorial measures to protect exhaustible natural resources was not "justifiable"; international agreement on the subject should be sought.

The standards of other nations have also been challenged as violations of WTO obligations. For example, the United States has challenged European Union bans of imports of meat from the United States, first for containing certain hormones, later for unsanitary conditions in U.S. meatpacking facilities. In the former controversy, the United States retaliated. In 1997, the WTO Appellate Body ruled against the EU ban on hormone-treated beef, citing the lack of an adequate scientific basis for the ban as required under the WTO Sanitary and Phyto–Sanitary (SPS) Agreement. (See discussion in Chapter 2.) There will certainly be further disputes with the EU in the future concerning genetically modified organisms (GMOs).

RESPONSES OF DOMESTIC
PRODUCERS TO IMPORT
COMPETITION

The duty payable on an imported item may be increased above that required normally by the posted tariff schedule because of certain "antidumping" measures or "countervailing duties" imposed by the country of importation (in the United States, imposed by the International Trade Commission in concert with the International Trade Administration). Antidumping duties are a trade response to what is considered to be a "dumping" of items into the country of importation at a price which is less than the price or value charged for comparable commodities in the country of origin, usually termed "less than fair value" (LTFV). Countervailing duties are a trade response to unfair "subsidies" given by another country to position its exports more competitively in the international market place. A third alternative for domestic producers responding to import competition is the escape clause or market disruption proceeding which is often added to antidumping and countervailing duty complaints as a shotgun approach to obtain protective relief.

Antidumping and countervailing duties are permitted by GATT 1994, and the criteria for them are largely derived from the WTO Covered Agreements. Under the Antidumping Code, each of these duties may be imposed on products of another Member only if two requirements are met. First, there must be an unfair trade practice, either dumping (sales at less than fair value) or prohibited or actionable subsidies. Second, there must be either "injury" or "adverse trade effects." Under U.S. law, these are proven by showing "material injury" to a domestic industry has actually occurred or is threatened, or the establishment of such an industry must be "materially retarded." Escape clause proceedings do not require a showing of any unfair trade practice, such as dumping or subsidies, so that the injury standard is higher, and the escape mechanism is available only when the imported products are a "substantial cause of *serious* injury, or the threat thereof" (emphasis added) to an established domestic industry.

NAFTA provides for resolution of antidumping and countervailing duty disputes through binational panels. Such panels apply the domestic law of the importing country, and provide a substitute for judicial review of the decisions of administrative agencies of the importing country.

It should be noted that none of these responses available to domestic producers have any relation to restricting goods from a nation because that nation does not allow our goods entry into its markets. Antidumping and countervailing duties deal only with unfair selling prices of the dutiable imported goods themselves, and the escape mechanism deals only with protecting the domestic competitors of the *imported* goods from serious harm.

DUMPING AND ANTIDUMPING DUTIES

The economics of dumping arise from a producer's opportunity to compartmentalize the overall market place for its goods, thus permitting it to offer the product for sale at different prices in different sectors of its market. Only if trade barriers or other factors insulate each market sector from other sectors of the market is there opportunity to vary substantially the product's price in different sectors of the overall product market. For example, a producer can "dump" its product in an overseas market at cheap prices and at high volume if it can be sure that the product market in its home country is immune from penetration by its products sold in its country by importers. The objective of dumping may be to increase long term marginal revenues or to ruin a competitor's market position. As pointed out earlier in this Chapter, dumping is the sale and export of products from one country to another country at less than fair value (LTFV). Such dumping contravenes Article VI of the GATT "if it causes or threatens material injury to an established industry in the territory of a contracting party or materially retards the establishment of a domestic industry."

One of the WTO covered Agreements is "The Agreement on Implementation of Article VI of GATT 1994," also known as the Antidumping Code. The Antidumping Code provides that a product is to be considered as being dumped if the export price of the product is less than the "normal value," the price which would be charged for the same or a similar product in the ordinary course of trade for domestic consumption in the exporting country. Thus, in evaluating whether an export price constitutes dumping, the best analytic tool is the domestic sales price of comparable goods in the exporting country.

However, such comparable sales may not be available, either because comparable products are not sold domestically, or because the usual retail transaction is not comparable (e.g., leasing rather than a sale). In that situation, the Antidumping Code provides a hierarchy of alternative computation methods to achieve an approximate evaluation. Among these alternatives, the preferred one uses the price for the same or a similar product in the ordinary course of trade for export to a third country. The next preferred alternative is to calculate the cost of production of the exported goods in the country of origin, plus a reasonable amount for profits and for administrative, selling and any general costs, and compare that to the export price of the product when sold for export to the United States.

United States objections to dumping were recorded as the subject of a protest by Secretary of the Treasury Alexander Hamilton in 1791, and have continued to be the subject of investigations. In general, U.S. antidumping statutes compare the price at which articles are imported or sold within the United States with the actual market value or wholesale price of such articles in the principal markets of the country of their production at the time of their export to the U.S. The approach was established by the Antidumping Act of 1916, a criminal statute, which was considered an unfair competition law, or price discrimination statute, and was functionally similar to the price discrimination statutes applicable to domestic business. The current U.S. antidumping provisions are set forth in 19 U.S.C.A. § 1673, *et seq.,* as amended, and now implement the WTO covered Agreements and the Antidumping Code.

Under 19 U.S.C.A. § 1673, "dumping" is the sale of imported goods at "less than fair value" (LTFV) or the difference between the product's export price or constructed export price and its "normal value." "Normal value", in turn, is usually determined by the amount charged for the goods in the exporter's *domestic* market (the "home market"). If such sales are both at LTFV and cause or threaten "material injury" to a domestic industry, or retard its development, then an antidumping duty "shall" be imposed. The antidumping duty levied is in addition to the usual customs charged on such products, and is in the amount of the difference between the price at which the goods are sold for export to the United States and the home market price.

Since the statute requires a determination of threatened or actual "material injury", or retardation of the establishment of a U.S. industry, much depends upon a workable definition of "material injury." The statutory definition is "harm which is not inconsequential, immaterial, or unimportant," and 19 U.S.C.A. § 1677(7) provides that, in making a determination of "material injury," the ITC "shall" consider the volume of imports involved, the effect of the imports on U.S. prices for "like products", and the impact of the imports on U.S. producers of "like products", but only in relation to production operations in the U.S. The ITC is directed to evaluate both the actual and potential declines not only in production, sales and profits, but also in market share and productivity of the domestic industry. It is also directed to evaluate actual and potential negative effects on employment, growth, ability to raise capital and investment. All effects are to be measured on an industrywide basis, and not in relation to an individual company; but a threat to a "major portion" of a national industry is sufficient.

The procedure for deciding whether to impose antidumping duties involves two governmental agencies: the International Trade Administration (ITA) and the International Trade Commission (ITC). The ITA is part of the Department of Commerce, which in turn is part of the Executive Branch. The ITC, on the other hand, is an independent agency, and was discussed previously in this Chapter. The ITA was originally designed to foster, promote and develop world trade, and to help American companies sell overseas by providing them with information concerning the "what, where, how and when" of imports and exports. It provides business data, educational programs, information sources, foreign license requirements, and procedures for starting a foreign business to individual businesses and trade groups. Since 1980, it has also decided whether import sales were at LTFV or benefitted from improper subsidies. The ITC was established by the Trade Act of 1974 (see 19 U.S.C.A. §§ 1330, 2231), and consists of six persons, appointed by the President with the advice and consent of the Senate, who have "qualifications requisite for developing expert knowledge of international trade problems".

In an antidumping proceeding, the ITA determines whether the imports are being sold at LTFV, and the ITC makes a separate determination concerning injury to a domestic industry. The proceeding may be initiated by either the Commerce Department or by an aggrieved business—or by a group or association of aggrieved businesses. However, the petition must be filed "on behalf of" the entire industry. The ITA then determines whether the petition "alleges the elements necessary for the imposition of a duty", based on the "best information available at the time" (19 U.S.C.A. § 1973a(c)). The ITC then makes a Preliminary Determination as to injury within 45 days "based on the best information available to it" at that time (19 U.S.C.A. § 1673b(a)). If the ITC makes such a finding, the ITA then makes a Preliminary Determination of whether there is "a reasonable basis to believe" that goods are being sold at LTFV (19 U.S.C.A. § 1673b(b)). If the ITA makes such a Preliminary Determination, it then proceeds to

make a "final determination" concerning sales at
LTFV. (19 U.S.C.A. § 1673d(a)). If sales at LTFV
are found by the ITA, the ITC then must make a
"final determination" concerning injury. (19
U.S.C.A. § 1673d(b)).

Any goods imported after an ITA *preliminary*
determination of sales at LTFV will be subject to
any antidumping duties imposed later, after final
determinations are made. Thus, this preliminary
determination tends to discourage imports, since
importers do not know what their liability for
duties will be. Foreign exporters are expected to
raise their "U.S. prices" to the level of home market prices soon after such a preliminary determination. If they do, the antidumping law will have
accomplished its purpose in eliminating dumping.

The ITA final determination of sales at LTFV
establishes the amount of any antidumping duties.
Since duties are not imposed to support any specific domestic price, they are set not to exceed the
"margin of dumping", or the amount the price for
domestic consumption in the exporting country exceeds the export price of the product in that country. The antidumping duty is to remain in force
only as long as the dumping occurs.

Congress enacted special rules to govern antidumping duty analysis of imports from nonmarket
economy countries (NMEs). 19 U.S.C.A. § 1677b(c).
The rules are based on the assumption that "normal value" cannot be determined by prices in a
NME which are bureaucratically determined, and

therefore are not sufficiently subject to the forces of competition to form an accurate standard for comparison. (Whether that assumption is accurate for all NMEs is beyond the scope of this Nutshell.) Instead, the ITA will "construct" a "normal value" by determining the factors of production (labor, materials, energy, capital) actually used by the NME to produce the imported goods, then value each of those factors in a market economy country "considered to be appropriate" by the ITA.

If a "normal value" cannot be constructed, an alternative is to use a comparable "surrogate" non-NME country which produces the imported product, and use its domestic price for the imported goods as the "normal value". The alternative construction was the primary method for valuation before 1988, but its results were not very reliable. Although the ITA sought a surrogate of comparable economic development and per capita gross national product, that was not always possible. Although the statutory definition refers to a "nonmarket economy country," which implies use of a single standard for a whole political unit, the ITA has recently begun to differentiate between different imports from China, based on whether particular factors of production are considered to be market driven or not.

SUBSIDIES AND COUNTERVAILING DUTIES

Duty payable on an imported item may be increased above the usual posted tariff schedule amount because of a "countervailing duty", levied as an offset by the country of importation, upon an imported item the production or export of which has been helped by an unfair "subsidy" in the country of origin. Subsidies come in many forms (e.g. tax rebates, investment tax credits, other tax holidays, subsidized financing); rapidly developing countries offer routinely to give some form of subsidy for initial foreign investment which may have an intended export aspect. In the United States, the Eximbank offers low cost loans to overseas buyers of products exported from the United States; other countries have similar programs.

In theory, the countervailing duty offsets exactly the unfair subsidy. Proponents of countervailing duties argue that they are necessary to keep imports from being unfairly competitive even though "fair" subsidies in other countries may be penalized in effect by the countervailing duty. Opponents of countervailing duties argue that there is no coherent standard of "fairness" vs. "unfairness" rationally to justify such duties. They point out that, absent a predatory motive by a foreign government, there is no more reason to justify government intervention in favor of a producer disadvantaged by foreign competition than disadvantaged by domestic competition because the result in each case is that the domestic resources used by the disadvantaged producer are shifted to their next highest value use and, viewing the world market as a unity, production efficiency worldwide is increased thereby. Opponents of countervailing duties point out also that it is often difficult to identify a subsidy.

International concern with unfair subsidies and countervailing duties is reflected in Articles VI, XVI, and XXIII of the GATT 1947 and in the "Agreement on Subsidies and Countervailing Measures" (the SCM Agreement), which is part of the Covered Agreements under WTO. The United States legislation implementing the SCM Agreement changed many concepts under U.S. law. Under the SCM Agreement, the authorities of the importing signatory have the power to impose a countervailing duty (CVD) in the amount of the subsidy for as long as the subsidy continues. The CVD may only be imposed after an investigation, begun on the request of the affected industry, has "demonstrated" the existence of (1) a subsidy; (2) adverse trade effects, such as injury to a domestic industry; and (3) a causal link between the subsidy and the alleged injury.

Under the SCM Agreement there is an attempt to shift the focus of subsidy rules from a national forum, as it was exclusively under GATT, to the multinational forum provided by the Subsidies Committee under WTO and the SCM Agreement. Subsidies complaints can now be brought either in the national forum or the WTO. There are now three classes of subsidies: (1) prohibited ("red light"); (2) permissible, but actionable if they cause adverse trade effects ("yellow light"); and (3) non-actionable and non-countervailable ("green light"). There are special rules which require LDCs to phase out their export subsidies and local content rules, but over 8 and 5 years, respectively. Transitional economies are also required to phase out both export subsidies and local content rules, but over a 7 year period.

The U.S. statutory provisions on countervailing duties on products imported from WTO Members is set forth in 19 U.S.C.A. § 1671, et seq. Duties may be imposed if it is found that the product is subsidized and that a U.S. industry is materially injured or threatened with such injury or its development is materially retarded.

A "subsidy" is defined as a "financial contribution" by a governmental entity which confers a benefit to the manufacturer of the subsidized product. 19 U.S.C.A. § 1677(5). It includes governmental grants, loans, equity infusions and loan guarantees, as well as tax credits and the failure to collect taxes. It can also include the governmental purchase or providing of goods or services on advantageous terms. Further, direct governmental action is not required; a subsidy can also be created if any of the above are provided through a private body. In addition to a "financial contribution" and a "benefit", a subsidy must be specific to a particular industry or enterprise. 19 U.S.C.A. § 1677(5)(A). Red light subsidies are "deemed" to be specific in WTO proceedings, and this concept is incorporated into the provisions on U.S. domestic proceedings for countervailing duties. 19 U.S.C.A. § 1677(5A)(A). However, specificity must be proven for other types of actionable subsidies.

"Red light" (prohibited) subsidies include financial contributions which are conditioned upon the export performance of the beneficiary, even where that condition is only one of several criteria (export subsidies). It includes both subsidies legally conditioned on export performance and also those which are in fact tied to actual or anticipated exportation or export earnings. It does not include, however, all financial contributions to all enterprises which happen to export. "Red light" subsidies also include financial contributions which are conditioned on the use of local goods (import substitution subsidies).

"Yellow light" (permissible, but actionable) subsidies are permissible under the SCM Agreement, but only so long as they do not cause "adverse trade effects." These subsidies include "financial contributions" which benefit specific enterprises or industries, but are not contingent upon export performance and are not insulated under "green light" criteria. Under U.S. law, such subsidies are subject to countervailing duties if they cause or threaten material injury to an industry in the United States, or materially retard the establishment of an industry in the United States. The definition of "material injury," or a threat thereof, or material retardation of establishment, is the same as in antidumping proceedings, discussed above. 19 U.S.C.A. § 1677(7). However, there are references in that U.S. definition to two provisions in the SCM Agreement—those dealing with "red light" and "dark amber" subsidies—with instructions that the ITC consider the nature of the subsidy in determining whether the subsidy imposes a material threat to an industry. 19 U.S.C.A. § 1677(7)(E)(1).

"Dark amber" subsidies are ones which exceed 5% of the cost basis of the product, or provide debt forgiveness, or cover the operating losses of a specific industry or of an enterprise more than once. This "dark amber" type of subsidy (halfway between "red" and "yellow") is a five year experiment under the SCM Agreement to provide "permissible, but actionable" subsidies in which there is a presumption of "adverse trade effects", and the subsidizing Member must rebut that presumption. At the end of the five year period, the Subsidies Committee must decide whether to continue, terminate or modify the "dark amber" provisions.

If a subsidy is either prohibited ("red light") or actionable ("yellow light"), it may be subject to either national or multinational actions. It will be subject to action within the U.S. legal system to impose a countervailing duty on imports of the subsidized product. It will also be subject to multilateral process within the WTO to obtain the withdrawal of the subsidy by the subsidizing Member.

The procedure for deciding whether to impose countervailing duties under domestic U.S. law is the same as that for antidumping duties, described previously, and involving both the ITA and ITC making both preliminary and final determinations. An ITA preliminary determination that a countervailable subsidy exists subjects any goods imported after that date to any countervailing duties imposed later, and therefore usually has the effect of reducing imports of such goods.

The Federal Circuit Court of Appeals has ruled that economic incentives given to encourage exportation by the government of a nonmarket economy (NME) cannot create a countervailable "subsidy." Georgetown Steel Corp. v. United States, 801 F.2d 1308 (Fed.Cir.1986). The court's rationale was that, even though an NME government provides export oriented benefits, the NME can direct sales to be at any set price, so the benefits themselves do not distort competition. The court also suggested that imports from NMEs with unreasonably low prices should be analyzed under antidumping duty provisions.

The multilateral procedure under WTO first provides for consultations between the complaining Member and the subsidizing Member. If these do not resolve the dispute within 30 days for a "red light" subsidy, or 60 days for a "yellow light" subsidy, either party is entitled to request that the DSB establish a panel to investigate the dispute and make a written report on it. The DSB panel will have 90 days (red light), or 120 days (yellow light), to investigate and prepare its report. The panel report is appealable on issues of law to the Appellate Body. The Appellate Body has 30 days (red light), or 60 days (yellow light), to decide the appeal. Panel and Appellate Body decisions are adopted without modification by the DSB unless rejected by an "inverted consensus."

If a prohibited or actionable subsidy is found to exist, the subsidizing Member is obligated under WTO to withdraw the subsidy. If the subsidy is not withdrawn within a six month period, the complaining Member can be authorized to take countermeasures. Such countermeasures may not be countervailing duties, but may instead comprise increased tariffs by the complaining Member on exports from the subsidizing Member to the complaining Member.

A new concept found in WTO, and incorporated in U.S. law, is the "green light" (non-actionable) subsidy. 19 U.S.C.A. § 1677(5B). Such subsidies are not subject to countervailing duties if they meet the rigorous criteria established in the SCM Agreement. Such subsidies are available for industrial research and development, regional development and adaptation of existing plant to new environmental standards. Green light subsidies are a five year experiment under the SCM Agreement to insulate certain governmental grants from countermeasures by other Members. At the end of the five year period the WTO Subsidies Committee must decide whether to continue, terminate or modify the green light provisions.

Research subsidies must be limited to no more than 75% of the cost of industrial research, or no more than 50% of the cost of pre-competitive development activity. Further, the subsidy must also be limited to the specific types of costs stated in 19 U.S.C.A. § 1677(5B)(B)(i).

Regional subsidies must be part of a general framework of regional development, and must be available to persons and enterprises in that region so as not to benefit specific enterprises or industries within the region. The region must be a clearly designated and contiguous geographic area, with an economic and administrative identity. The region must be designated as disadvantaged through neutral and objective criteria, which must be based in part on per capita income or unemployment rate statistics.

Environmental subsidies can be used only to adapt existing facilities to new environmental requirements. It must be available to all enterprises and industries on a non-specific basis. Such subsidies may subsidize only a maximum of 20% of the cost of the adaptation, and the cost calculations must reflect any manufacturing cost savings achieved by the new equipment. The subsidy must be a one-shot, non-recurring measure, and it cannot cover the subsequent cost of replacing any subsidized equipment.

A Member which undertakes to provide any of these three types of "green light" subsidies has the option to "notify" the WTO of the subsidy program and seek an evaluation of its features. The notification asks the WTO Secretariat to review the subsidy's provisions and determine whether they satisfy the criteria for "green light" subsidies. After the review, the Secretariat reports its findings to the Subsidies Committee, which reviews its findings. A Member which disagrees with the Subsidies Committee process may request binding arbitration to determine the matter.

If a "notified" subsidy is determined to satisfy the "green light" criteria, the subsidy cannot later be challenged, except through the Subsidies Committee. It cannot be challenged through the DSB procedure described above in relation to "red light" and "yellow light" subsidies. It also cannot be challenged under U.S. domestic countervailing duty proceedings before the ITA and the ITC, also described above. If a subsidy has been "notified" under the SCM Agreement, it is expressly exempted from investigation or review under U.S. CVD law. 19 U.S.C.A. § 1677(5B)(E).

However, if a Member believes that a "notified" subsidy is causing "serious adverse effects" to its domestic industry, it may request a review of that "green light" subsidy before the Subsidies Committee. Such a review is similar to the DSB reviews described above, except that it is heard by the Subsidies Committee (which earlier determined it to have "green light", or non-actionable, status), rather than by a DSB panel. If the Subsidies Committee finds that serious adverse effects exist, it "may" recommend that the subsidizing Member modify the subsidy to eliminate the adverse effects. If such a recommendation is made, the subsidizing Member must follow the recommendation within six months or be subject to appropriate countermeasures.

ESCAPE CLAUSE PROCEEDINGS

GATT Article XIX permits suspension of tariff concessions and MFN treatment if increased quantities of imports threaten or cause *serious* injury to a domestic industry. The suspension may be for such time as is necessary. Under U.S. law, such suspension of GATT tariff concessions causes the imported goods to become dutiable at the prohibitively high rates of the Smoot–Hawley Act of 1929, set forth in Column 2 of HTS.

In the United States, suspension of tariff concessions is obtained through "escape clause proceedings," also called Section 201 proceedings (19 U.S.C.A. §§ 2251–2253). In the United States, decisions about import adjustments are made by the President upon recommendation of the International Trade Commission (ITC), the successor to the United States Tariff Commission. A petition requesting import relief for the purpose of "facilitating positive adjustment to import competition may be filed with" the ITC by any entity which is "representative of an industry." Such entities may be an industry member firm, a trade association, a labor union or even a "group of workers," so long as they are representative of the industry. The petition must specify the purposes for which import relief is being sought, and ought to present the industry's plan for meeting import competition. The ITC then investigates to determine whether the increase in imports is "a substantial cause of serious injury", or threatens serious injury, to the domestic producers of the imported item.

The statutory criteria for these issues require the ITC to consider:

(A) with respect to serious injury, the significant idling of productive facilities in the domestic industry, the inability of a significant number of firms to carry out domestic production operations at a reasonable level of profit, and significant unemployment or underemployment within the domestic industry;

(B) with respect to threat of serious injury, a decline in sales or market share, a higher and growing inventory . . ., and a downward trend in production, profits, wages, or employment (or increasing underemployment) in the domestic industry concerned . . .; and

(C) with respect to substantial cause, an increase in imports (either actual or relative to domestic production) and a decline in the proportion of the domestic market supplied by domestic producers.

In responding to such a petition, the ITC will consider such economic factors as whether, for the entire industry, production and employment is declining or merely static, there is significant idle capacity, and a significant number of the firms operate at a reasonable level of profit. Even if serious injury is found, the imports must also be a "substantial cause" of that injury under 19 U.S.C.A. § 2252(b)(1). This "substantial cause" requirement means a cause which is important and not less than any other cause. Competing causes can include inept management, negative general economic or market trends, and technological innovations.

The statute requires the ITC to report its findings to the President within four months after the petition is filed. If the ITC finds that imports have increased, and that this increase has been a "substantial cause" of actual or threatened serious injury to the industry, the President "shall" take all appropriate and feasible action to facilitate efforts by the industry to make "a positive adjustment to import competition." Even though the word "shall" is used, there are many open provisions which allow the President to resist taking action. Thus, unlike antidumping and countervailing duty proceedings, the President has control over both whether any relief will be given in a Section 201 proceeding, and what form of relief will be granted.

One reason why protective escape clause relief is difficult to obtain is the fact that most trading partners of the United States are entitled to take compensatory action if the President decides to provide such relief. They are authorized to do this by the General Agreement on Tariffs and Trade. This is the case because escape clause proceedings do not concern any unfair trade practice. Rather, they are simply a reaction to the fact of increased import competition. This perspective helps explain why the President frequently decides that it is not in the national economic interest of the United States to impose escape clause relief.

If relief is given, it can be either protective relief or adjustment assistance. The former is directed toward the imported goods and can include increased tariffs, tariff rate quotas (tariffs which increase after reaching a certain quota), trade quotas or "orderly marketing agreements" (OMAs). The likelihood of action being taken against goods imported from their countries has prompted some countries to agree "voluntarily" to lessen pressure on the country of importation by restraining their exporters or otherwise entering into such "orderly market agreements". Japanese auto export restraints to the United States and Europe are two prime examples.

A GATT code on escape clause and related "gray area" protective measures was agreed upon during the Uruguay Round. This code was approved and implemented by Congress in December of 1994 under the Uruguay Round Agreements Act (URAA). One of its more important prohibitions is against seeking, undertaking or maintaining voluntary export or import restraint agreements (VERs and OMAs) with the exception of one such agreement which may last through 1999. Substantive and procedural escape clause rules are also established, notably on proof of "serious domestic injury," opportunities to present evidence and a maximum 4–year period of protection (extendable to 8 years). The right to retaliate when another country invokes escape clause relief is suspended for the first 3 years of such invocation. Special rules limit the use of escape clause measures to exports from developing nations and extend the potential for their use on imports by such nations.

Escape clause proceedings can also lead to adjustment assistance to workers and firms. This assistance is designed to accommodate the increased imports, not to prevent or reduce the imports. Escape clause relief assistance is always considered temporary, but adversely affected workers may be provided with "adjustment assistance" payments for up to one year. For example, automobile workers have been paid such assistance because foreign automobile manufacturers enjoyed great marketing success in the United States.

THE COURT OF INTERNATIONAL TRADE

Judicial review of any final determinations by the ITA and ITC concerning antidumping or countervailing duties or escape clause proceedings is by the Court of International Trade (CIT). The CIT was established in 1980 as the successor to the Court of Customs. The CIT is an Article III court, possessing all the legal and equity powers of a Federal District Court, including that of jury trial, but with three limitations. These limitations prohibit its issuance of injunctions or writs of mandamus in challenges to trade adjustment rulings, allow it to issue only declaratory relief in suits for accelerated review, and limit its power to order disclosure of confidential information to a narrowly defined class of cases.

The CIT has "exclusive" subject matter jurisdiction over suits against the United States, its agencies, or its officers arising from any law pertaining to revenue from imports, tariffs, duties or embargoes or enforcement of these and other regulations. The court's exclusive jurisdiction also includes any civil action commenced by the United States that arises out of an import transaction, as well as authority to review final agency decisions concerning antidumping and countervailing duty proceedings and trade adjustment assistance eligibility. The geographical jurisdiction of the CIT is nationwide, and it is even authorized to hold hearings in foreign countries. However, the CIT does not have jurisdiction over disputes involving public safety or health restrictions on imports, because of the need in such cases for uniformity of treatment of both domestically produced goods and imports, which can be insured only by referring such issues to U.S. District Courts.

CIT decisions are appealed, first, to the Court of Appeals for the Federal Circuit (formerly the Court of Customs and Patent Appeals), and, ultimately, to the United States Supreme Court.

CHAPTER FOUR

CONTROLS ON EXPORTS

A merchant in the United States wishing to export goods must consider all limitations on imports imposed by the importing nation which affect the proposed transaction. Any foreign import controls may or may not be similar to the United States import controls discussed above in Chapter Two. For nations which are members of the WTO, the controls are likely to be relatively similar. But the merchant in the United States must also consider that the United States may have *export* controls which affect the goods. Additionally, if there are any third party nation components in the goods to be exported, the export controls of that third nation must also be considered. For example, if a United States manufacturer of shirts made from materials from India wishes to export the finished shirts to Pakistan, it must consider whether India prohibits the trade of any of its products to the final destination of Pakistan. Another example is Cuba, which has been acquiring many products manufactured by foreign subsidiaries of United States companies, even though the United States has a trade embargo against Cuba.

Control of the reexport (including transshipment or diversion) of goods from a foreign nation is difficult to police and creates ill feeling on the part of the reexporting nation. Assume that India is engaged in a trade embargo against Canada and attempts to halt the export from the United States to Canada of the above mentioned shirts made in the United States from Indian sourced material. The United States government might ignore the Indian demand, just as Canada and Argentina have ignored demands by the United States to halt shipping to Cuba automobiles made in GM and Ford subsidiary plants in Canada and Argentina, respectively.

Why does a nation control exports? Exports earn revenue and create jobs. The above comments suggest that export controls are imposed more for political or foreign policy reasons, than for economic reasons. But sometimes the controls have a mixture of these reasons. For example, exports are limited for reasons of national security (military weapons, controlled by the Arms Export Control Act of 1976), fear of spread of nuclear components (partly controlled by Nuclear NonProliferation Act), preservation of natural resources (endangered species, subject to an international convention–CITES), reserving resources for domestic use (certain hardwoods for making furniture), or holding resources for sale at expected higher prices in the future (oil).

Export controls, which may assume such various forms as quotas, taxes (fees) or even prohibitions, are almost uniquely domestic rather than international. Export controls are mentioned in the GATT and WTO agreements, but as a practical matter there are no GATT or WTO obligations which affect significantly a country's use of export controls. GATT members expressed the need to reassess the GATT language regarding exports within the context of the entire international trade system and, in particular, the developing nations, but nothing of importance was accomplished in the creation of the WTO. The introductory language speaks of helping developing nations "share in the growth of international trade," which certainly must include exports. But the WTO Agreement is clearly an *import* trade rules document. It is thus to United States law that we turn to discover the framework for the governance of United States exports.

THE PRESIDENT VERSUS THE CONGRESS

The friction between the executive and legislative branches over export policy usually involves questions of *where* goods may be sent as opposed to *what* goods may be sent. There is usually less immediacy about controlling the nature of the goods as opposed to the destination of the goods. Restrictions on exports are usually introduced to punish nations for something which the Congress *and* the President, or the Congress *or* the President, find so distasteful that limits on United States exports to that country are justified, and more than offset the economic losses to United States businesses caused by the diminished exports. The President is in a better position than Congress to respond quickly to foreign acts which may justify immediate export controls. For example, the President took action in 1981 and 1982 after the Soviets imposed martial law in Poland, prohibiting the export of component parts for the USSR's Siberian oil pipeline. The President's decision generated substantial adverse reaction from several European nations which were the location of U.S. owned subsidiaries affected by the order.

Foreign actions which lead to controls may be either actions which are related to the exports themselves, such as their diversion from friendly to boycotted nations, or actions unrelated to the exports, such as the USSR martial law imposed in Poland. When a foreign nation's allegedly hostile acts persist, the Congress usually joins the President in limiting exports by enacting special legislation, such as the boycotts of Libya, Cuba and North Korea. This legislation tends to consist of controls implemented not by the Department of Commerce, but by the Department of the Treasury. Treasury controls currency, and without the ability to move currency across borders, trade is quickly diminished.

THE EXPORT ADMINISTRATION ACT AND REGULATIONS

United States exports are principally governed by the Export Administration Act (EAA), 50 U.S.C.A.App. § 2401 et seq., and the several hundred pages of associated regulations, 15 C.F.R.

Parts 730–774. The power to regulate exports as expressed in these laws originates in the Constitution, which grants to the federal Congress "Power ... To regulate Commerce with foreign Nations." Art. I, § 8, cl. 3. It is the same provision establishing authority to regulate imports. This Congressional power often conflicts with the President's conception of his Constitutional "foreign affairs" powers, and leads to disagreements with the executive branch over the extent to which Congress may restrict Presidential discretion in limiting exports to achieve foreign policy goals.'

The Export Administration Act is of limited duration, the last one enacted in 1979 was amended (extended) in 1985, but expired in 1994. Since that time the executive and legislative branches have not been able to agree on the substance of a new act. The President has vetoed one attempt (in 1990) to adopt a new EAA because he believed that his powers were unfairly restricted by Congress. In order to continue controls over exports, the President has extended the duration of the EAA by declaring a state of emergency under the International Emergency Economic Powers Act (IEEPA), 50 U.S.C.A. §§ 1701–1706.

The policy of the United States toward export controls is set forth in § 3 of the Export Administration Act of 1979, 50 U.S.C.A.App. § 2402, which provides, in part, that:

It is the policy of the United States to use export controls only after full consideration of the impact on the economy of the United States and only to the extent necessary—

(A) To restrict the export of goods and technology which would make a significant contribution to the military potential of any other country or combination of countries which would prove detrimental to the national security of the United States;

(B) to restrict the export of goods and technology where necessary to further significantly the foreign policy of the United States or to fulfill its declared international obligations; and

(C) to restrict the export of goods where necessary to protect the domestic economy from the excessive drain of scarce materials and to reduce the serious inflationary impact of foreign demand. . . .

* * *

It is the policy of the United States . . . to oppose restrictive trade practices or boycotts fostered or imposed by foreign countries against other countries friendly to the United States or against any United States person.

THE PROCESS OF LICENSING EXPORTS

United States merchant contemplating exporting their products must understand the licensing regulations. Prior to 1996 essentially *all* commercial exports had to be licensed. But that was deceptive.

Most exports required only a *general* license (i.e., one which did not require individual application and approval), which the exporter acquired by use of the Department of Commerce form "Shipper's Export Declaration." The exporter actually issued its own general license. But in some cases the exporter needed to obtain a *validated* license (i.e., one authorizing a specific export, issued after approval of an application). Time generated many variations of licenses, such as a general license GLV allowing shipments of limited value which otherwise would have required a validated license, or a validated license authorizing multiple exports to approved distributors or users in noncontrolled countries, or sales to foreign subsidiaries, or sales to an entire activity or project, or sales of replacement or spare parts for goods previously sold. The general and validated license framework was replaced in 1996, with an allegedly easier to use new process. Some critics suggest it does little but alter the labels, rather than change the substance of the process. That is probably an unfair evaluation, the process is easier.

Whether or not a license is required depends primarily on two issues; the type of goods or technology to be exported, and the destination country. The Bureau of Export Administration (BXA)(www.bxa.doc.gov) of the Department of Commerce maintains the Commerce Control List (CCL). 15 C.F.R. Part 738. This includes all items subject to export controls, except for those under the control of another branch of the government, such as the control of munitions by the Department of State. The CCL is divided into ten general categories (e.g., "3—electronics"). Within each category are five different groups of products, identified by letters A through E (e.g., "C—Materials"). Three further numbers identify the reasons for control (national security, possible use by terrorists, etc.). Together this makes a four digit and one letter Export Control Classification Number (ECCN, i.e., 3A001).

The Commerce Control List Supplement No. 1 (15 C.F.R. Part 774) includes the many variations of ECCNs. For each ECCN, this Supplement includes the License Requirements, the License Exceptions, and the List of Items Controlled. The 1996 revisions provide a fairly easily understood path through the maze of regulations, by means of a 29 step process to determine whether a license is needed, and if needed whether there are applicable exceptions. Use of the process involves reference to the Commerce Country Chart, which helps identify countries subject to controls for such reasons as national security, missile technology, UN or U.S. embargo, etc. For example, Country Group A includes several dozen nations with which the U.S. generally has good political trading relations. Country Group E, contrastingly, currently includes seven nations subject to either a UN or U.S. trade embargo, such as Angola, Cuba and Libya.

When a license is needed, application is made to the BXA in the Department of Commerce. The application must be approved and the license issued before the goods or technology may be exported. In many cases, a license will only be issued upon certain conditions, such as limiting the capability of the export product, restricting it to civilian use and prohibiting its use for any military or intelligence gathering purposes, or prohibiting resale to another controlled country. There is often a considerable negotiating process between the exporter and the BXA. When a license is issued, the exporter is responsible for the performance of all terms and conditions of the license, both by the foreign licensee and by foreign buyers or subsequent buyers. It is important for the exporter to know what conditions might be imposed on the license at the time the original contract is signed, so that such conditions may also be imposed in the contract on the foreign parties.

Speed may be important in processing an application for a license. But the administration of the EAA often has been characterized by delay, uncertainty and lack of accountability, as conflicts arise between national defense and export promotion policies. Many sensitive items have nevertheless evaded export controls, demonstrated by the 1980s sale to the USSR by Toshiba of Japan and Kongsberg of Norway of propeller milling machines and numerical controllers, respectively, which allowed the manufacture of submarine propellers which would function as quietly as U.S. submarines. The companies were subjected to sanctions prohibiting some trade to the United States.

EXPORT LICENSE APPLICATION REVIEW

Although delay is attendant to many export applications, there is a timetable which governs processing license applications. 50 U.S.C.A.App. § 2409. Within 10 days after proper submission, the Secretary of Commerce must acknowledge receipt of the application and advise about any other applicable procedures. Unless referral to another government department is necessary, the license should be granted formally or denied within 90 days. Even if referral is necessary, the statutory timetable requires issuance or denial within 180 days of the application.

Before its demise, a multilateral review by CO-COM might extend the review period to 240 days. COCOM was the Coordinating Committee of the Consultative Group on Export Controls. It was an informal multilateral organization of the U.S. and its military allies (NATO countries less Iceland, plus Japan) established to regulate certain strategic materials exports to communist countries. The United States rules were often more restrictive than were those of COCOM, and COCOM review was sometimes used as leverage to grant rather than to deny an application. COCOM members continually tried to convince the United States to relax some of its export rules. But the United States often acted alone in regulating sensitive exports, as it did in December, 1990, when the President announced the "Enhanced Proliferation Control Initiative," which expanded controls on items used in chemical and biological weapons. Following the changes in Eastern Europe and the breakup of the USSR, COCOM was abolished in 1994, with promises by many of its members to create a new organization for multilateral export review. The successor organization, established in 1995 and composed of about 28 nations, is the Wassenaar Arrangement on Export Controls for Conventional Arms and Dual–Use Goods and Technologies. Its purpose is similar to that of COCOM.

The statutory timetable of the EAA often is not met, despite Congressional attempts to mandate administrative conduct. Daedalus Enterprises, Inc. v. Baldrige, 563 F.Supp. 1345 (D.D.C.1983), illustrates the failure to comply with the timetables and an obvious frustration of a contemplated contract. The court permitted a suit to enjoin the Department of Commerce's noncompliance with the statutory timetable, but 29 months elapsed between the filing of the license application and the court ruling. Fortunately, more recent experience suggests a more rapid review process by Commerce.

SANCTIONS FOR EAA VIOLATIONS

Civil and criminal sanctions for violation of the EAA are formidable. 50 U.S.C.A.App. § 2410; 15 C.F.R. Part 764.3. A business which "willfully" violates any provision of the statute, its regulations or a license, knowing that the exports are destined for a controlled country or for its benefit, can be fined $1 million, or five times the value of the exports, whichever is *greater*. Fines of more than $1 million have been levied. An individual engaged in the same violation is subject to 10 years in prison or a fine of $250,000, or both. Similar sanctions may be applied to a business or an individual with a validated license who knows of a diversion of exported goods to military use by a controlled country and fails to report the diversion. The most feared sanction, however, is the ability of the Secretary of Commerce to suspend, revoke or deny the authority to export any goods which are subject to the EAA. This is considered an "administrative action" and is available whether or not the violation is willful.

BOYCOTT PROVISIONS AND THE EXPORT LAWS

Boycotts affect both exports and imports. The United States uses trade boycotts as a means to achieve political goals, although there is considerable debate regarding their effectiveness. A boycott by many nations, such as that imposed under UN auspices against South Africa in the 1970s and 1980s, was only questionably effective, and certainly caused a loss of jobs for those it was intended to benefit. But formal apartheid ended and the boycott deserves partial credit. When a boycott is by only one nation against another, contrastingly, such as the United States boycott of trade with Cuba, the likelihood of success in achieving a political goal is considerably diminished. The intention of the Cuban boycott has been to remove Fidel Castro from leadership. More than forty years later Mr. Castro continues in office.

United States boycotts which prohibit trade, both exports and imports, tend to be the subject of specific legislation directed towards identified countries. Enforcement is shifted from the Department of Commerce to the Department of the Treasury. The Office of Foreign Assets Control (OFAC) within Treasury is the responsible agency for controlling these specific boycotts. The pattern of governance is a broad assets control law with additional laws directed to specific countries, such as the Cuban Assets Control Regulations. 31 C.F.R. Part 515. The various country specific regulations prohibit specific transactions and transfers. By controlling the flow of currency, whether to pay for imports or be paid for exports, trade is thereby controlled. Terminating the flow of currency is intended to terminate trade. It works, but not completely, because considerable trade may take place through third nations. Many U.S. goods are sold in Cuba, transferred first to middle-men in such nations as Mexico or Panama. Unilateral boycotts which are unpopular in other nations are difficult to enforce.

United States boycott policy, as expressed in such laws as the Cuban Democracy Act of 1992, the Iran and Libya Sanctions Act of 1996 and the Cuban Liberty and Democratic Solidarity (Libertad) Act of 1996 ("Helms–Burton"), may attempt to reach the conduct of third party nations toward the boycotted country. Using such devices as exerting extraterritorial power over owned or controlled entities located in third nations, the United States attempts to draw into the boycott these third nations. It is not surprising that third nations have often responded with extremely strong criticism about interference with their sovereignty by the United States. Curiously, the United States is attempting to mandate conduct by these third party nations which it expressly rejects in the United States *anti*boycott provisions, when other nations attempt to have the United States assist in a foreign boycott.

ANTIBOYCOTT PROVISIONS OF THE EXPORT LAWS

While boycotts are governed as outlined above by regulations enforced by the Department of the Treasury, the Export Administration Act addresses a special problem relating to exports, *antiboycotts*. The provisions are a direct consequence of the Arab nations' economic boycott against Israel commenced initially in 1954. When the Arab boycott was extended beyond the primary level (no trading with Israel), to the secondary level (no trading with any nation's enterprise which trades with Israel), and to the tertiary level (no trading with any third party nation's enterprise trading with Israel if it obtained components from a nation trading with Israel), the United States Congress began to debate whether United States companies ought to be allowed to assist the boycott of a nation friendly to the United

States. After several years of debate and the failure of voluntary controls to have any effect, the EAA was amended to prohibit any United States person from complying with, furthering or supporting any boycott by a foreign nation against another foreign nation which is friendly to the United States. 50 U.S.C.A.App. § 2407.

The statute was intended to achieve a political end, that is to assist Israel, although the language of the law never refers to any country by name. The EAA provisions include broad language which directs the President to issue regulations prohibiting any United States person from doing business in a boycotted country; refusing to hire or discriminating against any United States person; furnishing a broad range of information; or paying, honoring or confirming letters of credit, where such action would comply with, further or support the boycott of a country friendly to the United States. But the provisions also require the regulations to recognize certain exceptions, such as compliance with various requirements of the boycotting country which are essentially nonsupportive of that nation's boycott. A further provision requires any United States person who receives requests which might provide information which would help the boycott to not only refuse such requests, but to report those requests to the Secretary of Commerce. The reporting requirements are extensive. A company is even denied the right to point out errors in the boycotting nation's policy, such as to note that the company is on the black list of the boycotting nation, even though it has never traded with the target nation of the boycott. Such a clarification is considered to support the boycott and is thus prohibited.

The regulations which have been issued in accordance with the EAA are extensive, providing both rules and (in very small print) numerous examples of acts which would or would not violate the law. The examples, when comprehensible, are not always consistent. But they provide some guidance as to the policy behind the regulations.

Since the 1977 amendments to the EAA which introduced the antiboycott provisions, relatively few cases have reached the courts. There have been many challenges by the Department of Commerce's Office of Antiboycott Compliance, but most have ended in a consent decree. The same severe sanctions as outlined above for violations of the United States export laws apply to violations of the antiboycott provisions, but consent decrees often have resulted in negotiating the minimum fines under the EAA, $10,000 per violation, substantially less than the costs and adverse publicity of litigation. Although the decreasing disharmony in the mid-East might suggest an end to the Arab boycott, the nations have not terminated the group boycott. The United States continues to proceed under the laws, illustrated by the 1995 agreement by United States subsidiaries (and a corporation counsel) of the French L'Oreal S.A. to pay fines of $1.4 million for allegedly furnishing or agreeing to furnish information by the subsidiaries to the French parent about business relationships with Israel. The penalties were among the highest negotiated under the laws.

Although the EAA and regulations have provided the teeth to attacking the Arab boycott of Israel, two other laws have also been used. The Internal Revenue Code denies certain tax benefits to a person "participating" in an international boycott, and the Sherman Act (antitrust laws) addresses refusals to deal as anticompetitive activity. But since the adoption of the EAA antiboycott provisions, the tax and antitrust laws have been infrequently applied.

FOREIGN CORRUPT PRACTICES ACT

One final issue of exports involves the practice of United States companies in making payments to foreign government officials or agents to encourage purchasing the company's products or services (or accept or extend its direct foreign investment). During the Watergate investigations of payments to United States political candidates, it was discovered that many United States companies had been making payments to foreign officials. The response was swift. The Foreign Corrupt Practices Act was passed in 1977. 15 U.S.C.A. §§ 78q(b), 78dd, 78fi(a). The original law included only three substantive sections, one establishing accounting standards which required disclosure of foreign payments, and two governing payments to foreign officials and to "other" persons, where those persons "knew or had reason to know" the payments would be passed on to a foreign official. The law included no definitions and only a brief exclusion for payments which were "ministerial" in nature. These were the familiar, minor "grease" payments so often necessary to pass goods through customs. The law was ambiguous, and from the beginning United States businesses requested that the Department of Justice issue guidelines. None were forthcoming. Like the anti-boycott laws discussed above, few cases reached the courts, most being settled with consent decrees and nominal fines, thus avoiding the label "corrupt payor."

Business interests continued to press for changes, which were finally forthcoming in the 1988 trade law. The most significant change was replacing the "reason to know" language with a requirement that any payment to a third person be made "knowing that" it would be passed on to a foreign official. But new definition provisions state that "knowing" may well include reason to know. Having "a firm belief" or being "aware" is sufficient to constitute "knowing." Another important amendment is the further clarification of permissible "grease" payments. Payments are allowed for a "routine government action", which includes obtaining permits to do business, processing papers, providing certain routine services such as police protection or telephone or power, and "actions of a similar nature." But it specifically does not include any decision by a foreign official regarding new business or retaining old business, decisions which are more than merely routine government actions. The law further includes an affirmative defense section which stipulates several payments which are not prohibited. They include payments permissible under the *written* laws of the other nation, and reasonable and bona fide expenditures such as travel and lodging if related to the promotion or performance of the contract. Other changes to the FCPA in 1988 include some clarification of the accounting provisions. A final change in 1988 removed what was known as the Eckhardt provision, which prohibited bringing a suit directly against an employee without first having received a judgment finding the employer in violation of the Act. See United States v. McLean, 738 F.2d 655 (5th Cir.1984). With the removal of the Eckhardt provision, corporate officers may find themselves scapegoats, and required to defend charges while the company remains free of any litigation.

A few individual nations have attempt to prohibit payments by their nations' entities, but some nations encourage such payments by allowing them to constitute deductions against taxes as ordinary business expenses. Attempts within the UN to govern payments to foreign officials on the international level failed. The United States Trade Representative began an intense effort in 1996 to gain agreement by other nations to prohibit such deductions. The international organization Transparency International urged adoption of laws prohibiting such payments, and has published annual lists of the most corrupt nations. Finally, efforts of the Organization for Economic Cooperation and Development (OECD) led to the 1997 OECD Convention on

Combating Bribery of Foreign Officials, which obligates signatories to criminalize bribery of foreign officials. The U.S. signed the Convention and amended the FCPA in 1998. The 1998 amendment slightly broadens the definition of wrongful conduct to include payments which "secure an advantage."

SECTION 301 AND SUPER 301

Section 301 of the Trade Act of 1974 is one of the most politically motivated provisions of United States trade laws. Basically, this section applies when United States rights or benefits under international trade agreements are at risk or when foreign nations engage in unjustifiable, unreasonable or discriminatory conduct. Thus Section 301 primarily focuses on the activities of foreign governments. Although it has been used to protect United States markets from foreign imports, Section 301 has been most notably applied to open up foreign markets to United States exports, investments and intellectual property rights. The focus has been on foreign market access for U.S. goods and services.

Section 301 of the Trade Act of 1974 authorizes and in some cases mandates unilateral United States retaliation if another nation is in breach of a trade agreement or engaging in unjustifiable, unreasonable or discriminatory conduct. Amendments contained in the Trade and Tariff Act of 1984 broadened the scope of Section 301 to include retaliatory action against foreign country practices in connection with *services*. Special remedies are allowed, including denial of "service sector access authorizations." Presumably, for example, the USTR (subject to presidential directives) could deny access to foreign banks by withholding licenses from federal authorities.

Petitions for action under Section 301 are filed with the United States Trade Representative, who undertakes appropriate relief after investigation, consultation with the relevant foreign country and other interested parties, and an affirmative determination of a Section 301 "offense." The USTR may self-initiate Section 301 proceedings, a practice increasingly undertaken since 1988. Remedies are mandatory (subject to various exceptions) when United States trade agreement rights are being denied or an unjustifiable foreign country practice is found. Remedies are discretionary when unreasonable or discriminatory practices are involved. The remedies available include suspending trade agreement concessions, various import restraints, and bilateral agreements with the offending country. The USTR chooses the remedy subject to presidential "direction." The remedy chosen need not have any connection with the complaints.

Perhaps the most critical difference between the Section 301 offenses concerns "international legal rights," which is part of the definition of unjustifiable practices. Discriminatory practices are those which deny national or MFN treatment, but there is no reference to doing so inconsistently with United States legal rights. Unreasonable practices are expressly not premised on international legal rights, and only need to be "unfair and inequitable." There is a long list of examples of unreasonable practices in Section 301(d)(3)(B).

The statutory definitions of unreasonableness were expanded in 1988. They include inequitable treatment in connection with market opportunities, investment and protection of intellectual property rights. There is no requirement that such behavior violate an international agreement to which the United States is a party. This has the advantage of not linking relief to international dispute settlement procedures. Thus, Section 301 is a statutory provision of remarkable breadth.

Most Section 301 proceedings have been resolved through negotiations leading to alteration of foreign country practices. Ultimately, if the President or the USTR is not satisfied with any negotiated result in connection with a Section 301 complaint, the United States may undertake unilateral retaliatory trade measures. Unlike subsidy, dumping, escape clause and market disruption proceedings, Section 301 of the Trade Act of 1974 has no origins in or other imprimatur of legitimacy from the GATT or World Trade Organization. Indeed, the unilateral nature of Section 301 is thought by many to run counter to the multilateral approach to trade relations embodied in the GATT and WTO. Brazil lodged but did not actively pursue a GATT complaint about Section 301 during the Uruguay Round negotiations.

Section 301 has received hostile responses from U.S. trade partners, especially after the amendments to Section 301 implemented in 1988 through the Omnibus Trade and Competitiveness Act. These amendments include the so-called "Super 301 procedures" which required the USTR in 1989 and 1990 (only) to initiate Section 301 proceedings against "priority practices" in "priority countries" identified by the USTR as most significant to United States exports. In May of 1989, the USTR initiated Super 301 procedures against the following:

(a) Japanese procurement restraints on purchases of United States supercomputers and space satellites, and Japanese technical barriers to trade in wood products;

(b) Brazilian import bans and licensing controls; and

(c) Indian barriers to foreign investment and foreign insurance.

Super 301 was timed to dovetail with the Uruguay Round of GATT negotiations on trade in services scheduled to end in late 1990. Some saw it as a clever United States bargaining chip. It was anticipated that intergovernmental negotiations concerning alleged unfair trading practices would be undertaken in the 12 to 18 months that followed. This proved to be true for Japan and Brazil, but not India, which refused to even discuss its Super 301 listing. Settlements were negotiated with Japan and

Brazil which significantly opened these markets to United States exporters.

The Super 301 procedures and designations created in Section 301 of the Trade Act of 1974 were limited in application to 1989 and 1990. Super 301 was perceived to be an acceptable alternative to the "Gephardt Amendment" which would have required 10 percent annual reductions in United States trade deficits with countries having excessive and unwarranted trade surpluses. Either way, Japan was clearly the main target of the Gephardt Amendment, Super 301 and continuing efforts to renew Super 301. These efforts, a notable rise in Japan's 1993 trade surplus with the United States and the failure of a trade summit early in 1994 all contributed to the revival of Super 301 in 1994 by President Clinton. This revival was undertaken for two years by executive order and (once again) may have forestalled more severe trade sanctions by Congress. The Uruguay Round Agreements Implementation Act in 1995 codified President Clinton's executive order. Executive orders have continued to give life to Super 301.

United States adherence to nearly all of the Uruguay Round agreements, including the Dispute Settlement Understanding (DSU), may reduce the frequency with which it unilaterally invokes Section 301. The DSU obligates its signatories to follow streamlined dispute settlement procedures under which unilateral retaliation is restrained until the offending nation has failed to conform to a World

Trade Organization panel ruling. However, disputes falling outside the scope of the Uruguay Round agreements to which the United States adheres remain vulnerable under Section 301, as the United States asserted in 1995 regarding Japanese restraints on imports of United States auto parts.

CHAPTER FIVE

VARIATIONS ON FOREIGN INVESTMENT

DEFINING THE FOREIGN INVESTMENT

Foreign investment commonly involves the *ownership* of some of the equity in a foreign business. It may also involve *control*. Ownership and control issues are often complex, especially in cross-border situations, as for example, when a corporation chartered in one nation has its center of management in a second nation and its owners (shareholders) are citizens of a third nation. While identifying the nation of the corporation's articles of incorporation (charter) is usually easy, it may not be easy to determine who owns or controls the entity, or even where that control occurs. Where the investor owns all the equity in the foreign investment, there is usually little question regarding who has ownership and control. But as the equity percentage owned by the foreign investor diminishes, the question of control arises. Ownership of a majority of the voting equity of the foreign entity usually means the entity is a subsidiary under the control of the investor.

If the investor from abroad has half the equity, who has control may be quite uncertain. No one has control by virtue of ownership of 50 percent, but one of the 50 percent owners may be able to exert control. It may depend on the existence of and ability to control proxies. Where the ownership is less than 50 percent, often the case of a joint venture where the foreign owner is limited to 49 percent equity, control is quite likely to be the result less of the equity split, than some form of management agreement. Few multinational corporations with foreign investments in many nations are willing to hold 49 percent equity without very substantial participation in management, if not assurance of absolute control.

As the discussion below will illustrate, some of the major issues involved with establishing a foreign investment relate to the issue of control and ownership. Restrictions on control and ownership are most likely to be part of the foreign investment legal and policy framework of developing and non-market economy nations. As developing and transitional nations join international trade organizations and regional economic groups, such as the WTO or the NAFTA, they are required to reduce or abolish restrictions on foreign investment. But they often are allowed reservations which allow reduction or abolition to occur over long periods of time, or even allow the permanent retention of certain restrictions.

REASONS FOR ESTABLISHING
A FOREIGN INVESTMENT

Foreign investments are initiated for many different reasons. Sometimes it is the natural succession
to a successful period of increasing export sales to a
foreign nation, when the company believes the foreign market is sufficiently large to justify foreign
production. Local, foreign production will reduce
transportation costs of finished products sold in the
domestic market of the foreign nation, and will
allow the use of local resources available at lower
cost, especially labor. Foreign investment may follow immediately after a successful period of export
sales, or follow a period of foreign production not by
means of a direct equity investment, but by licensing the technology for foreign production to a domestic firm in the foreign nation. An example is the
aircraft manufacturing industry. In order to assure
participation in sales in the increasing Asian market, especially China, United States aircraft manufacturing companies have moved the manufacture
of some parts to Asia, both by licensing and by new
direct foreign investment.

The multinational company may dislike transferring technology to a company owned by another,
foreign party, whether due to a fear of loss of that
technology, or an inability to control production
quality. The fear of loss of the technology is of
special concern when the technology consists of
knowhow, which often lacks the more specific pro-

tection provided patents, trademarks and copyrights. Such fear is particularly well founded with respect to nations which do not afford very strong protection to intellectual property rights. Even if a transfer of technology license to an unrelated company in another nation has resulted in a profitable relationship, the technology owning multinational may prefer to establish a wholly or majority owned subsidiary to take over the production of the goods or services. The multinational may not wish to share in the profits with the licensee when it could do the production itself, and, as noted above, keep better control over production quality.

The foreign investment which follows export sales or a transfer of technology tends to be *voluntary* in the sense that the company makes the decision for business reasons, not because the framework of laws and policies of the foreign government require local production. In some cases, however, especially in developing nations with balance of payments problems, the government may make it very difficult, if not impossible, for other nations' businesses to export to the country. High tariffs, quotas and other nontariff barriers may be used both to reduce imports and the consequent demand for scarce foreign currency to pay for the imports, and also to offer considerable protection to domestic industries. The answer for the multinational company may be to become one of those domestic industries by establishing a direct foreign investment. This would be to some degree an *involuntary* investment, in that it is not one of several alternatives available, but the only allowable form of doing business, although the final decision to invest is of course made by the foreign investor.

There is another voluntary/involuntary relationship with foreign investment, where the foreign investor establishes a joint venture. The joint venture decision may be totally voluntary on the part of the foreign investor, or a joint venture may be mandated by local law or policy. For whatever reasons a multinational decides to commence a direct foreign investment, it will face different rules in different countries. It is to some of those rules which we now turn.

RESTRICTIONS ON FOREIGN INVESTMENT—DEVELOPING NATIONS

Restrictions on the establishment of a foreign investment frequently limit the amount of equity and the amount of management control allowed to foreign investors. They may also restrict the way in which the investment is created, limiting or prohibiting investment by *acquisition* of an existing locally owned entity. Limitations on acquisitions and mandates for joint ventures are interrelated. When foreign investment by acquisition is prohibited, the joint venture mandates play no role. When foreign investment by acquisition is permitted, the joint venture laws may enter to limit the permissible amount of foreign equity which may be acquired.

Until the early 1970s, there were comparatively few restrictions on foreign ownership in market economy developing nations. During the 1960s, many large multinationals expanded abroad by opening new plants or by acquiring locally owned enterprises. The acquisition of existing enterprises in developing nations generated concern and often hostility, and led to the adoption of laws in many developing nations regulating foreign investment. Those laws tended to have fairly common approaches to foreign investment.

First, the acquisition of host nation enterprises was either limited or prohibited.

Second, new investment would be required to be permitted to own certain percentages of local equity participation. Some areas of investment, such as export oriented extractive industries, communications, transportation, banking, insurance and electricity, often were reserved for either exclusively state owned enterprises, or enterprises which were owned by nationals and excluded all foreign equity participation. Other areas of business, those not expressly designated for the above limits, could have specific levels of participation by foreign investors, usually a maximum of 49 percent. As in the case of the transfer of technology, a government agency would have to approve acquisitions or new investment. The agency usually was allowed discretion in granting exceptions, and frequently the statute provided a list of criteria for approving or disapproving the proposed investment. Common criteria, whether in those lists or in the unwritten policy of the approving agency, would include:

1. assisting in generating economic development,

2. agreeing on the number of workers to be employed,

3. considering the effect on existing national businesses,

4. considering the effect on balance of payments, i.e., mandating certain minimum levels of exports,

5. mandating the use of domestic materials and parts,

6. requiring financing be obtained from abroad,

7. contributing to host nation acquisition of advanced technology,

8. locating the plant in designated development zones, and

9. establishing research and development facilities in the nation.

Investment laws were often supplemented by regulations, guidelines and decisions of foreign investment registration and review agencies. Frequently the decisions of review agencies were not made available to the public, for example decisions of the Mexican National Commission on Foreign Investment. But attorneys occasionally gained access to these decisions through personal contacts in the government, and counsel with such access were better able to assist in predicting how the agencies were likely to respond to applications for exceptions to the restrictive investment laws. What thus confronts potential investors in developing nations are not only the restrictive investment laws on the books, but written and unwritten guidelines and policies which generally moderate many of the restrictions. It is the unwritten restrictions which create the most concern for the unknowing investors and their counsel.

Developing nation joint venture laws were quite different from joint venture laws in nonmarket economy nations. The latter were passed by nations which had long prohibited any foreign investment; new investment laws were intended to "attract" foreign investment, but initially only to a maximum level of 49 percent foreign ownership. Foreign equity was sometimes limited by constitutional provisions which placed the ownership of the means of production and distribution in the state. Developing nation joint venture laws, contrastingly, were intended to "restrict" new investment, and also to encourage, or coerce, existing wholly foreign owned investment to sell majority ownership to local individuals or entities owned by local investors or the state.

The laws were rarely retroactive by their terms, but they often contained features which made them retroactive in application. The Mexican 1973 Foreign Investment Law did not apply to existing companies, but a company could neither expand into new lines of products nor open new locations without "Mexicanizing" the entire company. That meant reducing the foreign equity to no more than 49 percent. Devices were created by the foreign investors to avoid this impact, such as fragmenting the manufacturing of products, by adopting the joint venture in new subsidiaries for the production of new products, but keeping the old enterprise wholly foreign owned.

Accompanying the mandates for local ownership were similar requirements for local management. Where foreign equity was limited to 49 percent, that same percentage would apply to the number of foreigners allowed on the board. But a minority in *numbers* does not necessarily mean a minority in *influence*, and the local board members usually were motivated by the same profit goals as the foreign parent appointees. Nationalism might arise among the board members, however, if the parent wanted the foreign affiliate to shift production to another nation, or take any action which appeared to benefit the company's activities in another nation at the expense of the entity in the host, developing nation.

Some developing countries, after several years of what must be labeled reasonable compliance with the host nations' restrictive rules by multinational enterprises, began to wonder why their nations had not increased their rate of development. No one gave much thought to the fact that developing nation private shareholders had the same aspirations of profit as developed nation shareholders, and developing nation directors acted in the same way as their counterparts in developed nations. Shifting ownership from foreign to domestic was no guarantee of economic development in the nation as a whole. To encourage more investment, many nations with restrictive laws began to allow total foreign ownership under written or unwritten "exception" provisions. The foreign investor was allowed to retain total ownership if it transferred the most modern technology to the host nation, or located the plant in an area of high unemployment or a zone designated for economic development, or exported a high percentage of its output, or located research and development facilities in the nation.

The IBM company is a good example. It has avoided joint ventures in its production abroad. In Mexico, IBM has expanded production considerably since the enactment of the strict investment law in 1973, by agreeing to produce the most recent models and by exporting a high percentage of production. But when told by the Indian government in the 1980s that it had to alter its structure to a joint venture, with no alternatives, IBM withdrew its investment.

After (1) the debt crisis in the early 1980s, (2) the opening to investment by many *non*market economies, and (3) the election of less "populist" governments in many developing nations, the rules of the game began to change dramatically in the 1980s and 1990s. Developing nations as well as nonmarket economies pushed aside the "myth of privatization" and began to take it seriously, selling off many state owned industries. Restrictive investment laws were interpreted in favor of foreign investors wishes, and subsequently replaced by laws more encouraging than restrictive of investment. But not all countries have been enthusiastic about opening to foreign investment. India, for example, remains a maze of restrictive laws and policies. But even the most investment encouraging nations retain restrictions. One of the most discouraging and enduring characteristics of investing abroad, in nonmarket as well as developing nations, is persistent and deeply rooted corruption. Government officials view openings to foreign investment as an opportunity to "cash in" on the enormous amounts of funds changing hands. Bribery is the blemish of business. Never legal but too often tolerated, it is one of the most difficult challenges to foreign investors, especially United States investors who confront the United States Foreign Corrupt Payments Act. (The FCPA is discussed in the previous chapter).

Foreign investment laws adopted since the 1980s usually allow total foreign ownership, but often restrict some areas for continued state ownership. Joint ventures are still encouraged, but when formed they tend to be more voluntary than involuntary. Sometimes continuing restrictions on foreign ownership of land induces a joint venture, as might risk analysis which suggests limiting equity participation, even though market studies encourage entering the market.

The ability under local law to form a foreign investment is now less the issue than the method chosen. For the host nation, the initiation of a new investment ("greenfields" investing) may be preferred over the acquisition of an existing one, and a joint venture preferred over total foreign ownership, but the foreign investor often is the one making the final choice. Many nations, including some developed nations, have some method of reviewing acquisitions, for such various reasons as national security or national economic interests.

Most developing nations encourage foreign investment to a greater degree than two or three decades ago, especially during the often hostile North–South dialogue era of the late 1960s and 1970s. Even nations slow to open to foreign investment, such as India, are more receptive to investment than during that troublesome era. What is essential to understand is that there is a *dynamic* process to investment attitudes among nations. The laws in place at one time ought not be viewed as representative of the legal framework a decade or two in the future. Investors must be prophets not in their own land, and be aware than the dynamic process of economic and political development and change is the engine which pulls the train of rules on trade and investment.

RESTRICTIONS ON FOREIGN INVESTMENT—NONMARKET AND TRANSITION ECONOMY NATIONS

Nonmarket economy nations are in most cases also developing nations. Thus nonmarket economy nations often have limitations on the initiation of foreign investment which parallel those described above for developing nations. But there are differences in the restrictions due to the nature of the nonmarket economy. As noted above, the restrictive rules on foreign investment were part of the political-economic Marxist philosophy adopted by most nonmarket economies, and expressed by the term *nonmarket economy.* But as nonmarket economy nations failed to achieve levels of growth occurring in market economies, and failed to produce internally or acquire from abroad advanced technology, they began to trade with and then admit some limited foreign investment.

They first attempted to obtain technology through transfers to local, state owned productive facilities. But they failed, usually because of inadequate legal protection of intellectual property. The lack of adequate protection was sometimes due to a stated belief that intellectual property was not subject to private ownership, but was the patrimony of mankind. Philosophical differences in who ought to own the means of production and distribution persist even as nonmarket economies enter the transition to market economies. Dealing with the bureaucracy is a major problem in investing in a nonmarket economy. Often there are no links of communication between foreign investors and the newly developing local business community. Labor has been vocal and sometimes well organized, and government ministries may continue to be the negotiators or lobbyists for local, private business.

Political interference is a continuing characteristic of investment in nonmarket economies. But it is a frustrating and elusive interference—the one who has the final say in the government is often "everyone and no-one".

Market economy nation companies do not wish to risk valuable technology and other intellectual property to Marxist principles of the patrimony of mankind. They would thus license technology only to wholly or majority owned subsidiaries, which local law often did not permit. Consequently, nonmarket economies were unable to gain access to very much advanced Western technology, because of their refusal to admit direct foreign equity investments, or provide protection to licensed technology. In the early 1970s, however, the desire for Western technology pushed some of the rigid Marxist theory to the back burner in several nonmarket economy nations.

Yugoslavia, Hungary and Romania each adopted joint venture laws. These new laws nevertheless limited the foreign equity participation to 49 percent. Since the nonmarket economies did not have equity share corporations, nor corporation or company laws governing the formation and operation of such entities, the two principal incidents of share ownership, management participation and profits, necessarily had to be creations of the joint venture *contract* rather than share certificates. Profits often would be taken in the form of some percentage of the production, to be sold in Western markets. Called *compensation* or *buy-back* agreements, they are included under the umbrella of *countertrade.* These arrangements have not been without difficulties, however, as the quality of nonmarket economy production has often been criticized. The criticism has often been supported by high percentages of returns of unacceptable products. Furthermore, unless the parent company expands its markets in the West, the nonmarket economy entity production taken as profit and sold in the West, will necessarily displace some Western production. What goodwill may have been created in the nonmarket economy may be lost in the Western nation affected by a loss of its production.

The second element of direct investment, participation in *control,* creates more philosophical problems than the problems of profit sharing, which are usually largely related to currency shortages. According to nonmarket economy political/economic theory, management is in the hands of the state, or, as practiced in the former Yugoslavia, under "workers' social property", directly in the hands of a plant's workers. Joint venture contracts sometimes provided for sharing major management decisions, but did not allow management to be dominated in numbers by foreign participants. A minority of a managing board, however, might be accepted by the majority as the influential management group. The philosophical participation of workers in ownership and control has influenced the role of unions as nonmarket nations have entered the transition phase. Governments often are not certain how to deal with their work force, but have tended to attempt to allow them to participate in ownership, and sometimes management representation, when state owned entities are privatized, and to allow them to organize in what in some countries are very strong unions. These unions often lack direction.

Joint venture laws varied significantly throughout the nonmarket economy world. The Eastern European laws developed over nearly two decades of experience, and were occasionally amended to accommodate new problems. China enacted a joint venture law in 1979, and within a decade there were some 2,500 established joint ventures. The Chinese law initially was brief and unclear, but underwent modifications in fact and in interpretation as the Chinese economy moved to adopt more market economy characteristics. By 1986, the Chinese were even allowing wholly owned subsidiaries. Contrastingly, the 1982 Cuban joint venture law generated little response from foreign investors (United States investors have not been permitted to invest in Cuba). The reason seemed long obvious to all but the Cuban government. The 1982 law was outmoded when it was enacted in comparison to the amendments occurring in Eastern European joint venture laws. Cuba wanted the benefits of foreign investment, without assuming any obligations of a host nation. But in 1995 a new law replaced the old, offering new concessions, but still a decade or more behind developments in those nations already well into the period of transition towards market economies.

With the development of joint ventures in Eastern Europe and the success in China, the major holdout, the USSR, created in 1987 a joint venture law. The Gorbachev era of glasnost included a major step in altering the tight control on the economy that existed for decades. The USSR joint venture law, like most initial nonmarket economy joint venture laws, was limited to creating a small opening to foreign direct equity investment which would likely lead to a small response, particularly were management of the joint venture to remain within Soviet hands. More recently, the newly independent states of the former USSR have been adopting much less restrictive investment laws, and even moving into the era of privatization.

If any label is merited by the nonmarket economies regarding the acceptance of foreign investment, it is that of "pragmatic accommodation." The most significant changes in the rules regarding foreign investment have occurred in those NME nations where there have been similarly meaningful changes in allowing free market elements to penetrate domestic trade. These changes are usually frustratingly slow, sometimes subject to periodic suspension, but they represent extraordinary alterations in the fundamental economic structures and attitudes of nations long satisfied with a place in the obscure recesses of the international trading community. Many of the nations in transition have moved well into the next phase, ridding the state of significant involvement of ownership of the nation's means of production and distribution. It is the era of privatization.

PRIVATIZATION: THE FOCUS OF THE 1990S

The lessening of state ownership of the means of production and distribution is being carried out principally by a process of privatization. While such conversion is a critical aspect of the transition of nonmarket economies to market economies, privatization is also occurring with vigor in many developing, *market* economy nations. The reason is partly shared by both forms of economy. State ownership of the means of production and distribution of goods and services is increasingly viewed as philosophically inappropriate as an activity for state ownership. More practically, most state enterprises have been unable to operate at a profit, causing a drain on state resources. Privatization is viewed as a means of reducing the drain on national revenue used to subsidize state owned enterprises, a way to raise revenue to improve national infrastructure, and a possible future source of revenue if private ownership means improving the efficiency of manufacture to the point of competing in world markets and increasing export revenue.

Additionally, privatization is thought to be a better way to provide goods and services demanded by a nation's population. This view extends to the largest developed nations. Britain, Italy, France and Germany have all privatized large state owned industries. In the United States, the privatization ideology has extended to highways, ports, wastewater facilities, gas utilities, and many local government services such as parking garages, and recreational facilities such as golf courses.

Not all enterprises have been placed on the market, but the NMEs often express a willingness to sell more large companies than some market economy developing nations in their own process of privatization. For example, Hungary has sold the telecommunications company, MATAV, the airline MALEV, and a large lighting products company, Tungsram. But developing market economy nations are not far behind. Argentina has sold 45% of the oil and gas company YPF, its airlines Aerolineas Argentinas, and the Telecom company. Some national companies are referred to as "untouchables". But even they are having parts sold. Mexico's previously untouchable oil enterprise, PEMEX, has sold retail outlets, and its petrochemical production. Only gas and oil production remain for the time-being "untouchable". Mexico's privatization of parts of PEMEX has not been without challenge and criticism; however, the process of privatization was at one time so sensitive in Mexico that it was referred to as "disincorporation."

As a comparatively new phenomenon, privatization has raised new issues for foreign investors. Privatization has become a process based on a mix of law and policy. The policy may be very pro-privatization, but backed by weak laws which do not answer many important questions. Most NMEs have adopted privatization laws which are periodically amended as more is learned about the issues confronting the process. Some of those issues include identifying businesses for sale, the role of workers in approving the sale, the valuation of the business, the level of foreign investment allowed in a sale, rights of nationals and/or employees to ownership preferences, method of financing, and the creation of an adequate legal infrastructure (corporation laws, securities laws, bankruptcy laws, etc.) to assist the process. In many cases these questions are not resolved in the written privatization laws of the nations. They must be dealt with in negotiations with the government.

One of the most difficult issue in privatization is how to value the business. Many nonmarket economy enterprises possess little of value for the new owner except the right to function as the business. Obsolete equipment must be replaced. New markets must be sought. Modern technology must be introduced. Work forces often must be reduced and the remaining workers trained in more efficient methods of production and the use of new technology. Accounting methods of the NMEs gave little attention to market economy concepts, and thus book value is generally useless. Since there was no share ownership there was no market value of ownership interests. The value issue in a privatization usually must be negotiated.

Even when a value has been established which seems generally acceptable, the absence of savings in the nonmarket economies probably means that foreign capital will be necessary to carry out the privatization. But there may be reservations about selling majority ownership and control to foreign investors. Additionally, the NMEs may offer their own nationals some preference in the way of certificates which may be exchanged for shares in privatized companies. This means that a foreign purchaser may obtain 80 percent of the equity of the enterprise, but be expected to pay for 100 percent of its value. At the head of the line of nationals seeking preferential treatment may be workers in the enterprise to be sold. Workers may have rights to purchase, also in the form of a kind of scrip exchangeable for shares.

The process of privatization has not been easy, and is only partly completed. It has been a dominant part of the process of alteration of the ownership of the means of production and distribution in NMEs throughout the 1990s, and will continue into the new century. It is a necessary concomitant to becoming market economies. If there is any doubt about the seriousness of nations to privatize, the figures speak loudly. The IFC of the World Bank reported that some 2,700 state owned enterprises were privatized between 1988 and 1993 in more than 95 countries, raising about $271 billion in revenue.

POLICY VERSUS LAW: DEALING WITH THE OPERATIONAL CODE OR THE WAY THINGS WORK

The written laws of the developing nations are the principal framework for regulating the foreign investor. Many developing and nonmarket economies have specific laws governing foreign investment, and the transfer of technology. These laws are what the public (and too often the foreign investor) believes comprise the *exclusive* framework for investment. But each nation has another level of law, that which is unwritten. It is the "way things work," an operational code. It consists of unpublished regulations and rulings which are applied in some cases, but not even mentioned in others. The Brazilians call them "drawer regulations." Investors in China are sometimes confronted with laws they have never heard of, and which they are told may not even be read by foreigners. This operational code allows the government to give different treatment to different investors. Fortunately, many local attorneys know what they are and how to use them. They are a reason for choosing local counsel wisely.

RESTRICTIONS ON FOREIGN INVESTMENT IN DEVELOPED, MARKET ECONOMY NATIONS

The enactment of laws affecting foreign investment is not limited to the developing nations and nonmarket economy nations. Investors attempting to establish equity investments in Japan confront numerous obstacles, although no written, restrictive foreign investment law exists. Many new foreign investors began to establish a base in the European Union for fear that a "Fortress Europe" would develop in 1992 (the consequence of the achievement of a "Europe Without *Internal* Frontiers") which would restrict foreign investment. Canada adopted a fairly restrictive foreign investment law in 1973, but following much criticism from abroad and debate within, the law was replaced with the far less restrictive Investment Canada Act in 1985. The 1985 law, which required review of large proposed investments, was incorporated into the 1989 Canada–United States Free Trade Agreement (CFTA), but with major exceptions for U.S. investors. The North American Free Trade Agreement Chapter 11 establishes investment rules, reflecting to some extent the provisions in the CFTA. France, Korea and other developed nations additionally review some foreign investment on national interest grounds. One ought not assume that control of foreign investment is limited to developing and non-market economy nations. Or assume that the United States does not control foreign investment in the United States.

The United States has long promoted an image of an investment encouraging nation, where only a few areas are subject to ownership and control limitations, such as national defense, nuclear energy and domestic air transportation. Upon occasion (fear of Japanese domination in the last decade) proposals have been introduced in the Congress to require some level of registration of foreign investment, but invariably they have been defeated as restrictive and discouraging of desirable job-creating foreign investment. A Committee on Foreign Investment in the United States (CFIUS), was created in 1975 to monitor foreign investment (www.treas.gov/oii). CFIUS became the presidential designee to monitor and review foreign investment when Congress in 1988 enacted the Exon–Florio Amendment of the Defense Production Act (DPA), as part of the Omnibus Trade and Competitiveness Act. 50 U.S.C.A.App. § 2170. The Exon–Florio law was partly the response to the proposed acquisition of Fairchild Semiconductor Corporation by the Japanese company Fujitsu, Ltd. Fairchild was engaged in defense manufacturing. CFIUS had reviewed this proposed acquisition (before the enactment of Exon–Florio) and determined that national security interests were at risk, but CFIUS had no authority to stop the acquisition. Fujitsu nevertheless terminated its proposed acquisition in the face of government pressure.

Although Exon–Florio expired October 20, 1990, with the lapsing of the DPA, new legislation in August, 1991, granted Exon–Florio permanent status. The first major amendment came in 1992, after Congressional dissatisfaction with the way the President and CFIUS handled the proposed takeover of part of LTV by Thomson–CSF, a conglomerate with majority ownership by the French government. The expected purchase by Thomson of LTV's missile division was terminated by Thomson when it believed it could not expect to gain approval under Exon–Florio from the Department of Defense. Congress had intervened because members were upset with the failure of the administration to act more strictly. Thomson's withdrawal led to litigation as well as to the 1992 amendments.

The Exon–Florio law gives the President (or designee—currently the CFIUS) authority to investigate effects on national security from mergers, acquisitions and takeovers which might result in foreign control. If national security is threatened, the President may prohibit the action. Under one of the major provisions of the 1992 amendments, the review *must* occur if the purchasing foreigner is "controlled by or acting on behalf of a foreign government". The second important amendment prohibits the sale of some United States companies to certain foreign investors, principally those involved with foreign governments.

Exon–Florio gives the President authority to block an acquisition within statutory guidelines. The review must commence within 30 days of receipt of notification of the proposed action, and must be completed within 45 days after the review commences. The President has 15 days to announce his decision after the investigation is completed. The presidential findings are not reviewable. He must find (1) "credible evidence" that foreign "control" might "impair the national security," and (2) that United States law (other than Exon–Florio and the IEEPA) does not provide adequate and appropriate authority for the President to protect national security. It is unclear what industries affect national security, although the law suggests (1) "domestic production needed for projected national defense requirements," (2) "capability and capacity of domestic industries to meet national defense requirements," and (3) "control ... by foreign citizens as it affects the capability and capacity of the United States to meet the requirements of national security." Certainly the defense industry, to the extent it may be defined, is included. Also included are nondefense industries which manufacture products which have strategic significance, particularly when they have a large share of the United States market and there are no easily located substitutes. What action the President may take is not included in the statute, which refers to "appropriate relief."

Prior to early 1991, the review could address any transfer of technology resulting from foreign investment. But the Treasury is thought by some to have adopted a policy (denied by Treasury) that CFIUS could only investigate the foreign acquisition of at least a majority of the equity of a United States company. That seems consistent with the language of the act, which mentions only "mergers, acquisitions and takeovers." Treasury argues that it is "control" rather than "equity percentage" which is the guide. But this alleged policy angered many members of Congress, who believed the law should be more extensively rather than less extensively applied. There have been (as of mid–1995) 959 notifications (voluntary system of reporting a proposed transaction) leading to 15 investigations, but only one blocked acquisition. The number of notifications has been decreasing each year, from a high of 295 in 1990 to 69 in 1994. The reason may be a combination of a reduced inflow of investment, and a better understanding of the scope of the law by practitioners.

Of the almost one thousand notifications presented to the executive under the voluntary reporting system, only 15 have proceeded to a formal investigation, causing critics to charge that the law is not being used to block investment as allegedly intended. A 1995 study by the European–American Chamber of Commerce suggested that European owned companies did not consider Exon–Florio to be a block to investment in the United States, but more an administrative annoyance. The Department of Defense, as might be expected, has become a major participant in requesting investigations. One example is where Defense joined the Departments of Energy, Treasury and Commerce to challenge the proposed acquisition of General Ceramics by the Japanese company, Tokuyama Soda Co., Ltd. General Ceramics manufactured ceramics used in nuclear weapon electronic circuits. There was evidence that Japan was urging its businesses to manipulate their acquisitions to avoid Exon–Florio challenges. It appeared likely that the acquisition would be blocked, and General Ceramics sold its defense related business to another company, leading CFIUS to find no objection to the acquisition.

The one case where a proposed acquisition led to a presidential order blocking the acquisition involved China's National Aero–Technology Import and Export Corp.'s (CATIC) proposed acquisition of MAMCO Mfg, a Seattle aircraft parts manufacturer. The investigation disclosed that the buyer CATIC had previously violated United States export control laws in purchases of General Electric aircraft engines. There were also concerns about CATIC's attempts to gain technology to build jet fighters able to refuel during flight, and carrying on some covert operations in the United States for the Chinese government. The Executive Order calling for divestment referred only to the threat to national security, providing no detailed supporting reasons.

Soon after the enactment of Exon–Florio, the Treasury Department was expected to issue regulations. Proposals were announced in July, 1989, but issuance of the final regulations was delayed until 1992. 31 C.F.R. Part 800, App. (1992). They were disappointing to those who expected the regulations to define "national security", and to provide a "bright-line" definition of what constitutes "foreign control". Nor did the regulations establish a "sunset" provision which limits the length of time a transaction not notified to CFIUS nevertheless remains subject to review.

Exon–Florio has increasingly been used by target corporations whose management is hostile to a proposed takeover. It is an unanticipated consequence of the enactment of Exon–Florio. The target company may use the 30 day post-notification review period to try to delay the takeover, even to the extent of providing misleading information to CFIUS. The intention would be to cause CFIUS to undertake an investigation, thus initiating the 45 day investigation period. Such delay may be enough to discourage the foreign would-be acquirer, even though there are no legitimate national security grounds to expect an ultimate presidential blockage. There are no clear sanctions for use of Exon–Florio to block a hostile takeover, but providing false or misleading information to CFIUS would seem to violate federal criminal statutes. If the United States intends to be receptive to foreign investment, including investment by way of acquisition, the misuse of Exon–Florio is counterproductive to that policy of openness.

Exon–Florio is viewed by many in Congress as the means by which Congress might increase control over foreign investment. The 1992 amendments did not solve all Congressional concerns. Remaining open to further consideration, in addition to clearer definitions and a time limit for filing notifications as noted above, are coverage of the acquisition of "critical" technologies with the test constituting the effect on "economic" versus "national" security; consideration of the concentration in the industry (it can be under antitrust laws), including as a factor whether the target company has received United States government funds; and transferring the chairmanship of CFIUS from Treasury to Commerce.

Proceeding against proposed foreign acquisitions of United States companies under Exon–Florio must be distinguished from proceeding on antitrust grounds. When the Justice Department filed suit in January, 1991, against Nippon Sanso's proposed acquisition of SemiGas Systems, Inc., of California, many thought it was a new policy of tough enforcement of Exon–Florio. It was not. The suit was initiated exclusively under the antitrust law because the proposal would give the Japanese acquirer too much control of the market of hazardous gases used in semiconductor manufacturing.

THE ROLE OF BILATERAL INVESTMENT TREATIES

International law has been slow to establish standards regarding how nations ought to treat foreign investment. The United Nations' efforts to draft a code of conduct for multinational enterprises did not include provisions regulating the conduct of host nations. The one-side efforts of the UN were thus quite unsatisfactory to foreign investors, who sought assistance from their home nations. Bilateral investment treaties (BITs) have provided some help. To promote national treatment and protect United States investors abroad, the United States embarked on the BIT program in the early 1980s. The BIT program followed earlier extensive use of Friendship, Commerce, and Navigation (FCNs) treaties. Unlike the FCNs, the model BIT distinguishes treatment for foreign owned, domestically incorporated subsidiaries and branches of foreign firms for some provisions, particularly employment.

As a result of the Sumitomo Shoji America, Inc. v. Avagliano, 457 U.S. 176 (1982) decision, the FCN treaty afforded no protection to a foreign company using its nationals in hiring. Under the typical BIT, explicit freedom to hire foreign nationals exists in a narrow range of management provisions. But investment screening mechanisms and key sectors often remain exempt from BIT protection, typically listed in the Annex to a BIT. While elimination of foreign investment screening and imposition of performance requirements has been an object of the BIT program, these provisions of the model BIT have been weakened in the treaties currently in force.

It is not only the United States which has emphasized these treaties, they are common features of most developed nations in their relations with host nations for foreign investment. For example, China has investment protection agreements with such nations as Australia, Austria, Belgium–Luxembourg, Denmark, France, Germany, Japan, the Netherlands, and the United Kingdom. A benefit of such an agreement is that its provisions prevail over domestic law, although the agreements usually allow for exceptions to investment protection when in the interests of national security.

The United States has entered into a number of bilateral investment treaties, as well as a number of less formal bilateral trade agreements. But a trade agreement may merely refer to investment as an area for further discussion, tending to deal only with tariff and nontariff barriers to trade. The bilateral investment treaties do address investment issues. They generally replace earlier Friendship, Commerce & Navigation treaties, to the extent that they apply to investments. While many of the first BITs were negotiated with small developing countries, more recently the United States has signed BITs with such important trading nations as Argentina. The Argentina–United States BIT follows the United States BIT prototype of addressing both investment protection and investor access to each other's markets.

The BITs do not prohibit nations from enacting investment laws, but provide that any such laws should not interfere with any rights in the treaty. The free access aspect of some BITs may not be perceived as a right. Thus investment laws might be enacted which limit access to certain areas, but would not create a right of the other party to challenge the law under the BIT.

One important provision the United States seeks to include in its BITs is the "prompt, adequate and effective" concept (if not always the language) of compensation following expropriation. Many of the nations which have recently agreed to this language disputed its appropriateness during the nationalistic North–South dialogue years of the 1960s and 1970s. But as they began to promote rather than restrict investment, these nations had to accept the idea that expropriated investment should be compensated reasonably soon after the taking ("prompt"), based on a fair valuation ("adequate"), and in a realistic form ("effective"). The Argentina–United States BIT uses language referring to the "fair market value ... immediately before the expropriatory action".

Most BITs do not include provisions for consultations when differences arise in the interpretation of the treaty. The Argentina–United States BIT is one of a very few exceptions. BITs do often provide for arbitration, sometimes with no necessary recourse to prior exhaustion of local remedies.

The BIT process is quite dynamic. Each successive agreement with a new country may include some new provisions. The United States has a prototype agreement, but it has been modified as host nations have sought new foreign investment and have been willing to sign a BIT to establish the most attractive conditions for that investment. It is certain that the BITs in existence today will not be identical to BITs executed in years ahead. BITs are an important contribution of the developed home nation to lessening the risk for their multinationals investing abroad. A BIT establishes some ground rules for investment on a bilateral, treaty basis which should not be unilaterally altered by the host nation to impose restrictions on the investments which are inconsistent with the BIT. Certainly, revolutionary governments have ignored similar agreements in the past and may in the future. But the BITs do provide some investment security, at least as long as the host governments remain relatively stable, and receptive to foreign investment. BITs are not likely to disappear with the completion of the GATT Uruguay Round and the creation of the WTO. The GATT/WTO rules regarding investment are a step in the right direction, but remain less specific than agreements among smaller groups of nations (such as the NAFTA), or bilateral agreements.

FOREIGN INVESTMENT UNDER THE NORTH AMERICAN FREE TRADE AGREEMENT

United States foreign investors in Canada and Mexico may benefit from the provisions of the North American Free Trade Agreement (NAFTA). Chapter 11 covers foreign investment. Section A includes provisions affecting Investment, while Section B addresses the Settlement of Disputes between a Party and an Investor of Another Party. The investment provisions in chapter 11 to some extent reflect provisions in the Canada–United States FTA, but there are some provisions unique to the NAFTA. For example, provisions for local management and control were important provisions in the 1973 Mexican Investment Law. NAFTA, as well as the newer 1993 Mexican Investment Law, prohibit mandating the nationality of senior management. But NAFTA does allow for requirements that the majority of the board of an enterprise which is a foreign investment be of a particular nationality, or resident in the territory, provided that such a requirement does not materially impair the investor's control over the investment. The provisions attempt to balance eliminating the distortions associated with mandating local management, with ensuring that host nation input is provided.

NAFTA investment rules are based on the concept of national treatment. Thus each nation must grant investors of the other member nations treatment no less favorable than is granted to domestic investors. Another central feature is the requirement that each member nation grant investors of the other member nations treatment no less favorable than it grants to any other nation outside NAFTA. Performance requirements are prohibited under NAFTA, and the provisions specifically list seven areas of prohibited performance requirements. But a nation may impose measures to meet protection of life or health, safety, or environmental rules. Incentives to invest also may not be conditioned on most performance requirements, but may be conditioned on location, provision of services, training or employing workers, constructing or expanding facilities, or undertaking research.

NAFTA allows investors to freely transfer profits, dividends, interest, capital, royalties, management and technical advice fees, and other fees, as well as proceeds from the sale of the investment and various payments (such as loan repayments). But limitations on transfers may be made involving certain bankruptcy actions, securities dealings, criminal acts, issues involving property, reporting of transfers, and to ensure satisfaction of judgments.

Each of the member nations of NAFTA listed exceptions to the investment rules, thus deviating from the basic principle of national treatment. Some exceptions were mandated by the nation's constitution, others by federal law. Where a nation has made exceptions which disallow foreign participation, it may either reserve the area for national ownership or exclusively for private domestic ownership. But it may also allow some foreign participation. Thus, some of the restrictive nature of earlier investment laws is preserved, but in a considerably more limited form.

FOREIGN INVESTMENT UNDER THE GATT/WORLD TRADE ORGANIZATION

Previous to the Uruguay Round the GATT did not address issues of foreign investment. But the Uruguay Round produced rules on foreign investment, referred to as Trade Related Aspects of Investment Measures, or TRIMs. These measures are considerably briefer than those in the NAFTA, and only one provision relates to dispute settlement. That article states that the provisions of the General Agreement relating to Consultation (XXII), and Nullification and Impairment (XXIII), and the Understanding on Rules and Procedures Governing the Settlement of Disputes under those articles, apply to consultations and dispute settlement under the TRIM provisions. Thus, there are no separate provisions directed to the uniqueness of investment disputes, as in the NAFTA. It will take time to determine how effective the WTO provisions are to resolving investment disputes.

The GATT Uruguay Round produced significant new investment rules. Prior to this Round, the GATT had not directly governed foreign investment. The new rules are thus quite an important development. But as must be expected with any large organization with divergent views, the investment provisions of the new WTO are not as comprehensive as those discussed above in the NAFTA.

The WTO investment rules or TRIMs first set forth a national treatment principal. TRIMs which are considered inconsistent with WTO obligations are listed in an annex, and include such performance requirements as minimum domestic content, imports limited or linked to exports, restrictions on access to foreign exchange to limit imports for use in the investment, etc. Developing countries are allowed to "deviate temporarily" from the national treatment concept, thus diminishing in value the effectiveness of the WTO investment provisions, and obviously discouraging investment in nations which have a history of imposing investment restrictions, and making such agreements as the NAFTA all the more useful and likely to spread.

The essence of the TRIMs is to establish the same principle of national treatment for investments as has been in effect for trade. TRIMs are incorporated in the overall structure of the WTO, alongside trade measures, rather than being treated as a quite distinct area. Because all the deficiencies of the WTO with regard to trade measures may apply to TRIMs, it remains to be seen how effective these measures will be in governing foreign investment. Because the measures are much less certain than those included in bilateral investment treaties, and small area free trade agreements, it is likely that much of the regulation of foreign investment will develop in the context of the latter rather than within the WTO.

THE OECD AND THE MULTILATERAL AGREEMENT ON INVESTMENT

Bilateral investment treaties have been present for several decades, but have been quite limited in scope. Regional agreements such as the NAFTA and the WTO are both more recent and more extensive in addressing foreign investment issues. The next development may be the adoption of the Multilateral Agreement on Investment (MAI) by the Organization for Economic Cooperation and Development (OECD). The nature of the OECD, dominated by developed nations and including only a few of the more advanced developing nations, such as Mexico, means the MAI is more likely to focus on concerns of the multinational corporations than the developing nations which host investment. But there has not been harmony in the negotiations, and hope for an early settlement of differences has diminished. Most of the OECD members wish to include limits on the extraterritorial application of laws, such as attempts to impose a nation's boycott on third nations, or govern the acts of foreign subsidiaries. The U.S. generally opposes such limitations on its use of extraterritorial application of laws. Conclusion of the MAI is likely, but the date remains uncertain.

THE SETTLEMENT OF INVESTMENT DISPUTES

Investment disputes often involve claims by the foreign investor that the host nation interfered with the investment to the degree that it constitutes a taking of property. A taking may violate international law, but that area is poorly defined in international law and disputed by different nations. Investors prefer to rely on other means for dispute settlement. Host nation law may include how investment disputes are to be resolved. Often the law provides for stages, beginning with a form of mediation, then arbitration, and if not satisfied through use of the courts. This may be unsatisfactory to the foreign investor if the membership of the mediation and arbitration panels, and the rules under which they operate, favor the host nation. A more neutral settlement process is usually preferred.

THE SETTLEMENT OF INVESTMENT DISPUTES: NAFTA

The NAFTA investment dispute scheme is extensive and complex. It essentially provides a mechanism to settle investment disputes by arbitration where a party to NAFTA has breached an obligation under Section A of Chapter 11 provisions relating to investment, or under provisions in Chapter 15 governing monopolies and state enterprises, and damage or loss has occurred from the breach. Investors of a party are allowed to submit the claim directly. The process first requires consultation and negotiation. If unsuccessful, it proceeds to arbitration. The rules to be applied are those of ICSID or UNCITRAL, depending on party participation in the ICSID Convention. The arbitrators are selected from "Chapter 11" panels established by each party, and the arbitration is enforceable. The process is to some degree a mini-ICSID procedure, with participation limited to disputants and arbitrators of the three NAFTA parties.

Two important reservations were made by Canada and Mexico to the investment dispute resolution provisions. A Canadian decision following a review under the Investment Canada Act regarding an acquisition is not subject to NAFTA dispute settlement provisions, nor is a Mexican National Commission on Foreign Investment decision on an acquisition subject to such provisions.

Several of the first Chapter 11 investment disputes have raised doubt about its appropriate use. Several U.S. challenges have been made to regulations adopted in Canada and Mexico which have prevented foreign investment from functioning. There is debate regarding whether the provisions constitute regulation or expropriation. A more contentious case, involving a Canadian funeral home chain subjected to a huge punitive damages decision in a Mississippi state court, has challenged aspects of the legal system, rather than traditional expropriatory measures. These decisions may lead to revisiting the Chapter 11 dispute procedure.

THE SETTLEMENT OF INVESTMENT DISPUTES: ICSID

Nearly 100 nations have become parties to the 1966 Convention on the Settlement of Investment Disputes Between States and Nationals of Other States. The Convention provided for the creation of the International Centre for the Settlement of Investment Disputes (ICSID) as part of the World Bank. The Convention and Centre provide for the arbitration of investment disputes, offering an institutional framework for the proceedings. Jurisdiction under the Convention extends to "any legal dispute arising directly out of an investment, between a Contracting State or ... any subdivision ... and a national of another Contracting State." But the parties must consent in writing to the submission of the dispute to the Centre. Once given, the consent may not be withdrawn.

Disputes regarding jurisdiction may be decided by the arbitration panel and appealed to a committee (ad hoc) created from the Panel of Arbitrators by the Administrative Council of the ICSID. The jurisdiction of the tribunal, challenged in a United States court, may well lead to a refusal to uphold the decision. Concern regarding the jurisdictional limitations led to the creation of the Additional Facility, which may conduct conciliations and arbitrations for what are rather special disputes. It was not created to deal with the ordinary investment dispute, but with disputes between parties with long-term special economic relationships involving substantial resource commitments. The Additional Facility may be used only with the blessing of the ICSID Secretary General.

Within the World Bank is another organization important to foreign investment, the Multilateral Investment Guarantee Agency (MIGA). MIGA provides investment insurance not unlike the United States Overseas Private Investment Corporation's (OPIC) insurance programs. Both MIGA and OPIC are discussed in Chapter 6.

CONCLUSION

The regulation of foreign investment is practiced by nearly every nation in the world, both market and nonmarket economies, and developed and developing nations. The motivation for regulation is always the protection of some domestic interest, whether national security, national economic interests or simply national interests. What is important to recognize is that such regulation is a dynamic process. The adoption of the joint venture as a mandatory vehicle for foreign investment by developing nations and nonmarket economies on the 1970s proved to be only one stage in the development process. Unfortunately it is not always recognized as a stage in an evolving process.

Some nations view what is a transitory stage in the development process as a permanent key to success. But the world has witnessed the development of foreign investment regulation move through stages of nationalizations and mandatory joint ventures to an era of privatization, as well as from import substitution promotion to export production promotion. Those nations which use investment controls carefully and sparingly, such as the Asian Four Tigers or Four Dragons, have achieved greater rates of growth than those nations which have incorrectly viewed strict foreign investment controls as a panacea for economic stagnation. Where the world is headed in investment regulation is always hard to predict. But as the new century unfolds, investment protection appears to be gaining a new justification—the protection of a nation's culture. Whether it proves to be truly a protection of important elements of culture, or another means of protecting inefficient domestic industry remains to be played out on the international trade stage in the coming years.

CHAPTER SIX

THE TAKING OF FOREIGN INVESTMENT PROPERTY BY GOVERNMENTS

Investment in foreign nations creates a risk that the host government may "take" the property and refuse to provide a "proper" compensation. What is a "taking" and what is "proper" compensation have long been debated. A taking may be abrupt and complete, or it may be what is sometimes called a "creeping" expropriation, where the host government chips away at the foreign investment until there is nothing of value left.

As to proper compensation, if some compensation is made, it may not be viewed by the investor as (1) paid with sufficient promptness, (2) adequate in amount or (3) paid in effective form, such as dollars or other exchangeable currency. Although the foreign investor obviously will be concerned by the taking itself, the right to take is difficult to challenge. Thus the issue usually becomes the proper compensation. One method of dealing with the compensation issue is to obtain insurance for expropriation and other political risks. Investment insurance is the subject of the following chapter. If the investment is not insured, the investor, after exhausting remedies in the taking nation, may seek to bring suit against that nation in a court in the United States. That litigation is likely to raise two defenses, sovereign immunity and the act of state. Both are subjects of chapters in the authors' International Business Transactions in a Nutshell (6th ed. 2000).

The terms most frequently used when referring to the taking of foreign property are not always clear in meaning. Nor are they consistently applied. The least intrusive stage in the process of taking property is called an *intervention*. That assumes the taking is temporary, and that the investment will be returned when the problems which motivated the taking, as viewed by the taking nation, are corrected. For example, the Cuban government in March, 1959, intervened in the operation of the Cuban Telephone Company. The company announced that there was no need to believe the action would lead to nationalization. But problems specific to the Company, such as allegedly excessive rates and inadequate expansion to meet demand, became less important than the general shift from private to state ownership of the means of production and distribution. If the property is not returned in some reasonable period of time, or, as in the Cuban case, it appears that the property will not be returned, the taking becomes at least a *nationalization*. The Cuban Telephone Company remained in a state of intervention for 16 months until July, 1960, when it was formally nationalized by decree.

The words *nationalization* and *expropriation* are often used interchangeably. They are usually intended to mean a taking followed by some form of compensation. But if no payment is made, or what would not be considered "proper" compensation, then the process may merit the label of *confiscation*. The absence of *any* payment would, with few exceptions, cause the taking to be viewed as a confiscation, or an expropriation in violation of international law. The more usual, and consequently more difficult, case is when there is a nationalization or expropriation followed by an offer of some payment, but there is disagreement between the taking nation and the foreign investor (and often the investor's government) over the terms of the payment. That disagreement involves whether the payment standard should be "just", "appropriate", "prompt, adequate and effective," or bear some other label. Each of these measures has a meaning, although they are not universally agreed to, nor are they always clearly defined.

NATIONALIZATIONS IN INTERNATIONAL PRACTICE

Foreign takings of property may be compared with common law concepts of condemnation or eminent domain. A city government takes property for a park. A state government takes property for a highway. The federal government takes property for a military base. In each case, *domestic* law mandates that compensation be paid. The source of law is often the nation's or state's constitution. To be a lawful taking, the government action must be for the public good. Usually the law also requires the payment of compensation, sometimes in advance of the taking. When governments take property of *foreign* investors who are from nations with such laws mandating compensation when property is taken for a public purpose, it is not surprising for the investors deprived of their property to wish to challenge *both* the public purpose and the adequacy of compensation elements. But it is difficult to challenge successfully the public purpose of another nation, even though many expropriations have been motivated by little more than revolutionary fervor, with little justification on any sound economic grounds. But the courts of one nation are not anxious to rule on the validity of the taking nation's satisfaction of the public purpose mandate. Not anxious, and probably not permitted to so rule under act of state theory.

Expropriation conflicts were rather frequent in the 1960s, beginning with the extensive takings by Cuba. But there were several expropriations of note in earlier years. Russia after the 1917 revolution, and Eastern European nations after World War II, eliminated private ownership of the means of production and distribution. United States and other nations' investors felt the impact of inadequate compensation following these conversions from market to nonmarket economies. Dutch nationals were similarly deprived after the Indonesian nationalizations in the 1950s. Some takings have been more selective, such as the Mexican expropriation of oil in 1938 and the Egyptian expropriation of the Suez Canal Company in 1956. When such selectivity is present, a separate issue arises, the possibility of *discrimination* by the taking nation of property of a particular foreign investor, or all the investors of a particular foreign nation. Separately, or along with discrimination, the act of taking might have been in *retaliation* for acts of the foreign investor or its government. Retaliation occurred when the United States in 1960 canceled the Cuban sugar quota and the following day the Cuban government expropriated a list of exclusively United States investor owned companies.

Nationalization of property has not been limited to acts by socialist or third world nations. The United Kingdom nationalized coal, steel, airline service and production, and other industries after World War II. France nationalized nearly all banks in 1982. (Many of the U.K. and French nationalized properties have been since returned to the private sector, through the process of privatization.) But in both the U.K. and France, the takings were of property owned nearly exclusively by nationals rather than by foreign investors. (A U.K. court suggested that a government might not be required to pay its own citizens as much compensation as it might have to pay to foreigners.) Many market economy nations have brought certain sectors of society into state ownership through the process of nationalization. The United States is not without its government's hand in the ownership of business.

Part of the nation's passenger rail service was
transferred to government ownership. But that instance involved an industry in severe financial dis-
tress. National ownership was viewed as a means of
saving a dying, vital service sector, rather than
entering an area successfully operated by the private sector. Nationalizations as an alternative to
bankruptcy are a special and separate classification
of property takings.

In the 1970s, the pace of nationalization slowed.
Many developing nations turned to a new "ization"
process, mandating the conversion of existing wholly foreign owned subsidiaries to joint ventures with
majority local ownership. This has been called Mexi-
canization, or Peruvianization, or Chileanization.
But even that process began to slow in the early
1980s, particularly after the debt shock in 1982 led
many developing nations to encourage more foreign
investment in the hope that exports would increase
and generate hard currency earnings to help pay
foreign debts. The next stage was privatization, the
reduction of state ownership by the sale of shares in
state owned enterprises, particularly those operating only because of government subsidies, to employees, to the general public, and even to foreign
investors. For example, many Mexican companies,
including the airlines, telephone company and
banks have been sold to private investors. This
direction in the late 1980s and early 1990s of an
emphasis on private ownership, has included some
restrictions on how much, if any, of the state owned
property to be privatized might be purchased by

foreign investors. The most significant privatizations of the final decade of the century have taken place in former nonmarket economy nations of Eastern Europe.

If nationalizations have not ended, and it is overly optimistic to suggest that the conflicts both causing them and flowing from them will never reappear, many of the "ization" process takings in the 1970s and early 1980s were less hostile to foreign investors than the earlier takings in Cuba, Chile, Indonesia and Peru. That may be because lessons were learned from those earlier hostile takings. President Castro of Cuba is alleged to have counseled President Torrijos of Panama to move cautiously in considering the expropriation of United Fruit Company properties—Cuba had paid a severe economic price for its massive takings of all, not just United States investor or even foreign investor owned, private property.

The most significant recent nationalizations were those by Iran in the late 1970s after the United States terminated diplomatic relations when the Iranian revolutionary government seized the United States embassy and many of its staff. Iran possessed very large bank accounts in the United States, which were frozen due to the hostilities. To obtain access to those funds Iran agreed to release the hostages and arbitrate all United States claims by establishing an Iran–United States Claims Tribunal at the Hague. The proceedings have provided a rich resource of claims procedures, and the development of substantive expropriation law.

Nationalizations *can* be amicably resolved. That is attested to by the Venezuelan and Saudi Arabian takeovers of foreign oil before the expiration of concessions, and the agreed upon post-nationalization contractual arrangements for marketing and technological support. Furthermore, there was almost no post-nationalization exodus of industry personnel. These takeovers were peaceful and orderly, and followed long negotiations between the governments of Venezuela and Saudi Arabia and the foreign investors.

In the instances noted above it was always clear that a nationalization had occurred. But some uncertainty may attach to a conclusion that a foreign investor's property has been subjected to a takeover. Government interference may involve a series of steps that amount to a disguised, constructive, defacto, or "creeping" expropriation. A taking may occur almost imperceptibly and often over a substantial period of time. Although some scholarly commentary discusses the extent to which there must be a specific governmental *mens rea* directed towards an investor and contemplation of a takeover, it is clear that taxes on an investment might be raised to a level which is confiscatory; mandatory labor legislation might serve as a vehicle to transfer the financial resources of an investment to nationals of the host country; remittances and repatriations might be blocked entirely or delayed to where host country inflation effectively consumes them; necessary government approvals might prove unobtainable; and other regulations dealing with various aspects of the investment might become burdensome to the point of constituting an overwhelming disincentive to continuing the investment.

For example, a foreign owned lumber mill may be "creepingly" expropriated if government permits are required before any trees may be cut and, following an initial permit to cut a specified number, the issuance of subsequent mandatory permits is so sporadic and so uncertain that the operation of the mill becomes prohibitively expensive. The Raytheon Company and Italy agreed to settle their dispute over the Italian government's alleged taking of Raytheon's Italian subsidiary. The ICJ chamber held in favor of Italy (4–1), that the U.S.-Italian FCN treaty had not been breached by Italy's interference with the liquidation of the subsidiary. Electtonica Sicula S.p.A. (ELST)(United States v. Italy) 1989 ICJ Rep.15. The most recent questions regarding the nature of a taking have arisen under Chapter 11 of the NAFTA, which appears to be expanding the concept of expropriation to include *regulatory* practices which impede a foreign investment.

ASSESSING THE RISK OF NATIONALIZATION

Causes which lead a country to nationalize a foreign owned commercial enterprise are difficult to predict. A taking of property may follow a change in administration, whether that results from revolution (Cuba, Indonesia, Iran, USSR) or election

(Chile). Or the taking may occur during an non-threatened administration (Mexico, Great Britain). Nationalism (pride in one's country and feeling that ownership of certain industries should be local) and a sense of exploitation by foreigners may generate a takeover. Or the taking may occur because other methods of ownership are viewed as economically unsound, or politically or socially inappropriate. They may also occur when a company manufacturing an essential product or providing an essential service is on the verge of bankruptcy. Most nationalizations are politically motivated; few have occurred within a stable government where a thorough economic study was undertaken that concluded that certain sectors of industry ought to be state owned, or at least owned by nationals rather than foreigners.

Predicting the risk of nationalization is sufficiently important to large multinationals that they have adopted techniques of inferential statistics, probability theory, and data collection about several hundred separate variables in trying to evaluate investment risk of loss. Some MNEs hire full-time political scientists and former Foreign Service Officers to calculate such risks. Some investors take advice from persons ("old hands") who are particularly knowledgeable about a country. Many make on-the-scene tours of a country from time-to-time.

A particular investment's susceptibility to being nationalized increases to the extent that it engages in what are viewed as essential national industries, such as extractive, export oriented natural resources, banking, insurance, international transportation (airlines), communications, national defense or agriculture. The entity is also more susceptible if it involves the use of people or processes that can be duplicated easily domestically; or if it consumes supplies which can be obtained easily from sources other than the affected investors; or if it does not have an essential value dependent upon the investor's goodwill or good name in the marketing of goods or services produced by the investment, and it has enough overall value to outweigh any bad press or other offsetting loss following a takeover.

Regardless of the predictive techniques employed, nationalization of an investment may be traumatic. Extracts from the Libyan Decree, effecting the takeover of Bunker Hunt oil interests in 1973, leave little room for misunderstanding the nature and scope of a discriminatory nationalization:

TEXT OF LIBYAN LAW NATIONALIZ- ING BUNKER HUNT INTERESTS

The Revolution Command Council yesterday issued Law No. 42 of [11 June] 1973 regarding the nationalization of the rights of Milton Bunker Hunt, owner of oil concession No. 65. The following is text of the law:

In the name of the people, the Revolution Command Council, after taking cognizance of [various laws authorizing nationalization and creating a national oil company] issues the following law:

Article 1. The rights of Milton Bunker Hunt under Concession Agreement No. 65 shall be nationalized and the ownership of all funds, rights, assets and shares of Milton Bunker Hunt related to the said concession agreement shall be turned over to the State. This particularly includes all the rights related to the installations and facilities of exploratory drilling, the extraction of oil and gas, and transportation, utilization, refining, storage, exploration and other assets and rights related to the said concession agreement.

Article 2. All funds, rights and assets of Milton Bunker Hunt, the ownership of which has been transferred in accordance with the provisions of the foregoing article, shall be transferred to Arab Gulf Exploration Company, ... The Arab Gulf Exploration Company shall replace Milton Bunker Hunt in all rights and obligations related to Oil Concession Agreement No. 65. The company shall not be answerable for previous obligations except within the limits of the funds, rights and assets transferred to the State on the date this law comes into effect.

Article 3. The Arab Gulf Exploration Company has the right to [word indistinct] current oil sale agreements concerning the rights related to the person concerned referred to in Article 1 in accordance with what it may deem to be in the public interest.

Article 4. The Arab Gulf Exploration Company shall pay to the State Treasury through the Oil

Ministry all the duties, land rent and additional duties and taxes which were imposed on Milton Bunker Hunt and which are due from the date this law comes into effect, in accordance with the provisions of the oil law and the concession agreement previously referred to and the agreements amending it.

Article 5. The State shall pay to the person concerned compensation for the funds, rights and assets transferred to it in accordance with Article 1. The compensation referred to shall be determined by a committee to be set up by the Oil Minister in the following manner:

A. A counselor of [word indistinct] courts, as chairman, to be nominated by the Justice Minister.

B. A representative of the National Oil Institute, as member, to be nominated by the Oil Minister.

C. A representative of the Treasury Minister, as member, to be nominated by the Treasury Minister.

The committee may seek assistance in carrying out its task as it may deem necessary by enlisting the help of employees and others.

Article 6. The sums necessary for the payment of duties and taxes and any other sums due to the State Treasury and related to the nationalized rights shall be deducted from the compensation due to [Bunker Hunt] in accordance with the foregoing article, within the limits of the total compensation.

Those to whom the debts, referred to in the clause above, are due must submit a statement indicating the dates of the debts, accompanied by related documents, to the committee provided for in Article 5 within a period not exceeding 30 days from the date of the decision setting it up.

Article 7. The committee provided for in Article 5 must issue a decision estimating the compensation and determining the [amount] to be deducted from it within a period not exceeding 3 months from the date of the decision setting it up. The committee decision shall include the reasons (musababan) and shall be final. It is not subject to any appeal. The Oil Minister shall inform the person concerned within 30 days of the date of its issue.

Article 8. The Arab Gulf Exploration Company has a right to [keep] the employees and workers of Milton Bunker Hunt of Libyan nationality. None have the right to leave their work or to refrain from it except by a decision of the company's management board. Foreign employees and workers have the option to continue or leave work. The national employees and workers and foreign employees and workers who choose to continue to work have a right to maintain their present wages and salaries.

Article 9. By a decision to be issued by the management board of the Arab Gulf Exploration

Company a committee shall be set up to take over funds, assets and rights of the person concerned referred to previously in Article 1.

Article 10. Every contract, action or measure contrary to the provisions of this law shall be considered absolutely null and void. Banks, corporations and individuals are prohibited from paying any sums or settling any claims and accounts due to the person concerned referred to in this law, except with the approval of the board of management of the company previously referred to. 13 *Int'l Legal Mat.* 58 (1974).

NATIONALIZATION AND EXPROPRIATION IN INTERNATIONAL LAW

A nationalization may appear to be legal under domestic law, but it may not pass scrutiny under international law. What constitutes the international law of expropriation, however, is not easy to discern, particularly since the third world in the late 1960s began to demand participation in formulating rules of international law applying to a nation's taking of property. Nations differ about what constitutes a public purpose and what is required compensation. They also differ regarding the unlawfulness of discriminatory nationalizations, when the property of only one nation is taken. Furthermore, some nations have presented lists of deductions to be applied to a multinational's valuation of its property, such as the Chilean deduction for what were considered excess profits for many past years of operation by foreign copper companies. Finally, and quite importantly, taking nations often reject the notion that any law other than *domestic* law should apply to a sovereign act of taking property, whether the property belongs to their own nationals or to foreigners. Different attitudes are sometimes ascribed to differences in colonial/colonialist political postures over the last two centuries, recency and rapidity of the country's industrial development, and differing attitudes toward public/private economic enterprise.

The right of a sovereign nation to full and permanent sovereignty over its natural resources and economic activities and the right to take privately owned property are long accepted concepts. That is true whether the property belongs to the country's own nationals or to foreigners. Most constitutions express that right. But the taking must be for a public purpose or in the public interest. What constitutes a lawful public purpose justifying the action of the nationalizing government is unlikely to be challenged in an international or foreign forum. Sovereignty is a shelter for many acts defined no more specifically than "for the social welfare or economic betterment of the nation." But the concept persists that a taking ought to be justified for some public purpose and if it is not, the taking should be viewed as improper. The difficulty of measurement, as well as the doubt that such measurement ought to be attempted outside the taking nation, have caused the public purpose element of expropriations to be relegated to obscurity in conflicts of the past few decades. The issue of importance has not been whether there was justification for the taking, but whether the question of compensation was properly addressed by the taking nation.

The United States government has repeatedly stated its position regarding nationalizations affecting the property of American nationals. The view stresses a "prompt, adequate and effective" standard of compensation as the prevailing rule of international law. However correctly "prompt, adequate and effective" may express what the Department of State believes ought to be the standard, it is a view with only minimal support from other governments, and from many jurists, arbitrators and international law scholars. The more commonly preferred terms are "just" or "appropriate" compensation. While the United States adherence to a "prompt, adequate and effective" standard may create obstacles in the settlement of an expropriation case, that standard is applied in determining whether certain benefits of United States laws may be extended to countries which carry out expropriations. For example, the President may not designate a nation as a beneficiary of the Generalized System of Preferences (GSP) program if that nation has nationalized property of United States nationals, and does not provide prompt, adequate and effective compensation. 19 U.S.C.A. § 2462.

The conflict regarding the proper standard of compensation, and the question of whether international law or domestic law applies to a taking, has its modern roots for the United States in the 1938

Mexican expropriation of foreign owned (largely British, Canadian and U.S.) petroleum investments. Subsequent to the Mexican action the United States informed Mexico that it recognized Mexico's sovereign right to take foreign property, but only upon payment of prompt, adequate and effective compensation according to international law. The Mexican response refuted both that alleged standard, and even the fundamental premise that international law rather than domestic law was the proper law to apply. Mexico said it would pay because the Mexican constitution required payment, and it would pay according to Mexican standards of compensation. A settlement was ultimately reached regarding payment, but no settlement was reached regarding the standard under which the payment ought to be made.

The next large scale nationalization of United States property was by Cuba in 1960. Cuba, like Mexico earlier, refuted the prompt, adequate and effective standard. The political hostility which continues today has prevented any settlement. Soon after the Cuban expropriations, the United Nations General Assembly passed the Resolution on Permanent Sovereignty Over Natural Resources (often referred to as Resolution 1803). 2 *Int'l Legal Mat.* 223 (1963). This Resolution affirms the right of nations to exercise permanent sovereignty over their resources and mandates the payment of "appropriate" compensation "in accordance with the rules in force in the State taking such measures in the exercise of its sovereignty and in accordance with international law." Although a General Assembly Resolution does not create international law, this Resolution appeared expressive of the customary international law of the day. A dozen years later, during which time the United Nations expanded with the addition of many newly independent nations, the General Assembly addressed the issue again in the Declaration on the Establishment of a New International Economic Order. 13 *Int'l Legal Mat.* 715 (1974). The Declaration was passed, but with reservations by Japan, West Germany, France, the U.K. and the U.S. Their concern was the absence of any reference to the application of international law in the settlement of nationalization compensation issues. Later that same year, the General Assembly passed the Charter of Economic Rights and Duties of States, with 16 votes (most of the major developed nations) against the article which stated that nationalization compensation was a *domestic* law matter. 14 *Int'l Legal Mat.* 251 (1975).

The view of the developing nations expressed in the U.N. resolutions was consistent with how they justified expropriations in practice. Chile expropriated the Kennecott Copper Company's holdings, offering to pay according to Chilean law, but only after deducting excess profits that Kennecott allegedly had withdrawn from its Chilean operation over a number of years. The profits conveniently totaled more than the value of the property, and Chile argued that it consequently owed nothing.

The kind of treatment accorded Kennecott by Chile is not the exception; similar refusals to compensate according to international standards have been expressed by many developing nations. Unfortunately, the International Court of Justice has produced no international standard. The narrow ruling in the *Barcelona Traction* decision did not reach the issues of expropriation. 1970 I.C.J. 3. The ICJ's predecessor, the Permanent Court of International Justice, held in 1928 in the often quoted *Chorzów Factory Case,* P.C.I.J., Ser. A, No. 17 (1928), that there was a duty of "payment of fair compensation", and the *Norwegian Shipowners' Claims,* 1 U.N.Rep.Int'l Arb.Awards 307 (1922), arbitration in 1922 adopted a "just" standard. More recently, there have been several arbitration and national court rulings which help determine the path of development of an international rule of compensation.

The *TOPCO–Libyan* arbitral award of 1977, declared the state of customary law to require "appropriate compensation", citing in support the above mentioned U.N. General Assembly Resolution 1803. 17 *Int'l Legal Mat.* 3, 29 (1978). In the U.S., the *Banco Nacional de Cuba v. Chase Manhattan Bank* decision in 1981, suggested that the consensus of nations was "appropriate compensation." 658 F.2d 875 (2d Cir.1981). A year later another arbitral award, *Aminoil–Kuwait,* also turned to Resolution 1803 and approved "appropriate" as the accepted international standard. 21 *Int'l Legal Mat.* 976 (1982). But the United States Department of State has continued to argue that the standard is prompt, adequate and effective. The American Law Institute rejected that as the standard in revising the Restatement on Foreign Relations Law, instead adopting in the Restatement (third) a standard of "just" compensation (§ 712). That standard is believed to avoid the possible inclusion of deductions under an "appropriate" standard.

The Iran–United States Claims Tribunal, which has been meeting at the Hague for more than a decade and a half, has not applied a "prompt, adequate and effective" compensation standard. Claims approved by the Tribunal nevertheless for the most part have been paid "promptly" from the funds established for such payment, and they have been paid in dollars, thus meeting any "effectiveness" standard. With respect to the "adequacy" element the tribunal has used various measurements of valuation which seem to satisfy any reasonable "adequacy" standard. Although this seems to support a "prompt, adequate and effective" standard as espoused by the United States government, the Iranian claims process is sui generis because of the vast funds which Iran possessed in the United States at the time of the nationalizations. Few massive nationals of foreign property have occurred where the taking country possessed significant assets in the country whose investments were expropriated.

If any conclusions can be made as to what is the current international law of compensation, it seems clear that it is not called prompt, adequate and effective, but rather appropriate or just. What those terms mean, and whether they reflect different criteria, must await further judicial or arbitral revelations.

FORUM FOR VALUATION OF NATIONALIZED PROPERTY

The expropriated property owner will have to establish the value of the property if there is a possibility of compensation. If the nationalizing country agrees to provide compensation, there likely will be direct negotiations with an agency of that government to establish the value. Alternatively, valuation might be decided by an arbitral panel, as in the case of the Iranian nationalizations. But if the taking state refuses any compensation, the issue of valuation may come before a court outside the taking state. That could be an international forum, or, more likely, a court either in the nation of the expropriated investor or in a third nation where the taking nation has assets. Because of lack of standing in the International Court of Justice, or reasons associated with defenses either of sovereign immunity or the act of state doctrine, or even because of possible obstacles to collecting under an insurance policy issued by the Overseas Private Investment Company, the satisfaction of the claim may have to wait for a considerable time, until the United States government has negotiated a lump sum settlement with the taking nation. The 1959–1960 Cuban nationalizations remain unresolved because of the continued absence of formal diplomatic relations and discussions of the claims.

Since 1948 several dozen nations have resolved claims brought by the United States by agreeing to lump sum settlements. When a lump sum settlement is made, the agreed amount is allocated among claimants according to rules developed by the United States Foreign Claims Settlement Commission. For example, disposition of investor claims arising out of expropriations of United States citizens' property following the 1917 Russian Revolution occurred in 1974, when the USSR offered a lump sum in settlement of all claims regardless of claimed value. In May of 1979, the People's Republic of China offered to pay $131 million over a six year period in satisfaction of investor claims arising out of the creation of the People's Republic in 1949, and the taking of U.S. property then valued at $197 million.

A special claims tribunal sits at The Hague in the Netherlands deciding claims of United States citizens against Iran. That tribunal is unique, however. Iran would not have agreed to the tribunal had there not been very considerable assets owned by Iran which had been frozen in United States banks as a consequence of the Iranian revolution and taking of United States hostages. Had Iran refused to settle claims accepted on a case-by-case basis before the tribunal, it is likely that a lump sum settlement would have been the method of resolution. There is one outstanding set of claims likely to be the subject of a lump sum settlement in the future. That is the approximately $2 billion of claims against Cuba from the 1959–1960 expropriation. Lump sum settlements are thus the way in which many expropriation claims are ultimately settled. Despite much debate over the proper international law standard for payment, the reality tends to be the use of the lump sum method of settlement.

Customary international law places no duty on a state to press claims of its investor nationals. But states often do espouse such claims. An aggrieved United States investor is likely to seek the assistance of the United States government. The government may make demands for payment, as mentioned above in the discussion of the exchange of notes between the United States and Mexico after the latter expropriated foreign petroleum investments in 1938. Where the expropriations are extensive, as in the case of Cuba, diplomatic relations may be terminated partly because of the expropriations. If substantial claims are present, the United States Foreign Claims Settlement Commission may play a major role in establishing claims *before* any settlement is reached, and thus in determining the proportions to be allocated to each claimant if a settlement is later achieved. Once payment is made to a nation which has negotiated the claims on behalf of its nationals, international law plays no role in how that sum is divided among claimants. That is left to the government receiving the agreed sum.

UNITED STATES FOREIGN CLAIMS SETTLEMENT COMMISSION

Created by the Reorganization Act of 1949 (68 Stat. 1279) and headquartered in Washington, D.C., the Foreign Claims Settlement Commission receives, examines, adjudicates, and renders a final decision with respect to claims against a foreign government, arising from nationalizations or other takings of property. The Commission gives public notice, in the Federal Register, of the time when and within which claims must be filed. All claims decisions are based on such evidence. Written legal contentions are submitted, and upon such independent investigations as the Commission may choose to make. Decisions are reduced to writing, supported by reasons, and constitute a full and final case disposition on law and fact which cannot be reviewed by any court unless violative of the United States Constitution.

Commission approved claims are certified to the Secretary of the Treasury and to the Secretary of State. When and if lump sum settlement money becomes available, approved claims are paid in full to the extent of the first $1,000 of each claim and, thereafter, in an amount which is proportional to the remaining principal balance of the claim, and reflects the same proportion as the aggregate unpaid principal balance of all claims bears to the total lump sum monies remaining for distribution to approved claimants. Payment of interest on approved claims is possible but quite unlikely.

COMPUTING THE VALUE OF
A TAKEN INVESTMENT

The reality that an investment may be expropriated abruptly and compensated for, if at all, only after a substantial period of time has elapsed, and in an amount which may represent less than full compensation, raises the importance of pre-planning for proof of investment value. To say that "prompt, adequate and effective" or "just" or "appropriate" compensation should be paid for a taking, or even that whatever measure of compensation is adopted must be equal to the value of property at the time of its taking, does not answer the valuation question. That question will be answered by the valuation method adopted by the determining body. Valuation methods may differ from country to country.

The need to agree on valuation procedures, when arising on the heels of a takeover, occurs usually within an unsettled and often adversarial atmosphere. Some possible approaches to valuation involve calculation of the investment's:

(1) book value (or adjusted book value)—this standard has been used for many years by the Foreign Claims Settlement Commission. Expropriating countries have noted that this approach uses the value recorded by an investor in prior official dealings with the expropriating administration, and possibly earlier administrations as well. To the extent that book value is the value of

total assets minus total liabilities, any manipulation of assets or any historical cost entries may distort an attempt to determine a truly accurate value of the investor's equity at the time of takeover. Adjusting the book value to reflect true values at the time of the taking may provide a more just figure.

(2) sale or market value—based on the price that the investment would bring under an agreement between a willing buyer and a willing seller, this standard has been favored by expropriating countries because a takeover may be viewed as a "coerced sale", and in many countries the government is the only likely buyer, even in the circumstances of a voluntary sale.

(3) replacement value—based on the amount it would cost the investor to replace fixed assets at the date of the takeover, this standard has been favored by investors. Investors and host countries have experienced some difficulty in agreeing about what assets should be considered in a determination of replacement value.

(4) going concern value—using a profit figure calculated for an agreed year or number of years, the profit figure is multiplied by another figure (e.g., 10 or more) to determine investment value. The Foreign Claims Settlement Commission has indicated a willingness to use this approach, but the likelihood that the approach will be useful in unanticipated, quick takeover situations is less predictable. Profits in any one year, or group of

years, are subject to manipulation by the investor and by the host country (e.g., through its taxing power), even if one concedes that past profits accurately measure the value of an investment. At least one United States court has declined to adopt this approach. Banco Nacional de Cuba v. Chase Manhattan Bank, 658 F.2d 875 (2d Cir. 1981).

Difficulty between an investor and the nationalizing government arises frequently in assigning value to contingent assets and contingent liabilities. One example is goodwill. As an item possessing compensable value following an expropriation, it has long received unsympathetic treatment by the Foreign Claims Settlement Commission. Another example involves possible deductions. Since the Chilean seizure of Kennecott's interests in the early 1970's, expropriating countries have talked about the extent to which additional deductions should be subtracted from ostensible investment value to determine the real value of the taken investment. Such deductions might include compensation for past instances of environmental damages, removing natural resources with payment at less than the world market rate for the resource, past inadequate employee compensation, excessive profit remittances and other examples of inadequate sensitivity to social needs in the expropriating country.

UNITED STATES LAWS AFFECTING THE NATIONALIZATION PROCESS

The United States Congress has enacted several laws which evidence a national position that expropriation must be accompanied by compensation, or, if not, the United States will use its powers to deny various benefits which the nationalizing country otherwise might receive from the United States. Treaty commitments and provisions of other international agreements between the United States and investor hosting nations may serve to narrow expropriation uncertainties, such as provisions in the earlier, frequently negotiated Treaties of Friendship, Commerce and Navigation, or the more recent bilateral investment treaties (BITs). But these agreements have not been reached with many third world nations where there is much foreign investment by United States nationals (e.g., India, Brazil).

In addition to provisions governing expropriation, the bilateral investment treaties have three other significant provisions dealing with (1) nondiscrimination in establishing and operating investments; (2) rights regarding transfers of investments; and (3) mandatory dispute resolution methods. Where these treaties do exist, however, there is always the threat that a successor government may reject them, however in violation of international law such action may be. They are important, nevertheless, and investors do gain an added challenge if their property is taken by a nation which has signed such a bilateral treaty with the United States.

The North American Free Trade Agreement (NAFTA) has a detailed provision governing the taking of investment property of a member nation. Article 1110 acknowledges the right to take property, but only where there is a public purpose, a nondiscriminatory taking, due process of law and minimum standards of treatment contained in the Agreement, and the payment of compensation. The compensation provisions do not refer to the prompt, adequate and effective standard urged by the United States, but quite clearly meet that standard by more specific language.

The new WTO Agreement on Trade–Related Investment Measures (TRIMs) are not as strict as those in the NAFTA, and do not include provisions governing the taking of investment property.

Other domestic laws of the United States apply to nations which have expropriated property of United States nationals and have failed to provide compensation or to illustrate a willingness to negotiate a compensation agreement. Subsequent to the Cuban nationalizations, the Hickenlooper Amendment to the Foreign Assistance Act was enacted. 22 U.S.C.A. § 2370(e). It provides, in part, that:

(e)(1) The President shall suspend assistance to the government of any country to which assistance is provided under this chapter or any other Act when the government of such country....

(A) has nationalized or expropriated or seized ownership or control of property owned by any United States citizen ...

(C) has imposed or enforced discriminatory taxes or other exactions, or restrictive maintenance or operational conditions, or has taken other actions, which have the effect of nationalizing, expropriating, or otherwise seizing ownership or control of property so owned, and such country, government agency, or government sub-division fails within a reasonable time … to take appropriate steps … to discharge its obligations under international law toward such citizen … including speedy compensation for such property in convertible foreign exchange, equivalent to the full value thereof, as required by international law, or fails to take steps designed to provide relief from such taxes, exactions, or conditions, as the case may be; and such suspension shall continue until the President is satisfied that appropriate steps are being taken.

The Sabbatino, or Second Hickenlooper, Amendment was passed by an angry Congress soon alter the United States Supreme Court held in Banco Nacional de Cuba v. Sabbatino, 376 U.S. 398 (1964), that the act of state doctrine prevented United States courts from hearing cases of foreign expropriation, even where there were allegations of violations of international law. The Congressional response reversed the presumption of *Sabbatino*, allowing United States courts to proceed unless the President stated that such adjudication would embarrass the conduct of foreign relations. 22 U.S.C.A. § 2370. Additional acts prohibit the United States from casting votes in organizations such as the

World Bank or IADB for loans to countries which
have expropriated property of United States nationals and refused compensation.

CHAPTER SEVEN

INSURING AGAINST THE RISKS OF FOREIGN INVESTMENT LOSSES

An investment in a foreign nation often is subject to risks which are not a significant concern for domestic investment. A domestic investor in the United States does not worry about damage to the business from military conflict, as foreign investors have suffered in recent decades in such areas as Bosnia, Iraq, Kuwait, Lebanon, Nicaragua, Northern Ireland, and Vietnam. Nor do domestic investors worry about losses from uncompensated expropriation, as foreign investors have suffered in China, Cuba, Indonesia, Peru, and the USSR and Eastern European nations. Nor about losses from currency which becomes inconvertible, as foreign investors have suffered in many developing nations. Because these risks are not present in the United States, nor in a number of developed, democratic nations such as Australia, Canada, Japan and many nations in Europe (and because they present sometimes impossible risk measurement problems), the *domestic* insurance industry generally has not developed insurance to cover such potential losses for investments abroad.

Very limited private insurance may be available for some of these risks, but it is to government investment programs that most foreign investors must turn to reduce the consequences of these risks through insurance. In the past few years insurers have been unable to keep up with the demand for political risk insurance. Markets have been opening in the former USSR, Eastern Europe, China, Southeast Asia and Latin America, creating a demand for insurance which has exhausted political risk insurer's per country underwriting limits. While the United States agency OPIC has entered most of these areas, it curtailed writing in China after the Tiananmen Square incidents in 1989, placing very substantial demands on the World Bank's agency MIGA, and on private insurers.

National insurance programs, such as the United States Overseas Private Investment Corporation (OPIC), usually exist to support government policies which encourage domestic industry to engage in investment abroad. There is consequently some element of government policy in the equation of premium calculation, which is absent in private insurance risk analysis. Private insurers tend to focus on the experience of the applicant and how carefully it has evaluated risks in past foreign investments. Private insurers also tend to be more concerned with the extent of the company's exposure in a single country. Critics of government "backed" insurance of United States investment abroad argue that the program encourages and subsidizes the transfer of productive facilities abroad, at the cost of jobs in the

United States. Proponents counter that OPIC does not offer subsidized rates, and cannot participate in projects that harm United States employment, such as runaway plants. They suggest that in projects supported, the jobs would move anyway, perhaps to lower investment nations, and that the United States benefits both by the return flow to the United States of profits on the foreign investment, and lower priced products for United States consumers.

There is a symbiotic relationship between providing financing and providing insurance. Although the latter is the subject of this chapter, sometimes organizations which are known principally to provide insurance also provide financing (OPIC), and sometimes organizations which are known principally to provide financing (or credits) also provide insurance. That insurance is often to insure exports rather than investment. But there may also be some investment insurance as well. For example, the 1982 Export Trading Company Act allows some banks to offer foreign investment insurance. As a condition of lending to a company for an investment abroad, a bank may require that the investor obtain insurance. In viewing OPIC's role over the past decades, more recently it has been involved in many contracts where both financing and insurance are provided. Clearly the financing side has become an important part of OPIC's business.

Some foreign nations have their own insurance schemes, designed to assist their own foreign investors and traders, and structured not unlike the United States OPIC. On a global basis, the World

Bank established the Multilateral Investment Guarantee Agency (MIGA) to offer foreign investment risk insurance not greatly dissimilar to that offered by the United States OPIC. OPIC has come under attack from some members of Congress who view investor insurance as a role for the private sector. OPIC's annual budget is often under attack, but as other industrialized nations support their own foreign investors with new OPIC-like programs, it may be hard for the United States to terminate the OPIC program. But MIGA may counter that argument to some degree, since it offers an alternative to OPIC. OPIC's growth nevertheless suggests that it provides a needed service, by mid–1999 it had supported foreign investments worth more than $121 billion. In late 1999, under the Export Enhancement Act of 1999, OPIC was reauthorized for four years, until September 30, 2003.

Insurance may not be an option for the foreign investor or trader. As noted above, United States banks may require insurance before they will lend, and a foreign host government may require that it be obtained from local, private insurers or from an agency of the government which issues insurance. Insuring by the host government's agency may be ineffective when it is usually the action of that very host government (often a successor regime) which creates the risk insured against.

Government insurers cover a variety of risks, such as short-term, import and export risks, or long-term risks involving direct investment. The United States Export–Import Bank (Eximbank) and the Overseas Private Investment Corporation (OPIC) provide these respective forms of coverage. OPIC has been the preeminent insurer of foreign investment risks. It frequently reiterates that it has functioned for over two decades without any net cost to the United States taxpayer. But its existence has often been somewhat tenuous. Many members of Congress believe its role should be assumed by the private sector. They are concerned both with the philosophical rejection of the government undertaking what the private sector might accomplish at lower cost, and the potential risk to United States taxpayers were many claims to be accepted. However, this attitude fails to acknowledge or accept the political policy role played by OPIC, which sets premiums partly by normal insurance risk analysis principles, and partly by foreign policy goals.

Were private insurance companies to be asked to replace the role played by OPIC, they would avoid assuming much of what OPIC insures, and likely charge higher rates. But the critics renew their concern in each session of Congress. Consequently, OPIC survives by successive legislative acquiescence, if not approval. The last major amendments to OPIC, in 1988, added provisions to enhance private political risk insurance programs. The amendments encouraged bringing the private sector into the area by cooperative risk sharing programs and the creation of an advisory group to help develop and implement cooperative programs. 22 U.S.C.A. § 2194b. Current suggestions are to merge

OPIC and the Export–Import Bank, to remain qua-si-independent entities under a new trade focused federal agency.

OPIC HISTORY AND STRUCTURE

OPIC owes its existence partly to the Marshall Plan created after World War II, and particularly to the Agency for International Development (AID). Until the creation of OPIC, AID was the primary organization through which the United States government issued risk insurance to United States investors in developing nations against risks of (1) expropriation, (2) inconvertibility of currency and (3) loss due to war, revolution or insurrection. Created as part of the Foreign Assistance Act of 1969, OPIC is an agency of the United States under the policy guidance of the Secretary of State. 22 U.S.C.A. § 2191. OPIC in 1971 assumed the insurance role earlier assigned to AID.

OPIC's mandate is to "mobilize and facilitate the participation of United States private capital and skills in the economic and social development of less developed countries and areas, and countries in transition from nonmarket to market economies, thereby complementing the development assistance objectives of the United States." 22 U.S.C.A. § 2191. Before 1992 insurance was limited to "less developed *friendly* countries and areas." The word *friendly* was as important as it was undefined. Rather than define it, Congress eliminated it with the new language above. But being friendly remains important. New insurance is halted when foreign relations become embittered with developing nations. When foreign relations with a nation become tenuous, if not hostile, the foreign nation is usually no longer a reasonable risk for investment insurance coverage. Private insurers obviously also consider the state of foreign relations in evaluating the risk abroad.

The difference between private insurers and OPIC, however, is that OPIC may insure certain risks that private insurers would reject, because United States foreign policy is to encourage investment in a certain nation for political reasons. OPIC also tends to enter an area sooner than private insurers. Not long after the USSR and the Eastern European countries shed communist governments, OPIC began to sign agreements with new more market oriented governments for OPIC eligibility, and the area is now a major focus of OPIC activities. OPIC has also increased its presence in the Middle East, including financing and insurance in Gaza and the West Bank. Because the number of nations which meet the *friendly* mandate has increased, especially with the transition to market economies by many former communist or socialist nations, OPIC has increased the number of eligible countries, and the amount of insurance and financial support.

Preferential consideration is given to investment projects in countries having a per capita income of $984 or less (in 1986 dollars). OPIC must restrict its activities in countries with per capita incomes of

$4,269 or more (in 1986 dollars). The President has some discretion in designating countries as beneficiaries. 19 U.S.C.A. § 2702. Otherwise qualifying countries may be denied OPIC insurance if they do not extend internationally recognized workers' rights to domestic workers, but presidential discretion may result in a waiver of this prohibition on national economic interest grounds. 22 U.S.C.A. § 2191a. Chile, where some 12 investments were insured between 1984 and 1986, was denied OPIC coverage between 1986 and 1990. In 1990, amid considerable controversy, the President determined that Chile had satisfactorily addressed workers' rights, and restored OPIC coverage. In 1992 amendments to the OPIC legislation added specific language that must be in any contract between OPIC and an investor that states:

> The investor agrees not to take actions to prevent employees of the foreign enterprise from lawfully exercising their right of association and their right to organize and bargain collectively. The investor further agrees to observe applicable laws relating to work with respect to minimum wages, hours of work, and occupational health and safety, and not to use forced labor. The investor is not responsible under this paragraph for the actions of a foreign government. 22 U.S.C.A. § 2191a(a)(1).

The Overseas Private Investment Corporation is intended to write insurance adhering to private insurance industry principles of risk management, and on a self-sustaining basis. Its insurance, however, is backed by the full faith and credit of the United States. The insurance portfolio amounted to $18.3 billion by mid–1999, with active projects in 96 countries. OPIC believes it has created 237,000 U.S. jobs and generated $58 billion in exports.

In addition to insuring investment risks, OPIC has limited financing authority. It provides loans which are sponsored by or significantly involve United States small businesses. These loans usually range from $500,000 to $6 million, but OPIC may loan up to $200 million per project. OPIC also may guarantee loans, regardless of the size of the company. Forty percent of OPIC financing is for investments in Latin America, but not in nations which do not have bilateral treaties with OPIC, thus eliminating Mexico and Cuba. There has been very significant recent financing in Eastern Europe and the new independent states, including $15 million for a Hyatt hotel project in Poland, $20 million for a hotel in Georgia, and $60 million to create an investment fund for Armenia, Azerbaijan and Georgia.

Another role of OPIC is support of private investment opportunities by helping to identify, assess, survey and promote private investment opportunities, such as underwriting a portion of the cost of a project feasibility study.

OPIC operates with a 15 member board of directors (three year terms) which includes eight appointed by the president (with advice and consent of the Senate) from outside the government. At least two of the eight must be experienced in small business, one each in organized labor and cooperatives. Other directors include the Director of the United States International Development Cooperation Agency (ex-officio chair) and the United States Trade Representative (ex-officio vice-chair; may designate Deputy USTR). Remaining directors come from government, including an official from the Department of Labor. The OPIC President and CEO is appointed by the President (with advice and consent of Senate), taking into account private business experience. It is this composition which causes OPIC to be referred to as a "quasi private/quasi public" organization.

INVESTOR ELIGIBILITY

OPIC is a United States program for United States business. Eligibility is limited to United States citizens, corporations, partnerships, or other associations "substantially beneficially owned" by United States citizens. "Substantial beneficial ownership" ordinarily means more than 50 percent of each class of issued and outstanding stock must be directly or beneficially owned by United States citizens. Foreign corporations, partnerships and other associations are also eligible if they are 95 percent owned by United States citizens. 22 U.S.C.A. § 2198(c). If it appears from all the circumstances that foreign creditors are able to exercise effective control over an otherwise eligible corporation, no insurance will be written.

OPIC INSURANCE PROGRAMS

Initially three principal risks were the reason for the creation of OPIC. They are risk of loss due to (1) inconvertibility, (2) expropriation or confiscation, or (3) war, revolution, insurrection or civil strife. 22 U.S.C.A. § 2194(a)(1). A fourth class has been added called "business interruption" caused by any of the principal three risks.

Before insurance against inconvertibility of currency is approved, the investor must obtain assurance from the host country that investor earnings will be convertible into dollars and that repatriation of capital is permitted. If the currency thereafter becomes inconvertible by act of the government, OPIC will accept the foreign currency, or a draft for the amount, and will provide the investor with United States dollars. Claims have been allowed readily where inconvertibility amounted to a discriminatory action by the host government against an investor.

Expropriation "includes, but is not limited to, any abrogation, repudiation, or impairment by a foreign government of its own contract with an investor with respect to a project, where such abrogation, repudiation, or impairment is not caused by the investor's own fault or misconduct, and materially adversely affects the continued operation of the project." 22 U.S.C.A. § 2198(b). OPIC contracts have followed a more specific and enumerative approach, because the law does not define more specifically what actions constitute expropriation. OPIC's standard insurance contract contains a lengthy description of what is considered to be expropriatory action sufficient to require OPIC payment. That definition may help an investor in drafting a contract with the foreign host government, because that government will have to deal with OPIC once OPIC has paid the investor's claim.

The investor must exhaust remedies before OPIC will be obligated to pay any claim. All reasonable action must be taken by the investor, including initiating administrative and judicial claims, to prevent or contest the challenged action by the host government. OPIC insurance contracts often stipulate that the investor is obligated to negotiate in good faith with the host government about compensation for expropriated property.

Prior to the receipt of payment of a claim, the investor usually will be required to transfer to OPIC all right, title and interest in the insured investment, including when the government expropriatory action consists of preventing the investor from exercising effective control over and withdrawing funds received from the foreign entity as dividends, interest or return of capital.

Upon payment of the claim, OPIC is subrogated to all rights to the investor's claim against the host government. The investor has an ongoing obligation to cooperate with the United States government in pressing claims against the host government. Because the United States must deal with the foreign government, OPIC will not write any insurance in a foreign country until that country agrees to accept OPIC insurance and thus to negotiate with OPIC after claims have been paid. Some governments have been reluctant to accept OPIC insurance because national leaders have been concerned that acceptance would constitute admission that the nation was susceptible to the various risks covered, particularly revolution and insurrection.

The third form of coverage, "war, revolution, insurrection, or civil strife," (political violence) is not defined by the statute. The usual OPIC contract provides protection against injury to the physical condition, destruction, disappearance or seizure and retention of Covered Property directly caused by war (whether or not under formal declaration) or by revolution or insurrection and includes injury to the physical condition, destruction, disappearance or seizure and retention of Covered Property as a direct result of actions taken in hindering, combating or defending against a pending or expected hostile act whether in war, revolution, or insurrection. OPIC Contract Article 1.07.

Civil strife is politically motivated violence (e.g., civil disturbances, riots, acts of sabotage, terrorism). Added to the OPIC statute in 1985 was a provision providing that:

> Before issuing insurance for the first time for loss due to business interruption, and in each subsequent instance in which a significant expansion is proposed in the type of risk to be insured under

the definition of "civil strife" or "business interruption", the Corporation shall ... submit to [Senate and House Committees] ... a report with respect to such insurance, including a thorough analysis of the risks to be covered, anticipated losses, and proposed rates and reserves and, in the case of insurance for loss due to business interruption, an explanation of the underwriting basis upon which the insurance to be offered. 22 U.S.C.A. § 2194(a)(4).

OPIC INVESTMENT INSURANCE TERMS

OPIC is authorized to issue up to $200 million in investment insurance for any one project. The maximum term is 20 years. While OPIC may not apply more than 10 percent of the maximum to any one investor, it would seem unjustified according to private insurance industry risk management principles to allocate anywhere near 10 percent to a single investor, especially if most of the investment were located in a single foreign nation. OPIC in 1990 insured General Electric Company's Hungarian investment for $141 million, which might be questioned were private industry risk management principles to actually govern OPIC investment insurance decisions. Hundred million dollar plus contracts are increasingly common for OPIC. In 1995 OPIC approved two contracts each for $200 million. In 1998 eight contracts were written for amount in excess of $100,000, the maximum being four written for $200 million (the maximum allowed).

Insurance premiums are based on the value of the investment. For example, OPIC charges to manufacturing or service projects a yearly premium of $.60 per $100 for expropriation, $.30 for inconvertibility and $.60 for political violence insurance.

ELIGIBLE INVESTMENTS

The creating legislation authorizes OPIC to carry out its functions "utilizing broad criteria". OPIC must consider investment eligibility in accordance with extensive guidelines which provide that OPIC conduct operations on a self-sustaining basis. It must consider the economic and financial soundness of the project; use private credit and investment institutions along with OPIC's guarantee authority; broaden private participation and revolve its funds through selling its direct investments to private investors; apply principles of risk management; give preferential consideration to projects involving small business (at least 30 percent of all projects); consider less developed nation receptiveness to private enterprise; foster competition and discourage monopolistic practices; further balance of payment objectives of the United States; support projects with positive trade benefits to the United States; advise and assist agencies of the United States and other public and private organizations interested in projects in less developed nations; avoid projects which diminish employment in the United States; and refuse projects which pose an unreasonable or major environmental, health, or safety hazard, or result in significant degradation of national parks and similar protected areas. OPIC must also operate consistently with the goals of United States law relating to protection of the environment and endangered species in less developed nations. 22 U.S.C.A. § 2191.

Additionally it must limit operations to nations which provide or are in the process of providing internationally recognized rights for workers. 22 U.S.C.A. § 2191a. Finally, OPIC must consider the host nation's observance of and respect for human rights. 22 U.S.C.A. § 2199(i). While the focus of OPIC for years has emphasized projects in Latin America and the Caribbean, the political and economic changes in Eastern European countries have resulted in considerable OPIC activity in that area. The 1994 amendments state that no law other than the OPIC provisions may prohibit OPIC programs in Yugoslavia, Poland, Hungary, or any other East European country, or the People's Republic of China, if the president views that allowing OPIC programs in those countries is important to the national interest. 22 U.S.C.A. § 2199(f). The area of least OPIC activity has been Africa, often not because of OPIC disinterest or lack of country eligibility, but lack of private investor interest.

OPIC participates only in new investments (loans or insurance) because its role is to encourage new investment, not facilitate existing investment. Each proposed investment is evaluated by OPIC to consider, in addition to the above eligibility requirements, the extent to which the United States participant has long-term management arrangements with the new enterprise, the extent of private participation and whether the project is likely to assist further development of the host nation's private sector. Loans or the contribution of goods or services to foreign governments will not be insured unless they are part of a construction contract. Nor will OPIC insure the credit or solvency of a foreign government. OPIC insures or provides a guaranty only for projects in countries which have signed an agreement with the United States for OPIC programs.

OPIC CLAIMS AND DISPUTE SETTLEMENT

Insured investors present claims to OPIC only after exhausting local remedies in the host nations. Claims are then "settled, and disputes arising as a result thereof may be arbitrated with the consent of the parties, on such terms and conditions as the Corporation may determine." 22 U.S.C.A. § 2197(i). OPIC insurance contracts have stated that "any controversy arising out of or relating to this Contract or the breach thereof shall be settled by arbitration in accordance with the then prevailing Commercial Arbitration Rules of the American Arbitration Association." Arbitration takes place in Washington, D.C., and all arbitral determinations are intended to be binding on the parties. The arbitration process is important; the Corporation has challenged a number of claims presented to it by United States companies claiming to have lost property through expropriations.

Under AID, prior to 1969, six investor expropriation claims and one inconvertibility claim were denied. Between 1969 and 1978, under OPIC, about eight percent of claims were denied for a variety of reasons, such as investor failure to fulfill contractual obligations to the OPIC, or insurance not in effect at the time of the expropriation. During that period at least eight expropriation and two inconvertibility claims were denied. Additionally, some five claims went to arbitration. Since 1978, OPIC has had the authority to deny loss claims if the investor, a controlling shareholder or any agent of the investor, has engaged in any act which resulted in a conviction under the 1977 Foreign Corrupt Practices Act, and such act has been the "preponderant" cause of the loss. 22 U.S.C.A. § 2197(1). There have been few convictions under the FCPA, however, since most charges lead at most to a consent decree.

Much of the value of expropriation claims which have been denied by OPIC is represented by a $95 million claim by ITT, $154 in two claims by Anaconda Copper Co., and a multi-million dollar claim by the Revere Copper and Brass Company. But in each case the resulting arbitration rejected OPIC's denial of liability.

ITT operations in Chile were expropriated in 1971. OPIC denied the ITT loss claim because ITT had failed to comply with a contractual obligation to disclose to OPIC facts material to the ITT claim, specifically its anti-Allende political activity in Chile. That activity, when discovered by the Allende

government, led to a breakdown in ITT–Chile negotiations. The arbitral tribunal held that ITT had
not violated its contractual obligations under the
written Agreement. 13 *Int'l Legal Mat.* 1307.

Anaconda operations in Chile also were expropriated in 1971. OPIC denied the claim on the basis
that the nationalization had actually occurred in
1969, when the company negotiated an agreement
with President Frei's government to sell 51 percent
of its ownership to the Chilean nation, and when
Anaconda's insurance had been on "standby" rather than in force. The arbitral tribunal rejected
OPIC's contentions, observing that:

> [o]n every point of contractual construction nec-
> essary for our decision, we find that the interpre-
> tation required to support the OPIC position is
> too strained for us to accept, even after giving due
> weight to the policy of the Foreign Assistance Act.
> OPIC could readily have drafted the contract
> forms so as to ensure in regard to each point the
> result it now contends for. But that was not done.
> It is not our proper function to rewrite the Con-
> tracts of Guaranty nor do we perceive any rea-
> sons of equity or statutory purpose for doing so.
> 14 *Int'l Legal Mat.* 1210, 1245.

In 1974–75 Revere Copper's Jamaican subsidiary
was subject to such increased taxation that it closed
because of what the parent called economic necessi-
ty. The Jamaican government in the original contract with Revere had promised not to increase
taxes on the subsidiary. Revere claimed that the

taxation amounted to expropriation. OPIC denied the claim. A divided arbitral tribunal held that the Jamaican action, along with other actions, amounted to a repudiation of the original investment and therefore constituted an expropriation.

OPIC AND PRIVATE INSURERS

OPIC continues to investigate methods of transferring its insurance coverage to private insurers. Most recently, it has been instructed by Congress to study the possibility of total privatization. But relatively few private insurers have been interested in investment risk policies. As might be expected, Lloyds of London does write some investment risk coverage. Since 1975 an Overseas Investment Insurance Group of private insurers has assisted OPIC with insuring against inconvertibility and expropriation risks. In more recent years, the group has expanded and helped to cover OPIC exposure in some countries. The 1985 amendments to the OPIC laws created a facultative reinsurance program allowing the Corporation to associate with the private sector by reinsuring risks underwritten by the private sector.

The 1988 amendments replaced the facultative reinsurance program with provisions relating to enhancing private political risk insurance, including risk sharing and the creation of an advisory group to help develop and implement cooperative programs. Even though many Congressional members view insurance of private investment abroad as best allocated to the private sector, it seems likely that OPIC will survive because its programs provide insurance of risks not broadly acceptable to the private insurance industry, and there are foreign policy considerations which may conflict with traditional risk management principles in establishing insurance premium rates. By the mid–1990s, however, OPIC's budget was being diminished, and the administration required to study privatization of the agency.

Private insurance for risks of foreign investment, when available, tends to be for short terms, such as 3–5 years. It may be obtained for expropriation (including creeping expropriation), or for arbitrary recall of credit, repudiation of contracts (such as the cancellation of a license), currency blockages, some commercial losses, embargoes and revocation of export/import permits and political diversions of investment assets (e.g., caused by hijacking). Lloyds of London plays a major role in issuing insurance against investment risks by private insurers. Lloyds is joined by a few United States private insurers in offering investment risk insurance.

More limited insurance directed to the sale of goods rather than investment is offered by the Foreign Credit Insurance Association (FCIA is a New York based group of some fifty insurers), which issues export credit insurance to United States exporters to protect against the short-term risk of foreign buyers failing to pay for the goods as agreed. The use of letters of credit diminishes the need for such insurance, however, since the letter of credit provides assurance of payment well before receipt of the goods by the foreign buyer. Either form may help the seller obtain attractive financing to cover the costs of providing or manufacturing such goods for export.

Information about private investment insurance is available from several organizations, such as the International Insurance Advisory Council of the United States Chamber of Commerce, the Insurance Committee of the OECD, and the United Nations Committee on Trade and Development's (UNCTAD) Committee on Invisibles and Financing Related to Trade (CIFT).

THE MULTILATERAL INVESTMENT GUARANTEE AGENCY: OPIC THEORY ON AN INTERNATIONAL LEVEL

OPIC insurance, which is limited to United States investors, has led to the establishment of similar insurance on an international level by the World Bank's creation of the Multilateral Investment Guarantee Agency (MIGA). See *www.miga.org.* MIGA's charge is to encourage increased investment in the developing nations. The MIGA Convention was opened for signatures in October, 1985, and came into force when five industrial and 15 developing nations ratified the Convention. Voting power is equally divided between the industrial and developing nations. By mid–1999, the MIGA Convention had been signed by 165 nations, with 149 having completed membership requirements. The only major nations which are not subscribers are Mexico and New Zealand.

Risks covered by MIGA are noncommercial and include inconvertibility, deprivation of ownership or control by governmental actions, breach of contract by the government where there is no recourse to a judicial or arbitral forum, and loss from military action or civil disturbance. The insurance may cover equity investments or loans made or guaranteed by holders of equity (probably including service and management contracts), and also licensing, franchising and production sharing agreements. In 1994, the World Bank approved expanding the role of the IBRD's (International Bank for Reconstruction and Development) guarantee authority to help large infrastructure projects in developing nations, especially privatizations. This new guarantee authority would not guarantee equity capital, which is a role of MIGA, it would rather guarantee commercial debt financing to public or private entities in developing nations. This is critically needed to help developing nations invest in their infrastructures. The developing nation governments do not have the resources to significantly improve their infrastructures, and to encourage foreign private lending and multilateral development banks to assist in their development, new forms of guarantees are needed. Further foreign investment in productive facilities, which may benefit from MIGA guarantees, may diminish if the infrastructures are not improved.

Investors must be from a member country, and only foreign investors qualify. With Agency approval, however, domestic investors may receive coverage for projects where they bring assets back to their nation. This special allowance is intended to promote the return of capital transferred to safe havens during times of political or economic uncertainty. The location of approved investments will mostly be developing nations, not necessarily those which are MIGA members, but only nations which approve the insurance. There was considerable discussion regarding insuring only in developing nations which adopted standards for protecting foreign investment, but the final Convention did not include any such conditions. Standards may nevertheless be a factor in writing insurance, if any measure of risk management principles is to be followed. The highest percentage of coverage is in Latin America and the Caribbean, followed by Asia, and then Europe and Central Asia. Africa (combined with the Middle East) receives the least coverage.

MIGA commenced with an authorized capital of $1.082 billion US. Fifty-three percent of the authorized capital was initially subscribed to by 42 World Bank members. Ten percent was required to be paid in, with the remaining 90 percent subject to call. Actually, most of the subscribed capital has been paid in. Shares are proportional to member nations' shares of World Bank capital. MIGA first was allowed to write guarantee coverage for up to 150 percent of its capital and reserves. That was subsequently increased by 1995 to 350 percent. Because of an increased demand for MIGA guarantees, but a slower growing amount of capital and reserves, MIGA needed to further increase its capital and reserves to avoid continuing to increase the allowable percentage of risk coverage to a point where the Agency had too great exposure for its capital and reserves. It responded in 1999 by nearly doubling the capital to more than $2 billion.

Since the viability of MIGA is dependent both on its care in selecting risks to insure, and its ability to negotiate settlements after paying claims, the right of subrogation is extremely important. Unlike national programs, such as OPIC, MIGA has the force of a large group of nations behind it when it presses a claim. Only experience will disclose the extent to which politics (and particularly the North–South dialogue) will enter the claims procedures. The clear intention of MIGA is to avoid political interference and consider the process solely as creating legal issues. MIGA has yet to face claims experience. If over time the risks MIGA (and other programs such as OPIC) insure substantially diminish, the use of such insurance will decrease. If on the other hand the risks become reality, the effectiveness of the claims procedures will become evident.

Creating MIGA within the World Bank structure offers benefits a separate international organization would lack. MIGA has access to World Bank data on nations' economic and social status, thus helping the assessment of risks. The World Bank has considerable credibility which favors MIGA, and encourages broad participation. It is not certain how MIGA will affect national programs, such as OPIC.

A United States company, for example, might prefer dealing with OPIC because of greater confidence of claims being paid, of maintaining information confidentiality, and benefitting from legal processes established in bilateral investment treaties. Experience to date suggests that United States investors very much approve the establishment of MIGA, and that MIGA's insurance is compatible with that of OPIC, acting to some degree as a gap filler for United States investors when OPIC insurance is not available or inadequate for the project. In mid–1995, MIGA issued its first policy in Vietnam, a $13.5 million guarantee for the Citibank Hanoi branch, covering expropriation, currency transfer restrictions, and war and civil disturbance. Other coverage has been written for such United States entity projects as a Honeywell Inc. joint venture in China; Citibank expansions in China, Costa Rica, and Pakistan; First National Bank of Boston in Brazil; and a Marriott hotel in Costa Rica.

Investors in nations without adequate national insurance programs certainly have welcomed MIGA's creation. But even some of the newly industrializing nations, such as India and Korea, have adopted national programs. MIGA's success will likely be where it fills gaps rather than where it competes with established and successful national insurance programs. Its real test will be when claims are made—the past decade has not been witness to the kind of expropriations which tested the viability of OPIC in the 1970s.

CHAPTER EIGHT

THE EUROPEAN UNION[1]

The European Union (EU), often called the Common Market, is a supranational legal regime with its own legislative, administrative, treaty-making and judicial procedures. To create this regime, fifteen European nations have surrendered substantial sovereignty to the EU. European Union law has replaced national law in many areas and the EU legal system operates as an umbrella over the legal systems of the member states.

The original six member states of Belgium, France, Italy, Luxembourg, the Netherlands, and West Germany, were joined by Denmark, Ireland and the United Kingdom in 1973, Greece in 1981, Portugal and Spain in 1986, and Austria, Finland and Sweden in 1995. Norway failed to join as planned in 1973 and again in 1995 after national referenda. Greenland (admitted with Denmark) withdrew in 1983. The Norwegians and Greenlanders strongly disliked the Union's Common Fisheries Policy. This Policy regulates the type and number of fish that can be caught in European waters, significantly subsidizes the fishing industry, and protects it from foreign competition. Its most con-

1. For much more extensive coverage, see Folsom's *European Union Law in A Nutshell.*

troversial feature requires common access to all fishing grounds beyond six (sometimes twelve) miles.

Turkey, an Associate for many years, formally applied for membership in 1987. It may be unable to join because of Greek hostility and the requirement of a unanimous Council vote on new members. There are also questions as to Turkey's commitment to democracy and its "European" status. Turkey's candidacy as an EU member state has also been diluted by the rush of Central European applicants after the fall of the Soviet Union. Formal negotiations for entry are now underway with Estonia, Poland, the Czech Republic, Hungary, Slovenia, Malta, Lithuania, Latvia, Slovakia, Romania, Bulgaria and Cyprus. These nations (and possibly Turkey) are expected to join the European Union in waves commencing in about 2004.

THREE COMMUNITIES

Technically, there are three European economic communities within the European Union: the European Coal and Steel Community (ECSC) established in 1952, and the European Economic Community (now the European Community) (EC) and the European Atomic Energy Community (EURATOM), both established by Treaties of Rome in 1957. Each community has its own founding treaty and secondary law. The EC must take pride of place in importance and effect on the lives of the citizens of the member states. In common parlance, references to the EU or the Common Market generally include the EC, the ECSC and EURATOM.

While each community originally had an organization separate from the other, since a Merger Treaty of 1965, all three communities have had common institutions: The Council of Ministers, the Commission, the European Parliament, and the European Court of Justice (ECJ). A Court of First Instance was created in 1989 to reduce the caseload of the ECJ.

The ECSC was formed in direct response to World War II and waning Allied control of German steel and coal production. Whereas the EC Treaty specifies that it is of unlimited duration, the ECSC Treaty expires in 2002. Nevertheless, it was the Coal and Steel Community that gave birth to the major institutions of European economic integration. The ECSC is a curious combination of French regulatory "dirigisme" (price and output controls, tariff protection, investment subsidies) and more market oriented policies (internal free trade, competition rules, adjustment assistance). Many European coal and steel firms are government owned, which has generally tended to cause the ECSC to protect these industries from world market forces. The ECSC levies taxes directly upon coal and steel companies, a power not found in the EC Treaty.

EURATOM was formed to promote the peaceful use of nuclear energy. It has sponsored research and development, joint ventures and free movement of related products and persons. EURATOM is rarely in the news, but played an important role when the EU revised its regulations after Chernobyl.

The European Union has an aggregate population exceeding 375 million and a gross "national" (Union) product exceeding $7000 billion. It is the largest market for exports from the United States. No other regional legal regime rivals Europe in detail of rulemaking and the extent to which its member states have achieved integration. Anyone doing business with Common Market nations will have contact with EU law, which is vast and intricate. There are law school courses devoted entirely to a study of the European Union.

EUROPE WITHOUT INTERNAL FRONTIERS

The EC Treaty is intended to achieve the harmonious development of economic activities of member states through: (1) the pursuit of trade and economic growth, a common customs tariff and commercial policy towards third countries, and an elimination of tariffs and quotas within the Community; (2) the abolition of internal obstacles to the free movement of persons, services and capital; (3) the adoption of common agricultural, fishery and transport policies; (4) the fostering of a system of "nondistorted competition"; and (5) the approximation (harmonization) of laws of member states so far as required for the proper functioning of the Common Market. Specific areas of policy include rules on competition, taxation, government contracts, state monopolies, free movement, transportation, the customs union, agriculture, dumping practices, state subsidies, regional development, monetary policy, trade relations, commercial policy, social policy and the European Investment Bank.

Development of the Common Market has not been easy. National interests and laws have often frustrated treaty rules and regional policies. This "hardening of the arteries" of trade and growth caused major revisions to the EC Treaty in 1987. These were undertaken through the Single European Act. Their principal focus was on nontariff trade barriers to trade and free movement. Enhanced policies for worker health and safety, foreign policy cooperation, research and development and the environment were also anticipated. The goal was, by the end of 1992, to establish a Europe "without internal frontiers". Hundreds of new legislative acts have been adopted in pursuit of a truly Common Market.

Realization of the goal of a Europe without internal frontiers *for people* has proved harder to achieve. The Benelux states, Germany, Italy, Spain, Greece, Portugal and France agreed to remove their internal frontier controls on people under the 1990 "Schengen Accord." This accord is the product of intergovernmental agreement, not legislation. It is not expected that Denmark, Ireland and the United Kingdom will participate. The Schengen Accord covers such sensitive issues as visas, asylum, immigration, gun controls, extradition and police rights of "hot pursuit." The main points of contention were cross-border traffic of immigrants and criminals, especially terrorists and drug dealers. These issues were resolved largely by promises of greater inter-governmental cooperation, notably through computer linkages. The Schengen Accord finally became operational in 1995.

In 1993, the EC Treaty was amended substantially by the Treaty on European Union (TEU). The tasks of the Union thereafter included creation of an economic and monetary union with emphasis upon price stability. The listing of activities in pursuit of that goal was expanded to include environmental, social, research and development, trans-European network, health, education, development aid, consumer protection, energy, civil protection, internal market, visas and other policy endeavors. On the other hand, the TEU sought to limit regional activities to those areas where the results are best achieved at the European (versus national) level. This is known as the "subsidiarity principle" and is the subject of intense controversy.

The Treaty on European Union also added what amount to side agreements ("separate pillars" in Eurospeak) on a common foreign and security policy and cooperation regarding justice and home affairs. Like the 1987 Single European Act's provisions on foreign policy, these side agreements did not amend the EC Treaty and stand on their own as separate international agreements. As such, they are not subject to the judicial review of the Court of Justice.

The Maastricht Treaty on European Union of 1993 called for yet another round of intergovernmental negotiations to revise both the TEU and the Treaty of Rome. Late in 1997, these negotiations bore fruit in the Amsterdam Treaty, which then faced national referenda and court challenges during the ratification process.

The Amsterdam Treaty of 1999 is in many respects best known for what it did not accomplish, namely major institutional and agricultural policy reforms in anticipation of European Union membership expansions. The Treaty did significantly extend Parliament's co-decision legislative powers, and institutionalized procedures to deal with "serious and persistent" member state violations of democracy, human rights and the rule of law. It authorized legislative action to secure "freedom, security and justice"(an effective transfer of much of the TEU justice and home affairs power), including asylum, extradition and the essentials of the Schengen Accord, all subject to Court of Justice review but also British, Danish and Irish opt outs.

Additional legislative powers cover employment incentives, public health,fraud prevention, customs cooperation, transparency principles and social policy (formerly the Social Protocol). A complex provision on "flexibility" seeks to allow, subject to detailed controls, some member states to establish "closer cooperation" than others. This provision appears to reflect the realities of less than comprehensive participation in existing policies and programs such as defense, the common currency, the

Schengen Accord and the like. Lastly, the Amsterdam Treaty adds a special protocol on the principles of subsidiarity and proportionality, and attempts to secure greater support for common foreign and security policies.

THE COUNCIL OF MINISTERS

The Council consists of representatives of the ruling governments of the member states. Specialized Ministers from national governments routinely meet (e.g., Economic and Finance Ministers, Foreign Ministers). Collectively, such Ministers comprise the Council when they act on regional affairs. The principal function of the Council is to coordinate the economic policies of the member states in fulfillment of the objectives of the Treaty of Rome. It exercises important power in approving legislation and international agreements. Since the Council often has the final word on such matters, it possesses considerable power to advance or retard European integration.

Most provisions of the EC Treaty state specifically which legislative steps and powers are conferred on the Council. However, there is a general enabling power entitling the Council, acting on a proposal from the Commission and after consulting the Parliament, to take action. This power may be used only where the powers necessary to attain one of the objectives of the Treaty of Rome have not been provided. Environmental regulations and directives, for example, were originally a product of unspecified Treaty law.

The Treaty requires the Council to act by a qualified majority on some matters and with unanimity on others. These requirements institutionalize an element of political agreement among the member states. In 1966, the Council adopted the "Luxembourg Accord". Regardless of the provisions of the Treaty. on very important questions the Council should try to act with unanimity. This accord vested each member state with a veto power. Adopting EC legislation became more and more difficult, especially as the number of member states increased. In recent years, the Council has frequently departed from the rule of unanimity. The Single European Act (effective July, 1987) the Maastricht Treaty on European Union (effective November, 1993) and the Amsterdam Treaty (effective May 1999) amended the EC Treaty to allow majority voting in many instances (most notably concerning the establishment of the internal free market). The Luxembourg Accord has been eclipsed by these developments.

The Committee of Permanent Representatives (COREPER) (established by the 1965 Merger Treaty) is a subordinate institution composed of member states' "civil servants", usually at the ambassadorial level. Its main function is to prepare the work of the Council and to maintain close communication with the Commission and with civil servants in member states. In practice, COREPER undertakes to make all noncontentious decisions for the Council, leaving to the Council only the task of formal adoption.

THE COMMISSION AND LAW–MAKING

A principal European institution is the Commission, which is located in Brussels, Belgium. Since 1958, hundreds of Commission decisions and regulations in economic and social areas have moved the Common Market toward closer union. The Commission is independent of the member states. Its 20 Commissioners (two from France, Spain, Germany, Italy and the U.K.—one from each of the other member states) are selected by Council appointment. They do not represent member states or take orders from member state governments. The Commission is charged with the duty of acting only in the best interests of the region, and serves as the guardian of the treaties. Each Commissioner supervises specific Directorates (Departments) administering regional policies: Agriculture, External Relations, Competition, etc. And each has an extensive staff of highly paid and tax sheltered Eurocrats.

Member states with special interests in certain policies usually are able, by common accord in the Council, to have "their" Commissioner supervise the Directorate in which they are most interested. Hence, a French Commissioner is often the head of the Agriculture Directorate, a British Commissioner often heads the Directorate for External Relations, and so on. Commissioners serve four-year terms and are frequently reappointed. However, in recent years, there have been some failures to reappoint Commissioners who lose the faith of their home governments. Prime Minister Thatcher, in particular, refused to renew a British Commissioner who had "gone native" (became too much of a European Union enthusiast).

One Commission function is to ensure that the provisions of the treaties are carried out. To do so, it has power to render law enforcement decisions and to formulate legislative proposals (regulations, directives) for the Council. It also exercises powers conferred upon it by the Council. Moreover, the Commission has asserted a power to act without express Council authority in situations involving overriding public interest. The EC Treaty enables the Commission to enforce, through the Court of Justice, the observance of Treaty provisions and secondary law by individuals, other regional institutions and by member states. In this capacity, the Commission has been an aggressive prosecutor of European law.

The Commission maintains relations with many international organizations such as the GATT and WTO. With Council mandates, it negotiates most commercial treaties on behalf of the Union. The EU has an extensive network of trade treaties, especially in the Mediterranean basin and in Central and Eastern Europe, and with former colonies of member states.

The Commission has an important function as the only institution which proposes and drafts European legislation. Proposed legislation is submitted to the Council for adoption. The Council may amend Commission proposals only by unanimous vote. The Council is obliged to consult and in some cases cooperate or co-decide with the European Parliament before enacting legislation. Cooperation procedures often result in adoption of amendments proposed by Parliament. Co-decision procedures give Parliament a veto over legislative proposals. Such mandatory procedures are the linchpin around which dynamic changes in structure are emerging. Slowly, the European Parliament is becoming a principal legislative body. This institutional power struggle and policy debate has lasted for years.

The Commission's exclusive power to draft legislation has made it the focal point of lobbying activities in which United States counsel often participate. For example, U.S. lobbying in connection with the European computer software directive is said to have been extremely heavy. More recently, Parliament's ever increasing roles in the legislative process have made it another lobbying center.

THE EUROPEAN PARLIAMENT

The European Parliament is an institution in the course of change. The European Parliament historically played an advisory role. Since 1979 its members have been elected directly by the citizens of the member states (prior to 1979 appointment was by nomination of the national legislatures of member states). The number of MEPs correspond roughly to the populations of each country except united Germany. MEPs serve five year terms, and are presently divided into transnational political groups. The European Parliament is a kaleidoscope of European politics.

The Parliament has the power to put questions to the Commission and the Council concerning regional affairs. It also has the power to censure the Commission, in which event all the Commissioners are required to resign as a body. In 1999, in the midst of controversy over fraud and mismanagement, the threat of such a censure combined with an investigatory report caused the commission to resign en mass. In the event of inaction by another institution, the Parliament can bring an action against that institution in the Court of Justice. For example, the Parliament sued the Council for failing to act on establishing a common regional transport policy, prevailing as a matter of law (but not remedy) before the European Court. The Council failure to act on transport policy was not enforceable since the duty to act was too imprecise.

At a minimum, the Parliament has a right to be consulted and to give an "opinion" as part of the legislative process. That opinion is not binding upon the Commission or Council, but it may prove awkward if that opinion is disregarded. For example, the Court of Justice has held that the Council acts illegally if it legislates without waiting for the Parliament's opinion. Left unanswered is how long Parliament may delay the giving of an opinion.

Parliament's limited consultative role still applies to agricultural and tax measures.

The Single European Act (1987) granted Parliament a greater "cooperative" voice in developing selected policies (e.g., free movement of workers, the right to establish a business, the freedom to provide services throughout the Common Market).

Basically, when the Treaty of Rome required adherence to cooperative procedures, the Parliament often proposed amendments. By an absolute majority, the Commission re-examined the legislative proposal in their light. If the Commission rejected the amendments suggested by the Parliament, they were excluded from the legislative proposal but transmitted to the Council with the Commission's opinion on them. In either case, unanimity within the Council was required to alter the legislative proposal. Again, in either case, a qualified majority vote in the Council in most cases adopted the measure into law. One 1989 study indicates that Parliament introduced nearly 1,000 amendments after the cooperation procedure was adopted in 1987. Of these, 72 percent were accepted by the Commission and 42 percent ultimately adopted by the Council.

The "cooperation procedure" applied selectively. Most significantly, it applied to nearly all internal market measures. With the development of the cooperation procedure, and success in persuading the Commission and Council to adopt its amendments, Parliament advanced its legislative agenda.

The European Parliament acquired significant powers under the Maastricht Treaty on European Union (1993) and Amsterdam Treaty (1999). On legislation, under the "co-decision" procedure, it has what amounts to a legislative veto over selected matters if conciliation through direct negotiations with the Council cannot be achieved. Co-decision applies, for example, to single market, education, culture, health, consumer protection, environmental, transportation and research affairs. The Amsterdam Treaty considerably expanded the number areas subject to co-decision. Thus, there are now three distinct European Union legislative processes, each defined in terms of the role Parliament plays: consultative, cooperative and co-decisional. After the Amsterdam Treaty, co-decision is the most prevalent legislative process.

Significantly, the EC Treaty gives the Parliament power to amend or propose changes in the budget, drafted by the Council, regarding treaty-mandated matters. This has increased Parliamentary influence over "compulsory expenditures" (mostly agricultural subsidies). Since 1975, Parliament has had ultimate control over "non-compulsory" expenditures, about 40 percent of the budget. As a practical matter, this gives the Parliament influence over expenditures in many of the new and important policy areas. However, Parliamentary amendments to the Council's draft budget cannot exceed the maximum rate of increase allowed under the Treaty. This maximum involves a complex calculation by the Commission of regional inflation and gross domestic product (GDP) rates as well as national budget variations. Parliament, at the end of a laborious process with multiple communications to the Council, adopts the final budget.

Parliament and the Council often quarrel over creation of the budget, with Parliament prevailing more and more. Parliament and the Council review how the Commission has implemented the budget. Upon Council recommendation, Parliament gives the Commission a "discharge" of its budgetary duties. The Court of Auditors assists the Parliament and Council in these tasks, which are reasonably routine. Parliament has refused to discharge the Commission, resulting in tighter controls thereafter. Parliament's power over the purse is increasing and its President reportedly remarked: "As long as Parliament does not have more power in other fields, there will be conflicts on the budget."

THE EUROPEAN COURT OF JUSTICE AND COURT OF FIRST INSTANCE

The European Court of Justice is to ensure that in the interpretation and application of the EC Treaty "the law" is observed. The Court has construed this assignment to include enforcement of international and customary law as well as regional law. The Court of Justice has also created new law, such as in the area of fundamental human rights, by analyzing the "general principles of law common to member states." This development is consistent with (but not specifically authorized by) the 1977 Joint Declaration on Fundamental Rights of the Council, Commission and Parliament. The Declaration commits Europe to safeguarding representative democracy, the rule of law, social justice and respect for human rights.

Fifteen Justices (one from each state) comprise the European Court of Justice in Luxembourg. They are appointed for six year terms by the common accord of the member states and are routinely reappointed to the Court. Most of the Justices and most of the lawyers appearing before the Court (who must be members of the national bars) have been trained in the civil not common law tradition. This imparts a distinctly Continental approach to the Court's procedures and the style of its opinions. For example, the *Court* (not the parties) may call witnesses, hire experts, and order documents produced (limited cross-examination rights are permitted). Thus, appeals to the European Court of Justice can review questions of both law and fact.

The Court has several Advocates–General, a position not found in Britain or the United States. These are civil service lawyers who evaluate cases before the Court and give advice in public opinions. The Court receives written and oral argument by counsel, and then hears the opinion of the Advocate–General, which it may adopt or reject. Lawyers working with European law often refer to such opinions for more extensive legal and policy reasoning than ordinarily appears in the judgments of the European Court. Advocate–General opinions are especially helpful in attempting to project trends or new developments in the law, since they often raise hypotheticals extending beyond the facts of the case.

The brief judgments of the Court of Justice are written in the civil law tradition without dissenting opinions, thus masking divisions within the Court. The Court of Justice has demonstrated a preference for following and citing its own precedents, but has not hesitated to reverse itself as needed. Americans may be comfortable with this approach, but it has caused some consternation in British circles where a strict attitude toward the binding nature of precedent prevails and nothing less than amazement on the Continent.

The Court is independent of other European institutions and of the member states. It acts in a number of different capacities—civil, administrative, constitutional—and has jurisdiction over European matters throughout the member states. The Court has a powerful voice in the interpretation of regional law. National courts must observe and enforce European law, but the Court of Justice is its final arbiter. Perhaps the most useful channel for assuring this result is the ability of the Court to give "preliminary rulings" on questions referred directly to it by any court of a member state. Lower courts may in their discretion (not the litigants' prerogative) make such references. Courts of last resort in the member states *must* refer regional legal issues to the European Court of Justice. However, courts of last resort sometimes avoid references by invocation of the French administrative law doctrine of "acte clair" or its equivalent. They argue that the law is so clear as to not warrant a referral. This doctrine has now been refined and adopted by the European Court as part of its law.

The Court is frequently called upon to review acts or the failure to act of regional institutions. Interested persons, member states and other institutions may raise such challenges before the Court. But the Parliament can as a rule only challenge failures to act, not the myriad of legislative and administrative acts pouring forth from the Council and Commission. Appeals to annul existing acts are limited. For example, the party against whom a Commission law enforcement decision (including decisions to impose fines or penalties) is taken may appeal to the Court. And Europe's institutions can litigate their power struggles before the Court by challenging regulations, directives, decisions and failures to act. These struggles have led to a series of provocative cases entitled Commission v. Council, Parliament v. Council, etc.

National courts and law enforcement institutions are responsible for implementing judgments of the Court of Justice, e.g., collection of fines and penalties levied under competition law against enterprises. When a member state refuses to comply with European law, the Court is often called on to render judgment against that state in actions commenced by the Commission. Its opinions have authority and respect, but prior to 1993 no practical means of enforcement against member states. Noncompliance is a problem, and states have been known to exhaust all their appeal rights and drag their feet before complying. The Maastricht Treaty on European Union authorizes the Court to levy fines and penalties against recalcitrant member states.

The European Court of First Instance (CFI) was authorized by Single European Act amendments to the Treaty of Rome in 1987. The CFI is "attached" to the European Court and its jurisdiction is limited to actions or proceedings by individuals or legal persons. Thus the Court of First Instance cannot hear prosecutions of member states by the Commission, references of European legal issues from national courts, nor challenges of Council or Commission acts or failures to act when these are initiated by member states or other regional institutions. It can hear such challenges and related "pleas of illegality" when they are privately initiated. Additional grants of jurisdiction to the CFI cover the dumping and external subsidies law fields.

The purpose, in general, behind creation of the Court of First Instance (CFI) was to relieve the European Court of some of its caseload. It commenced doing this in November of 1989. However, there is a right of appeal on points of law from the CFI to the European Court. The Council Decision establishing the CFI indicates that such appeals lie on grounds of lack of competence, procedural failures that adversely affect the appellants' interests, and infringement of European law by the CFI. Any failure by the CFI to follow prior ECJ decisions could amount to such an infringement.

Judges of the European Court of Justice and Court of First Instance are of noted calibre and the court is held in high esteem.

THE NATURE OF EUROPEAN LAW

The treaties establishing the European communities are more than international treaties among contracting sovereign states. They transfer sovereign rights concerning legislative, administrative and judicial powers from member states to regional institutions. For example, the EC Treaty grants the power to enter into international agreements and treaties. In areas where member states have clearly transferred "competence" to the region, international agreements may be made only by the European Union. Since the EC Treaty is broad in scope and more transfers of competence occur each year, this theoretically amounts to a substantial transfer of national sovereignty.

European law includes the EC, ECSC, EURATOM and TEU treaties and all subordinate legislation made thereunder. Member states have adopted much of this law as national law. For example, upon the entry of the United Kingdom, the UK Parliament enacted the European Communities Act of 1972. Section 2(1) of that Act provides that "all such rights, powers, liabilities, obligations ... created or arising by or under the Treaties ... are without further enactment to be given legal effect ... in the United Kingdom".

Europe's institutions normally legislate through regulations and directives. The EC Treaty empowers both the Council and the Commission, or (less frequently) the Commission acting with Council authority or the Council and the Parliament acting together, to create such law in most areas of regional policy. A regulation has general application, is binding in its entirety, and is applicable directly in all member states. Normally, a regulation is self-executing and creates rights and obligations for member states, and for their citizens as well. Most regulations concern the common agricultural policy, but they are also important in competition law.

A directive is binding, as to intended result and timing, upon the member state to which it is addressed but leaves to the state the choice of form and method of implementation. Thus, member states must enact or amend their laws or regulations, or do whatever is needed, to carry out directives. Directives have frequently been used to harmonize national policies of concern to the Common Market, e.g., tax systems, company law, customs, investment control, mobility of labor, recognition of professionals, products liability (using a strict liability standard), environmental law, etc.

European law can affect citizens of member states directly without the intervention of the national legislatures of the member states. This is only true of *directly effective* law. National courts are obliged to enforce directly effective European law, and citizens may invoke such law in national courts. EC regulations are always directly applicable. The

Court of Justice ultimately determines which of the many Treaty terms, international treaty obligations and Council directives are directly effective law. It has, for example, decided that equal pay for equal work is a directly effective Treaty provision. This decision allows individuals to challenge pay discrimination in public and private sector jobs. A flight attendant for Sabena Airlines was thus able to allege illegal discrimination on the basis of regional law before a Belgian work tribunal. Indeed, European law in this area enshrines the principle of "comparable worth," a controversial issue in United States employment law.

Directives issued to implement the equal pay for equal work mandate job classifications to measure the comparable worth of one job with another. The Commission successfully enforced one such directive in a prosecution before the European Court of Justice against the United Kingdom. The British Sex Discrimination Act of 1975 did not meet the directive's standards because employers could block the introduction of job classification systems. Danish law's failure to cover non-unionized workers also breached the directive on equal pay for equal work. Dutch law allowing for compulsory retirement of women at age 60 and men at age 65 violated the directive. But implementation of these directives under German law, notably by constitutional provisions, sufficed to meet regional standards. The case law on equal pay and (more broadly) equal treatment is vast.

The Court of Justice has consistently held that when Treaty provisions are clearly defined and intended to impose concrete legal obligations and rights upon individuals, member states and regional institutions, they are directly effective law. Various EC Treaty provisions concerning tariffs, quotas, state monopolies, competition, nondiscrimination on grounds of nationality and others have been held to have this effect. Such provisions can be contrasted with the more numerous "aspirational" Treaty terms which do not establish directly effective legal norms. Similar criteria govern the legal consequences of international treaty obligations and regional directives. The Court has held, for example, that Article 11 of GATT (which broadly prohibits quotas in international trade) is binding but not directly effective law. In the Court's view, GATT rules were not intended to create legal rights and obligations for individuals, only governments. Thus a Dutch importer could not challenge regulations applying quotas to apples from outside the Common Market.

LAW ENFORCEMENT

Both the Council and the Commission are empowered to render law enforcement decisions, which are binding upon the persons addressed. The Commission undertakes most prosecutions for violations of European law by member states, institutions, individuals and enterprises. Such decisions, and regulations and directives, must state the reasons upon which they are based. They are subject to judicial review by the European Court of Justice or Court of First Instance. In the exercise of its power of review, the Court may declare a Council or Commission act void on four grounds: (1) lack of competence; (2) infringement of an essential procedural requirement; (3) infringement of the Treaty or any rule of law relating to its application; and (4) misuse of powers.

These grounds for appeal originate in French administrative law, which should be consulted to amplify their meaning. They also illustrate the significance of different official languages to the law. When first commenced, English was not an official language of the Common Market. Attorneys operating prior to 1973 (the membership date of the UK and Eire) worked in German, Dutch, Italian and French.

It is still standard procedure in analyzing European law to compare text in various official languages to uncover nuances and arguments not always apparent in English. This is especially helpful when dealing with pre–1973 law (now officially translated into English), including the Treaties. For example, the appeal ground translated from as "misuse of powers" is much better understood as "détournement de pouvoir", a narrow term of art in French administrative law. Furthermore, "misuse of powers" (a term of art in British administrative law), while broader than "détournement de pouvoir," is not as broad as "abuse of powers or abuse of discretion" in United States law. Hence, American attorneys should avoid projections of their legal concepts into European law.

If a conflict arises between regional law and the domestic law of a member state, the Court of Justice has held that the former prevails. The Treaty binds member states in an identical way, not subject to the particularities of domestic law. There is no supremacy clause, but the Court has ruled that *supremacy of European law* is absolutely necessary to make the Common Market work and is implied by the very existence and structure of the EC Treaty. For the most part, national courts have followed this interpretation. However, several national courts have held that conflicts between European law and national *constitutional* rights should be resolved in favor of the latter. These rulings have not significantly affected the operation of the Common Market, but serve as a reminder that its law on human rights needs development.

It is often said that the doctrines of direct effect and supremacy represent the twin pillars of the European Court's integrationist jurisprudence. Without the cooperation of national courts, especially in using the preliminary ruling reference procedure and in following the rulings of the Court, this jurisprudence would lack widespread, effective implementation.

European law and domestic law co-exist in the sense that they are both enforced through the national courts. It is even possible for regional law and domestic law to apply simultaneously in connection

with the same business transaction (possibly causing multiple liabilities), but only to the extent that
uniform implementation of European law is not
prejudiced. For example, certain rights and powers
came into question because of a Council regulation
which made it obligatory upon member states to
install recording tachygraphs on trucks. The United
Kingdom government failed to make such installation mandatory. The Commission issued a decision
ordering the installation, but the UK government
did not comply. The Commission brought the matter before the Court of Justice. The UK government
argued that: (a) to introduce mandatory legislation
would cause political difficulties and great economic
damage; (b) the costs were prohibitive compared
with benefits; and (c) the regulation should not
apply to trucks not involved in international trade
because no other member states would be prejudiced. The Court rejected all these arguments and
considered them directly contrary to the legal force
of an EC regulation. That the objectives of the
regulation could have been achieved by other means
was irrelevant.

FREE MOVEMENT OF GOODS

The EC Treaty attempts to achieve free movement of goods by establishment of a customs union
to eliminate, between the member states, customs
duties and all other charges having "equivalent
effect." This elimination applies both to goods having their origin within member states and to those

emanating from elsewhere which are in "free circulation." Thus, potatoes from Canada in free circulation in Britain may not be subjected to Irish import licenses. The elimination of internal tariffs was actually completed ahead of schedule, and is being phased in for new members.

A common customs tariff (CCT) with the outside world has also been established. This was originally derived by arithmetically averaging the tariffs of the member states. CCT customs duties are now negotiated by reciprocal agreement with third countries, most often through the GATT by the Commission. The combined effect of the removal of internal tariffs and the creation of the CCT has been to increase trade among member states and reduce trade with non-member states. For example, Britain's trade with Europe increased from 33 to 41 percent of its total trade volume in the first eight years of membership. This increase came largely at the expense of Britain's formerly extensive Commonwealth trade.

Quantitative restrictions on imports between member states and measures having an equivalent effect are also prohibited. A number of Commission directives and Court rulings have stringently enforced this provision against trading rules even remotely capable of hindering regional trade. For example, the Court of Justice ruled that the Belgian Royal Decree mandating cubic package sales of margarine was a measure equivalent to a quantitative restriction upon imports because of its capacity to hinder trade.

In a famous case, the Court of Justice held that Belgium could not block the importation via France of Scotch whiskey lacking a British certificate of origin as required by Belgian customs law. The Court of Justice decided that any national rule directly or indirectly, actually or potentially capable of hindering internal trade is generally forbidden as a measure of equivalent effect to a quota. However, *if* European law has not developed appropriate rules in the area concerned (here designations of origin), the member states may enact "reasonable" and "proportional" (no broader than necessary) regulations to ensure that the public is not harmed. Products meeting reasonable national criteria may be freely traded elsewhere in the region. This is the origin of the innovative "mutual reciprocity" principle used in significant parts of the single market legislative campaign.

The Court has used a Rule of Reason analysis for national fiscal regulations, public health measures, laws governing the fairness of commercial transactions, and consumer protection. Environmental protection and occupational safety laws of the member states have been similarly treated. Under this approach, for example, a Danish "bottle bill" requiring returnable soft drink and beer containers was generally upheld. The Danes successfully argued that this law was environmentally necessary and reasonable.

The Court of Justice has made it clear that all of the Rule of Reason justifications for national laws are temporary. Adoption of Common Market legislation in any of these areas would eliminate national authority to regulate trading conditions. These judicial mandates, none of which are specified in the Treaty of Rome, vividly illustrate the powers of the Court of Justice to expansively interpret the Treaty and to rule on the validity under regional law of national legislation affecting internal trade in goods.

Nontariff trade barriers (NTBs) are frequently the subject of intense negotiation and remain the most troublesome feature of the customs union. Some progress has been made. For example, various directives have reduced NTBs in the auto industry, e.g., safety plate glass standards, minimum axle strength, etc. Automobiles meeting these standards can be freely sold. Progress in other areas has been less visible and endless national rules on safety, health, the environment, standards, taxation and the like continue to inhibit a completely free trade of goods.

While not intended to promote or justify NTBs, the free movement of goods within the Common Market is qualified by the EC Treaty. National prohibitions or restrictions on imports and exports may be justified on grounds of public morality, public policy or public security, including: health and safety laws, measures to safeguard national treasures, and industrial and commercial property protection laws. However, such prohibitions or restrictions may not "constitute a means of arbitrary discrimination or a disguised restriction on trade between member states." The public health "escape clause" has attracted headlines in some culturally symbolic litigation. Germany sought to invoke it to keep out beer from other member states that did not meet its "pure" standards. Likewise, Italy tried to block trade in impure pasta (pasta not made with durum wheat). The European Court had relatively little trouble in rejecting these arguments. Free internal trade prevailed.

INTELLECTUAL PROPERTY

The Court of Justice has frequently issued significant opinions concerning industrial and intellectual property rights. Such rights are territorially based. Thus, for example, a U.S. manufacturer will typically hold a basket of national patent, copyright and trademark rights in the Common Market. The territoriality of these rights threatens free trade within the Common Market because manufacturers can often sue for infringement and other relief in the national courts whenever goods to which those rights apply cross borders. However, the Court has in most cases eliminated this possibility in favor of greater "intrabrand" trade and competition. Patented, copyrighted and trademarked goods, once sold in the Common Market with authorization, are said to "exhaust" the intellectual property rights with which they are associated. In the Court's view, blocking parallel imports through infringement actions was not intended to be part of the package of essential rights given by national laws. Even if so intended (as seems likely), the Court has ruled that the exercise of these rights would often amount to a means of arbitrary discrimination or disguised restrictions on trade. Thus, existing legal rights have been modified by the Court to promote the goal of Common Market integration.

A good example of this result is Centrafarm v. Sterling Drug (1974) Eur.Comm.Rep. 1147. A New York pharmaceutical company, Sterling Drug, held patent rights for several of its products throughout Europe. The products were produced under license by subsidiaries in Britain and Germany but not Holland. In Holland, an exclusive distributorship for Sterling Drug products was established. A Dutch importer (not the exclusive distributor) purchased certain of these drugs from UK and German third party suppliers at about half the price in the Netherlands. Sterling Drug sued the importer for infringement of its Dutch patent and trademark rights. Employing the preliminary ruling procedure, the Dutch High Court (Hoge Raad) sought the opinion of the European Court on the use of clearly existing legal rights to block trade in pharmaceuticals. The Court ruled that Sterling Drug's intellectual property rights had been exhausted upon sale of the goods in the UK and Germany. The rights existed as a matter of Dutch law, but they could not be exercised as a matter of European law. To allow them to be exercised would have the practical effect of giving to Sterling Drug the power to divide upon the Common Market.

FREE MOVEMENT OF WORKERS

The EC Treaty distinguishes the "free movement of workers" (blue collar workers and artisans) from the "right of establishment" and "freedom to provide services." Regarding workers, the Treaty prohibits any discrimination based on nationality between workers of the member states as regards employment, remuneration and other conditions of work and employment. This is subject to limitations justified upon grounds of public policy, security or health, and *excludes* the public service. In general, the exceptions to the right of free movement of workers have been limited strictly by the Court of Justice. Restraints based on prior convictions, for example, cannot justify exclusion of a worker unless there is an immediate threat of criminal behavior.

A Council regulation clarifies the rights of workers' families. It provides that workers from other member states must enjoy the same social and tax advantages, the same access to vocational schools and training centers, and the same right to join labor unions and to receive housing as do citizens of the host member state. Social security and pension rights have also been safeguarded by Council regulation. As a result, workers may move freely from job to job within the region and then retire with full pension benefits in their home country.

It is illegal for a member state, despite a pledge to maintain full employment for its citizens, to institute quotas or work permit requirements for incom-

ing citizens of other member states. The existence
of such a prohibition may well intensify job restrictions upon migrants from non-member states, e.g.,
the large numbers of Turks in Germany or Al-
gerians and Moroccans in France. There are also
Council directives dealing with unemployment and
safeguarding the rights of employees when businesses are transferred. The extensive provision for
European workers' rights has no counterpart in
NAFTA.

RIGHT OF ESTABLISHMENT

Free movement of self-employed persons and of
services across member state boundaries is aided by
the right of establishment. The freedom of establishment includes the right to take up and pursue
business activities throughout the Common Market
under the same conditions laid down for nationals.
It includes the right of self-employed persons to set-
up and manage undertakings, branches, agencies or
subsidiaries. Differences in company law have, to
some degree, inhibited exercise of the right of establishment. To remove these inhibitions, the Council
and Commission have embarked on a program of
directives intended to harmonize the company laws
of member states. This effort, insofar as it applies to
the self-employed, has had mixed results. The right
of establishment is perhaps most evidently exercised by restaurant owners who have opened for
business in other states. It has also been invoked by
professionals moving within Europe.

FREEDOM TO PROVIDE SERVICES

Restrictions on the freedom to provide services across borders without local establishment are being abolished progressively, and the EC Treaty contains a grant of authority to extend the relevant provisions to non-member state nationals. Removal of restrictions has been relatively simple where the subject activity is much the same in each member state. For example, the Council has adopted directives about freedom to supply services in the case of travel agents, tour operators, air brokers, freight forwarders, ship brokers, air cargo agents, shipping agents, and hairdressers. Similarly, it has been relatively easy to deal with those professions (e.g., medicine and accounting) in which diplomas and other evidence of formal qualifications relate to equivalent competence in the same skill. It did, however, take 17 years to negotiate the directive on free movement of veterinarians. And litigation over the implementation of these directives continues. It took a Commission prosecution to remove the French requirement that doctors and dentists give up their home country professional registrations before being licensed in France.

Where the profession is concerned with matters like law, considerable difficulty has been encountered in lifting restrictions within member states on the freedom to provide services. For example, within the legal profession there may be only a small amount of training or required knowledge held in common by a "lawyer" from a civil law jurisdiction (e.g., an avocat from France), and by a "lawyer" from a common law jurisdiction (e.g., a solicitor from England). As a result, the directive relating to lawyers' services takes a delicate approach to the question of freedom to provide legal services. The directive allows a lawyer from one member state, under that lawyer's national title (e.g., rechtsanwalt, barrister), to provide services in other member states. This has given rise to lawyer identity cards issued under the auspices of *Commission Consultative des Barreaux Europeens* (C.C.B.E.).

Admission to the practice of law is still governed by the rules of the legal profession of each member state. However, several European Court judgments have upheld the right of lawyer applicants to be free from discrimination on grounds of nationality, residence or retention of the right to practice in home jurisdictions. By joining the bar in another country, lawyers acquire the right to establish themselves in more than one nation. This right is now generally secured by a directive providing for the mutual recognition of all diplomas after three years of study. However, host country competence tests and additional training in the law of that country may still be required.

The multinational law firm, pioneered by Baker and McKenzie in the United States, has only a few regional counterparts in the practice of European law. Slowly, however, attorneys from member states are establishing affiliations and sometimes partnerships which reflect and service the economic and social integration of Europe. Ironically, one of the most rapidly integrating forces is the emergence throughout Europe of multinational accounting firms as providers and employers of legal services. Such growth is hampered in the United States by rules against unauthorized practice of law. "European law firms" often compete with existing branches of U.S. multinational firms for the lucrative practice of Common Market law.

FREE MOVEMENT OF CAPITAL

The EC Treaty requires the removal of national restrictions on the free movement of capital belonging to persons of member states to the extent necessary to insure the proper functioning of the Common Market. However, member states were initially just required to be "as liberal as possible" in granting authorizations under national exchange controls for capital transfers. The free movement of personal and investment capital should be distinguished from the free movement of payments necessary to trade. Current payments are, as a rule, treated more liberally and indeed are essential to the free movement of goods and services in the Common Market.

The free movement of capital goals of the Treaty of Rome have been much delayed. It was not until the implementation of the Europe without internal frontiers campaign that new legislative acts firmly entrenched the right of individuals and companies to move capital across borders without substantial limitation. Short term monetary and exchange rate national safeguards are preserved, but subject to Commission controls. Capital movements to and from Europe as a whole are expected to be similarly liberalized. This capital movements legislation, when combined with the various banking reforms, promises to bring forth a remarkable new financial sector.

Late in 1991 an historic agreement was reached at the Maastricht Summit to establish a common currency governed by a European central bank. To participate, member states had to meet relatively strict economic criteria. The common currency (the EURO) took effect in 1999 for eleven nations. Britain, Denmark and Sweden negotiated special rights to participate only when and if they wish. Greece failed to qualify for "EUROLAND".

COMMON TRANSPORT POLICY

The Common Transport Policy envisioned by the EC Treaty has taken a long time to materialize. The European Court of Justice ruled in 1985 that the state of the overall transport policy amounted to a "failure to act" by Council in violation of the Treaty. This ruling was sought by the European Parliament and promised greater development in the future.

A major issue is when transport may be operated within a member state by a national of another member state. The Commission has considered a general policy covering all aspects of transport (including ships and airlines), but a piece-meal approach has proved more practicable. Progress has been by small steps, representing difficult negotiations and compromises within the Council. By the end of 1992, for example, truckers were able to move freely without quotas. Directives have been issued to abolish discriminations arising from different road transport rates and from conditions applied to like goods in like circumstances. Directives deal also with common rules for international road carriage, restrictions upon drivers' hours, and installation of tachygraphs that record such hours. Differences among the member states about road taxes, and truck weights and dimensions have been mostly resolved. Considerable progress has also been made on liberalizing air, rail and sea transport.

COMMON AGRICULTURAL POLICY

The special place of agriculture within the Common Market has led to the creation of the controversial Common Agricultural Policy (CAP). The objectives of the CAP stated in the EC Treaty include the increase of productivity, the maintenance of a fair standard of living for the agricultural community, the stabilization of markets and the provision of consumer goods at reasonable prices. In practice, the CAP has heavily subsidized production and exports of agricultural goods, and it consumes about two-thirds of the regional budget (which is largely financed by the common customs tariff, agricultural levies and value-added tax revenues). Target prices for many commodities (e.g., grain) are established periodically and maintained through market purchases and "variable import levies." These levies are periodically changed to ensure that imports do not disrupt the CAP. They are of enormous consequence to U.S. agricultural exporters.

Equally significant are "export refunds" on agricultural commodities, refunds that affect the opportunities of U.S. exporters in other parts of the world. The United States has consistently argued that these refunds violate the GATT rules on subsidies. The results have been mixed and agricultural trade wars between the U.S. and the EU frequent. Indeed, agriculture (more than any other topic) explains why the Uruguay Round of GATT negotiations failed to reach closure on time at the end of 1990. Europeans were simply unwilling to substantially alter the CAP.

In most years, the net effect of the CAP is to substantially raise European food prices above world price levels. The CAP has also generated a significant amount of fraud to obtain subsidy payments. Despite its costs, the CAP is one of the political cornerstones of the European Union. France and Italy might not have joined without it, Greece, Spain and Portugal eagerly looked forward to it, and Germany (joined to a lesser extent by the UK) continues to pay heavily for it. On the other hand, Germany is the major beneficiary of industrial free trade in the Common Market.

Like the United States, Europe seems unable to effectively control the level of its agricultural subsidies, resulting in overproduction ("butter mountains", "wine lakes") and frequent commodity trade wars. More recently, the Europeans adopted rules designed ultimately to reduce agricultural expenditures by linking total expenditures to the rates of economic growth, establishing automatic price cuts when production ceilings are reached, and creating land set-aside and early retirement programs for farmers. These rules are reinforced by the 1994 Uruguay Round Agreement on Agriculture and the reality of the need to reform the CAP prior to admission of Poland, Hungary and other nations in 2003.

TAXATION

The EC Treaty deals with many other areas of economic and social life in member states. These include taxation, which must neither be discriminatory nor protective as between products of different member states. With considerable effort the Europeans have adopted a common tax system—*value-added taxation*. But different revenue needs and tax policies cause different levels of VAT to apply to like items in the various member states. In the UK, for example, VAT had generally been collected at one "egalitarian" rate. In France, on the other hand, different levels of VAT apply to basic goods, middle level items and luxuries. Negotiations to harmonize VAT levels and agreements on the goods and services to which they should apply have progressed slowly.

Many consider the ability of Europe to achieve a consensus as to the proper levels of VAT and excise taxation, or at least to reduce the degree of differences in such taxation among the member states, to be the litmus test of the campaign for a fully integrated market. The Council has agreed to the gradual alignment of VAT rates around a standard rate band of 15 percent. A reduced rate band of 5 to 9 percent is anticipated for selected products. Existing zero or less than 5 percent rates are grandfathered. The tax frontiers have been eliminated by imposing VAT reporting and collection duties on importers and exporters using the destination principle on VAT rates. The excise tax frontier has been eliminated by moving to a system of interlinked bonded warehouses between which goods can move easily. As with the VAT, excise taxation follows the destination principle. The Commission would prefer taxation on the basis of origin principles.

TRADE RELATIONS

The Treaty requires member states to coordinate and implement a *common commercial policy* toward non-member states. This policy is based upon uniform principles regarding tariff and trade agreements, fishing rights, export policy and other matters of external concern. The EU, for example, regularly negotiates as a bloc within the GATT and WTO and subscribes to various GATT Codes (e.g., the Dumping and Subsidies Codes) and GATT programs (e.g., the generalized system of tariff preferences for developing countries).

The European Union has established special tariff and commodity support preferences for third world nations (mostly former colonies) participating in the Lomé Conventions. These Conventions establish innovative commodity export earnings protection programs known as STABEX and MINEX, benefiting Lomé nations. The Union also has negotiated preferential trade treaties with Mediterranean basin nations, much as the United States has done in the Caribbean basin. Europe's trade relations can create duty free import opportunities for goods originating in favored nations.

The Commission generally negotiates common external commercial policies, subject to a mandate from and ultimate control by the Council. Throughout 1986, for example, Europe and the United States vigorously disputed the amount of trade compensation that the U.S. was entitled to under the GATT as a result of the expansion of the Common Market to include Spain and Portugal. After a series of threats and counterthreats to increase tariffs, this dispute was finally resolved mainly by preserving substantial U.S. agricultural exports to Spain. United States officials dealt primarily with Commissioners and staff in reaching this accord. Similar negotiations were replayed in 1995 when Austria, Finland and Sweden joined the Union.

EU CONVENTIONS

The European Union has adopted two conventions of considerable importance to international traders: The Convention on Law Applicable to Contractual Obligations (Choice of Law) (1980) and the Convention on Jurisdiction and Enforcement of Judgments in Civil and Commercial Matters (1968). The Contractual Obligations Convention affirms the right of parties to commercial contracts to designate the law which will govern those contracts. The Enforcement of Judgments Convention is an extremely detailed agreement generally allowing enforcement of civil and commercial judgments of the courts of the member states in the courts of other member states.

The Judgments Convention *denies* enforcement by European domiciliaries against European domiciliaries of certain judgments deemed to be based on "extraordinary jurisdiction" (e.g., French jurisdiction based solely on French citizenship of the plaintiff). But, in a discriminatory measure of importance, it permits European domiciliaries to enforce judgments based on extraordinary jurisdiction against non-European domiciliaries e.g., U.S. companies. The Enforcement of Judgments Convention has been extensively construed by the European Court of Justice.

BUSINESS ORGANIZATIONS LAW

The cumulative effect which European Union law has had upon persons doing business with or within member states is very substantial. Special attention should be paid to the Common Market rules on competition ("antitrust") outlined in Chapter 9. This section briefly surveys company and securities law.

Several important directives have been adopted in the securities field. These concern admission of securities to stock exchange listings (1979), the issuance of a prospectus (1980), regular information disclosures by publicly traded firms (1982), and a directive on insider trading (1989). This directive prohibits trading on the basis of inside information by primary and secondary insiders. Inside information is defined as non-public information which if made public would be "likely to have a significant effect on the price" of securities. Many perceive that the insider trading directive closely parallels U.S. securities' law principles.

The Council has adopted a number of non-controversial directives advancing company law. The first sets out requirements for standardization of liability (including pre-incorporation liability) of companies and publication of particulars. The second deals with the classification, subscription and maintenance of capital of public and large companies. The third concerns the internal merger of public companies. The sixth directive governs sales of assets of public companies, including certain share-holder, creditor and workers' rights. The fourth standardizes the treatment of annual accounts of public and large companies (e.g., in presentation, content, valuation and publication). In this directive, there is a permissive provision relating to inflation or current cost accounting. Accounts are to show a "true and fair view" of the enterprise. There is some doubt about the degree of relation to similar requirements of, for example, the United Kingdom accounting bodies or "generally accepted accounting practices" of the United States. The fourth directive is followed by the seventh concerning requirements for accounts of groups of companies. The eighth provides certain minimum standards and qualifications for auditors of company accounts.

Innovative company law proposals include those for a European Company Statute (SE) and a European Economic Interest Grouping (EEIG). The former is intended to create a corporate entity, overcoming the transnational problems associated with existing methods of incorporation within member states. The EEIG, adopted in 1985, is a vehicle with legal capacity formed in the manner of an international partnership of member state companies. The EEIG is prohibited from offering proprietary interests to the public and is a nonprofit enterprise. Limited liability is not obtained. The EEIG is intended for small or medium sized research and development or marketing ventures.

CHAPTER NINE

BUSINESS COMPETITION RULES—EXTRATERRITORIAL ANTITRUST LAWS

The European Common Market has accomplished among other things, an institutionalization of competitive market doctrines. The role of the Court of Justice and Court of First Instance in interpreting Articles 81 and 82 (formerly Articles 85 and 86) of the EC Treaty is one example of the movement toward greater union. In that sense, these articles assume some of the function of the interstate commerce clause of the United States Constitution. Articles 81 and 82 of the Treaty of Rome have a mandatory effect upon any international trade or investment touched by their reach. The articles evidence the degree of rule-making complexity and detail achieved in one area of law. Recent Court of Justice and Court of First Instance rulings about their application to persons, things and events beyond the territorial limits of the Union serve to introduce the larger issue of extraterritorial laws and international business transactions.

In general, Article 81(1) aims to prohibit "arms length" competitors from agreeing between themselves to prevent, restrain or distort competition.

Article 81(1) is roughly analogous to the prohibition against restraints of trade in Section 1 of the U.S. Sherman Antitrust Act. Broadly speaking, Article 82 prohibits dominant enterprises from abusing their position to the prejudice of competitors or consumers. This prohibition is more encompassing than monopolization as an offense under Section 2 of the Sherman Act.

Articles 81 and 82 are complicated and elastic. Although each article lists certain proscribed business practices, much of their specific, substantive content has been generated by Commission and Court interpretations. Numerous treatises (including several multi-volume works) are devoted to European competition law. A notable feature is their applicability to publicly owned enterprises (of which there are many). For example, the European Court affirmed the applicability of Article 82 to RAI, the Italian state broadcasting monopoly, provided that such application would not obstruct its tasks.

The terms of Articles 81 and 82 are enforced, in the first instance, by the Commission. The Commission has the power to investigate, *sua sponte* or upon complaint by interested persons or member states, possible violations of Articles 81 and 82. The Commission may obtain information from national authorities as part of its investigatory process and it may require those authorities to conduct investigations for it. The Commission may require enterprises to produce records or documents necessary to its investigation. When there is a failure or refusal to comply with a Commission investigation or enforcement decision, the Commission may seek a compliance order from the Court. Several procedural requirements for Commission investigations and hearings have been discussed by the Court of Justice. One notable Court decision upheld the authority of the Commission to conduct searches of corporate offices without notice or warrant when it has reason to believe that pertinent evidence may be lost. Another notable decision permitted a Swiss "whistle blower" who once worked for Hoffman–La Roche (a defendant in competition law proceedings) to sue in tort for disclosure of his identity as an informant.

The subject matter of Articles 81 and 82 is commerce, yet their impact is as political as commercial. Astute observers have noted that a significant number of the leading "test cases" have involved defendants from Japan, the United States, Switzerland and other non-members. It is, of course, politically much more acceptable when Articles 81 and 82 are applied to foreign firms. But they have also been applied extensively to European enterprises. The quantity and significance of competition law is sufficient to have generated a growing number of lawyers who specialize in giving advice about the effects of Articles 81 and 82 on transactions in the Common Market.

A person who ignores the reach of Articles 81 and 82 may experience severe consequences, but nothing comparable to the felony criminal sanctions and private treble damages actions found in United States antitrust law. Article 81(2) renders offending business agreements null and void. Nullity is most often raised as a defense to enforcement of contracts, licenses and joint ventures in national legal proceedings. Fines may be levied by the Commission for supplying false or misleading information or for holding back information in connection with inquiries about the applicability of the articles, and further fines may be levied if persons or activities are found to have contravened Article 81 or 82.

For example, the Belgian and French subsidiary enterprises of the Japanese electrical and electronic group, Matsushita, were fined by the Commission for supplying it with false information about whether Matsushita recommended retail prices for its products. Furthermore, offending activity may be penalized per day until there is compliance with a Commission order. All Commission decisions imposing fines or penalties under competition law are subject to judicial review by the Court of First Instance. In early years the Court of Justice tended to reduce the amounts involved because of the developmental state of Article 81 and 82 law. In more recent decisions, the Court upheld substantial fines and penalties imposed by the Commission in competition law proceedings.

Article 81 and 82 fines are reducible to judgment in the courts of any member state. Because regional law supercedes only inconsistent laws in any of the members states, violating Article 81 or 82 may not preclude additional sanctions for breach of a member state's business competition laws (e.g., laws which may authorize an aggrieved person to receive damages). Indeed it is possible, as several examples suggest, that multiple liability under British or German competition law (the most vigorous in the Common Market), European law and U.S. antitrust law can simultaneously occur. With such a high level of risk, law in this area is ignored only at great peril to international business.

ARTICLE 81 AND ITS EXEMPTIONS

In term-of-art language, Article 81(1) declares as prohibited, and therefore null and void, agreements, decisions and concerted practices which may affect, directly or indirectly, trade between the territories of member states in the Common Market *and* which have, as an object or potential effect, the prevention, restriction or distortion of competition within the Common Market. The Court of Justice has pointed out that Article 81(1) prohibits any restriction on competition at any trading level between the manufacturer and the ultimate consumer. An offending agreement need not be a contract; "recommendations," "informal undertakings" and "concerted practices" may suffice. It must be possible to foresee, with a sufficient degree of probability on the basis of a set of objective factors of law or fact, that the agreement, decision or concerted practice may have an influence, direct or indirect, actual or potential, on the pattern of trade between member states. This requirement is analogous to the "interstate commerce" test of the Sherman Antitrust Act. The effect on competition must be significant. Article 81(1) does not proscribe activities with effects which are negligible on trade between member states and thus are not appreciable in impact on market conditions.

The Commission has taken the position that the concept of a "concerted practice" refers to a form of coordination between undertakings which knowingly substitutes for the risks of competition a practical cooperation between them leading to conditions of competition which do not correspond to normal market conditions. As with "conspiracies" under the Sherman Act or "arrangements" under the UK Restrictive Trade Practices Act, "concerted practices" are most often proved by circumstantial evidence falling short of a formal agreement to restrict competition. For example, price fixing by a European chemical dyestuffs cartel was held illegal in a major concerted practices opinion of the Court of Justice. I.C.I. v. Commission (1972) Eur.Comm.Rep. 619. The circumstantial evidence supporting this conclusion included: (1) a series of nearly identical, simultaneous price increases by ten dyestuffs producers; (2) the uniformity of the price increases over thousands of different dyes; (3) the use of the same price increase instruction manuals by all ten firms; and (4) the existence of informal contacts and occasional meetings between the dyestuffs companies.

Not all anticompetitive agreements violate Article 81(1). By operation of Article 81(3), Article 81(1) may not apply to an agreement, decision or concerted practice which contributes to an improvement of production or distribution of goods, or which promotes technical or economic progress (while allowing consumers a fair share of the resulting benefit), *provided* the agreement or concerted practice does not serve to eliminate competition in a substantial part of the products in question. Interested parties may petition ("notify") the Commission to obtain a declaration of the inapplicability of Article 81(1) to their activities under the terms of Article 81(3). These are known as "individual exemptions" and are discussed *infra*.

Council and Commission regulations operate to exclude from Article 81(1) certain exclusive purchasing and distribution agreements, categories of research and development agreements, certain agreements or concerted practices in the technology transfer area, and horizontal agreements among smaller firms for specialization in the manufacture of products. Also exempted by regulation are certain franchising and motor vehicle distribution and servicing agreements. These regulations are known as "block exemptions" since they are based upon the legal criteria of Article 81(3). They have the practical effect of dramatically reducing the Commission's workload because it is not necessary to apply for a block exemption. Parties need only conform their conduct to the terms of these regulations.

Lawyers representing clients doing business in Europe usually prefer to structure contracts and other arrangements in accordance with block exemptions since this preserves confidentiality. Voluntary adherence to block exemptions has become a successful, cost-effective way of implementing Article 81. The meaning of the regulations is better understood by a review of the leading cases previously brought by the Commission to test its authority in each of these fields. Lines drawn in the block exemptions may later be reviewed in private litigation or public enforcement proceedings.

Other competition law exemptions also exist. Article 81(1) has not traditionally been extended to the transportation industry, but this is rapidly changing. Airlines, for example, are now generally subject to Articles 81 and 82. A Commission notice removes exclusive commercial agency agreements from the coverage of Article 81(1). Finally, Article 81(1) has not been applied to agricultural agreements authorized in connection with the Union's common agricultural policy.

These exemptions notwithstanding, Article 81(1) is presently and potentially of wide application. By way of illustration, the article expressly prohibits agreements and concerted practices which:

    1.   even indirectly fix prices of purchase or sale or any other trading conditions;

    2.   limit or control production, markets, technical development or investment;

    3.   allocate markets or sources of supply;

    4.   apply unequal terms to parties furnishing equivalent consideration, thereby placing them at a competitive disadvantage; or

5. make a contract's formation turn upon acceptance of certain additional obligations having, according to commercial usage, no connection with the subject matter of the contract ("tying arrangements").

Some of these illustrations have parallels in Sherman Act law establishing per se illegal restraints of trade. Reference to United States antitrust principles in European competition law cases occurs. Commission and Court rulings frequently deal with practices which are not specifically mentioned in Article 81(1) but fall within its broad language: sales information exchanges between competitors, export bans, reciprocal exclusive dealing, exclusive licensing, group boycotts, price discrimination, franchising, joint venture royalties, contractor/sub-contractor agreements, anticompetitive joint ventures, joint selling, delivery and sales quotas, price discounts, promises not to challenge the validity of patents, and the use of trademarks or copyrights to restrain competition. Selective distribution agreements, by which sales at various distribution stages are limited only to appointed dealers, are also watched closely by the Commission.

Particularly in the case of exclusive patent licenses, the Commission has demonstrated an active interest in four types of clauses: covenants not to compete, obligations of licensees to use the licensor's trademark, prohibitions against use of licensor know-how after an agreement has terminated, and mandatory royalty payments beyond the patent's expiration date. The Court of Justice has held that an exclusive license, which does not affect the position of third parties such as parallel import-ers and licensees for other territories, is not in itself incompatible with Article 81(1) of the Treaty. Thus, an exclusive patent license does not violate Article 81(1) if the licensor undertakes merely not to grant other licenses in the same territory and not to compete with the licensee in that territory. But if the license in any way blocks third party trade in the goods concerned it violates Article 81(1). These principles are now incorporated in the technology transfer block exemption.

Such agreements and concerted practices are only a partial list of Council, Commission and Court regulatory concerns under Articles 81 and 82. In 1987 the Court of Justice ruled that Article 81 applies to mergers and acquisitions, activities previ-ously thought to fall only under Article 82. This decision is yet another indication of the significance of competition law to those drafting distribution contracts, licensing agreements, joint ventures and other business arrangements. Counsel should be especially circumspect about any contractual or li-censing term that may tend to divide up the Com-mon Market by allocating territories or customers. Since great effort has been made to create the Common Market, private market division arrange-ments inhibiting competition in goods or services are practically "per se" offenses under Articles 81 and 82. This is true even of intrabrand vertical market division restraints, which are now frequently permitted under the Rule of Reason approach to U.S. restraint of trade law.

ARTICLE 82

Article 82 complements the regulatory scope of Article 81 and provides that it is unlawful for one or more enterprises, having a dominant market position within at least a substantial part of the Common Market, to abuse that position if trade between member states may be affected. Use of the words "dominant", "market", "substantial", "abuse" and "one or more enterprises" virtually guarantees Article 82 an interpretative life as long and lively as that of Section 2 of the Sherman Act.

In *Continental Can* the Commission took the position that:

> "Enterprises are in a dominant position when they have the power to behave independently without taking into account, to any substantial extent, their competitors, purchasers and suppliers.... This power does not necessarily have to derive from an absolute domination enabling the dominant enterprise to disregard the wishes of other enterprises participating in the market.... It suffices that it is strong enough to ensure an overall independence of behavior, even if there are differences in the intensity and the extent of their influence on the different submarkets." 11 *Common Mkt.L.Rep.* D27 (1972).

This position was affirmed by the Court of Justice. The Court has subsequently held that a market share of 40 percent may constitute dominance under Article 82. Such a percentage is well below the threshold market share associated with monopolization cases under Section 2 of the Sherman Antitrust Act. While the Court has said that a market share of 5 to 10 percent would ordinarily rule out the existence of a dominance, exceptional circumstances could show such a position. Moreover, a large market share (say 50 percent or more) is presumptive proof of a dominant position.

The "relevant market" in which a dominant position is found may prove to be quite a narrow segment of the overall Common Market. For example, one Commission decision held the market for making vitamin B-2 separate from another market for making vitamin B-6. The relevant product market in Article 82 law includes identical products and products which, by reason of their characteristics, price and use for which intended, may be regarded as similar by the consumer. For example, the Court in *Continental Can* held that metal lids for glass jars constituted a "relevant market" and stated that the definition of product markets, in large part, takes into account the consideration of special production features that make a product suited for its particular purposes. A market limited geographically to one member state or parts thereof has been considered by the Court sufficient to constitute the requisite "substantial part of the Common Market" within the regulatory purview of Article 82. The narrower the relevant product and geographic markets under Article 82, the more likely the defendant will be found to have a dominant position in that market. Thus, the case law on defining the relevant market has created an expansive scope for Article 82.

Article 82 seeks to curb abuses, which by its language include:

1.   directly or indirectly imposing unfair purchase or selling prices or other unfair trading conditions;

2.   limiting production, markets or technical development to the prejudice of consumers;

3.   applying unequal conditions to equivalent transactions with other trading parties, to their competitive disadvantage; or

4.   making the conclusion of a contract turn upon the other party's acceptance of additional obligations which, either by nature or commercial usage, have no connection with the subject of such a contract ("tying practices").

Activity constituting an abuse of a dominant position has been said by the Commission to include any action which reduces supplies to comparable purchasers in different ways without objective justification, thereby creating competitive disadvantage. In short, conduct of an enterprise amounts to an abuse if, from an objective viewpoint and in light of goals set forth in the Treaty, the activity must be characterized as misconduct. The Court of Justice has indicated that any conduct that is not "normal competition," and which hinders the maintenance or growth of competition, is abusive.

This open-ended legal concept is similar to determination of "acts of monopolization" under Sherman Act law. For example, the mere strengthening of an enterprise's dominant position (by contract, licensing, merger, joint venture or other practices) can constitute an abuse if competition may be substantially lessened. The European Court, in the famous *United Brands* case, (1978 Eur. Comm. Rep. 207), found that price discrimination in banana sales to distributors in six member states could not be justified by cost-to-market differences, and thus violated Article 82. The Commission indicated subsequently that price differences of even five percent are scrutinized. In some sales, the banana prices were considered "excessive," an abuse leading to review of profit levels at United Brands. On the other hand, banana prices which were below cost and which served to drive competitors out of business were also condemned. Thus, most pricing decisions by United Brands were abusive: some prices were too high, others too low, many unlawfully discriminatory.

The Court of Justice has held that predatory pricing can constitute an abuse of a dominant position in violation of Article 82. Predatory pricing below average total cost (as well as below average variable cost) may be abusive if undertaken to eliminate a competitor. Regarding the former, pricing below average total cost could drive out competitors as efficient as the dominant firm but lacking its extensive financial resources.

Abuses of dominant positions have been prohibited in a variety of different contexts. A dominant enterprise's requirement that all future copyrights, as well as present ones, be assigned to it in return for the supply of certain services constituted an abuse. A particular production and marketing practice by which a supplier, in a position of dominance, would supply only to customers who re-sold to certain persons was also an abuse. Outright refusal to sell to a customer unless certain conditions are present has also prompted Commission action, as has the use of seller fidelity rebates given to certain purchasers in return for a promise to continue purchases only from that seller. As a practical matter, therefore, once a dominant position is found, the Commission and Court review the entire range of business practices of the defendant in search of misconduct (abuses). Very few companies have survived such a scrutiny unscathed.

NEGATIVE CLEARANCES AND INDIVIDUAL EXEMPTIONS

Council Regulation 17 gives the Commission authority to declare that an enterprise activity, existing or planned, is not prohibited by Articles 81 and 82, and thus merits a "negative clearance". Regulation 17 also prescribes the terms, conditions and procedures by which such a declaration can be obtained. It further provides that the Commission may certify, upon appropriate application and on the basis of facts in its possession, that there are no grounds under Article 81(1) or Article 82 for enforcement or other action on its part. Negative clearances are often granted when the activities in question are of *de minimis* trade or competitive consequence. A negative clearance is similar in result to passage through the antitrust "business review procedure" of the U.S. Justice Department or Federal Trade Commission.

When an agreement, decision or concerted practice offends Article 81(1) of the EC Treaty, it must be "notified" to the Commission. The Commission, subject to review by the Court, may declare that the notified activity is "individually exempt" under Article 81(3). Such activity is thus permissible for a specified time and subject to such conditions and obligations (e.g., reporting requirements) as the Commission may attach. Individual exemptions can only be obtained from and renewed by the Commission. The exemption may cover a five to ten-year period from the notification date. The Commission may revoke or amend its decision or prohibit specific acts by those granted the exemption if any facts, basic to the decision to exempt, have changed or if the decision has been based upon incorrect information or has been induced by deceit. If those who are granted the exemption breach an attached obligation or condition, or otherwise abuse the exemption, the exemption may be terminated.

Restrictions permitted upon issuance of an individual exemption are sometimes denied at a later stage in renewal proceedings. Thus, obtaining an individual exemption commences an ongoing regulatory process. It is not surprising, therefore, that counsel to parties involved in regional trade and investment much prefer less visible self-reliance on block exemptions.

The procedure for obtaining negative clearances and individual exemptions has been set forth by the Commission. Where the request deals with the applicability of Article 81(1), the Commission requires that application Form A/B be completed. This form is typically used to petition for a negative clearance or, in the alternative, an individual exemption under Article 81(3). This is the equivalent of first arguing that Article 81(1) does not apply, but if it does, then the applicant is entitled to an exemption. There is no prescribed form when clearance is sought from the applicability of Article 82, for which (by its terms) there are no individual exemptions. Negative clearance applications relating to Article 82 must contain a full statement of the facts and specify, in particular, the practice concerned and the market position of the applicant within the Common Market or a substantial part thereof.

The filing of a Form A/B notification is not an admission that Article 81(1) is applicable. Likewise, notification does not, by itself, work to validate restrictive arrangements. During the time between notification and Commission action, the agreement, decision or concerted practice under review is immune from the imposition of any fines. If the Commission grants a negative clearance, there is no legal risk. Individual exemptions usually are retro-active to the filing date of the notification; all parts of an agreement purporting to exist before that date which violate Article 81(1) are null and void and subject to the imposition of fines.

The Commission often publishes Form A/B notifications, and its proposed decision to grant a negative clearance or an exemption, in order to gain the comments of interested third parties. The Commission may initiate certain investigations and ultimately declare that Article 81(1) is applicable and that no exemption will be granted under Article 81(3). Indeed, it may then proceed to levy fines and penalties if the offending agreement has already been put into place.

When the Commission has manifested an objection and before an adverse decision is made, the applicant is entitled to a hearing. The Commission's position must be communicated to the applicant. Publication in the *Official Journal of the European Communities* is deemed adequate notice. The applicant must submit written reply comments and may offer oral argument with or without the assistance of lawyers accredited before the Court. The Court of Justice has held that the Commission has discretion whether to hear oral argument on negative clearance and individual exemption applications. Third persons may have access to the hearing process on showing a legitimate interest. The hearing is private, and a written record is made. The Commission must give written reasons to explain whatever final decision is taken, although the Court of Justice has held that the Commission need not discuss every fact or law issue raised during the proceedings.

Appeal may be taken to the Court of First Instance on the limited grounds specified in Article 230 of the EC Treaty: lack of competence, infringement of essential procedural requirements, infringement of the Treaty or EC law, or misuse of powers. The issuance of an Article 81(3) exemption does not foreclose the possibility of a prosecution under Article 82.

The Commission has developed a "comfort letter" practice in connection with applications for 81(3) exemptions and requests for negative clearances. This practice avoids the delays inherent in the process of reaching formal exemption or clearance decisions. Comfort letters are issued only when the businesses concerned wish to have them. They signal that the Commission's file is closed without issuance of a negative clearance or an 81(3) exemption. Comfort letters state that the Commission sees no reason to intervene in opposition to the activities notified. The parties then typically proceed to implement their agreement. In the absence of a change of circumstances, the Commission cannot alter its position and is precluded from fining the recipient. However, national courts are not bound by the comfort letter in their determinations of Article 81 violations.

Individual and block exemptions have no real parallel in United States antitrust procedures. European competition law procedure is much more reliant upon administrative reviews, exemptions and sanctions than U.S. antitrust law. Nevertheless, private actions before the courts of Member States commonly raise Article 81 and 82 issues. Sometimes these suits seek damages relief under torts principles.

COMMISSION REGULATION OF CONCENTRATIONS

In December of 1989, the Council of Ministers unanimously adopted Regulation No. 4064/89 on the Control of Concentrations Between Undertakings ("Mergers Regulation"). This regulation became effective Sept. 21, 1990. It vests in the Commission the power to oppose large-scale mergers and acquisitions of competitive consequence to the Common Market. The control process established by the Mergers Regulation commences when a concentration must be notified to the Commission. The duty to notify is triggered only when the concentration involves enterprises with a combined worldwide turnover of at least 5 billion EUROS (approximately $6 billion) *and* two of them have an aggregate region-wide turnover of 250 million EUROS (approximately $300 million).

As a general rule, concentrations meeting these criteria cannot be put into effect and fall exclusively within the Commission's domain. The effort here is to create a "one-stop" regulatory system. However, certain exceptions apply so as to allow national authorities to challenge some mergers. For example, this may occur under national law when two-thirds of the activities of each of the companies involved take place in the *same* member state. The member states can also oppose mergers when their public security is at stake, to preserve plurality in media ownership, when financial institutions are involved or other legitimate interests are at risk. If the threshold criteria of the Mergers Regulation are not met, member states can ask the Commission to investigate mergers that create or strengthen a dominant position in that state. States that lack national merger controls seem likely to do this.

Once a concentration is notified to the Commission, it has one month to decide to investigate the merger. If a formal investigation is commenced, the Commission ordinarily then has four months to challenge or approve the merger. During these months, in most cases, the concentration cannot be put into effect. It is on hold.

The Commission evaluates mergers in terms of their "compatibility" with the Common Market. Using language reminiscent of *Continental Can,* the Mergers Regulation states that if the concentration creates or strengthens a dominant position such that competition is "significantly impeded," it is incompatible. The Commission is authorized to consider in its evaluation the interests of consumers and the "development of technical and economic progress." These considerations suggest an analysis like that followed under Article 81(3).

During a mergers investigation, the Commission can obtain information and records from the parties, and request member states to help with the investigation. Fines and penalties back up the Commission's powers to obtain what it needs from the parties. If the concentration has already taken effect, the Commission can issue a "hold-separate" order. This requires the corporations or assets acquired to be separated and not, operationally speaking, merged. Approval of the merger may involve modifications of its terms or promises by the parties aimed at diminishing its anticompetitive potential. Negotiations with the Commission to obtain such clearances may follow the pattern of Article 81(3) individual exemptions. If the Commission ultimately decides to oppose the merger in a timely manner, it can order its termination by whatever means are appropriate to restore conditions of effective competition. Such decisions can be appealed to the Court of First Instance.

The first merger actually blocked by the Commission on competition law grounds was the attempted acquisition of a Canadian aircraft manufacturer (DeHaviland—owned by Boeing) by two European companies (Aerospatiale SNI of France and Alenia e Selenia Spa of Italy). Prior to this rejection in late 1991, the Commission had approved over 50 mergers, obtaining modifications in a few instances. The Commission, in the DeHaviland case, took the position that the merger would have created an unassailable dominant position in the world and European market for turbo prop or commuter aircraft. If completed, the merged entity would have had 50 percent of the world and 67 percent of the European market for such aircraft.

In 1997, the Commission dramatically demonstrated its extraterritorial jurisdiction over the Boeing–McDonnell Douglas merger. This merger had already been cleared by the U.S. Federal Trade Commission. The European Commission, however, demanded and got(at the risk of a trade war)important concessions from Boeing. These included abandonment of exclusive supply contracts with three U.S. airlines and licensing of technology derived from McDonnell Douglas' military programs at reasonable royalty rates. The Commission's success in this case was widely perceived in the United States as pro-Airbus.

THE EXTRATERRITORIAL REACH
OF ARTICLES 81 AND 82

There is a question about the extent to which the competition rules extend to activity anywhere in the world, including activity occurring entirely or in part within the territorial limits of the United States. Decisions by the Commission and the Court of Justice suggest that the territorial reach of Articles 81 and 82 is expanding and may well extend to an international business transaction occurring within the United States.

For an agreement to be incompatible with the Common Market and prohibited under Article 81(1), it must be "likely to affect trade between member states" and have "the object or effect" of impairing "competition within the Common Market". The Court has repeatedly held that the fact that one of the parties to an agreement is domiciled in a third country does not preclude the applicability of Article 81(1) if the agreement is effective in the territory of the Common Market. Swiss and British companies, for example, argued that the Commission was not competent to impose competition law fines for acts committed in Switzerland and Britain (before joining the EU) by enterprises domiciled outside the Union solely because the acts had effects within the Common Market. Nevertheless, the Court held those companies in violation of Article 81 because they owned subsidiary companies within the Union and controlled their behavior. The foreign parent and its subsidiaries were treated as a "single enterprise" for purposes of service of process, judgment and collection of fines and penalties. In doing so, the Court observed that the fact that a subsidiary company has its own legal personality does not rule out the possibility that its conduct is attributable to the parent company.

The Court has extended its reasoning to the extraterritorial application of Article 82. A United States parent company, for example, was held potentially liable for acquisitions by its Italian subsidiary which affected market conditions within Europe. In another case, the Court held that a Maryland company's refusal to sell its product to a competitor of its affiliate company within the Union was a result of united "single enterprise" action. It proceeded to state that extraterritorial conduct merely having "repercussions on competitive structures" in the Common Market fell within the parameters of Article 82. The Court ordered the U.S. company, through its Italian affiliate, to supply the competitor at reasonable prices.

In 1988, the Court of Justice widened the extraterritorial reach of Article 81 in a case where wood pulp producers from the U.S., Canada, Sweden and Finland were fined for price fixing activities affecting Common Market trade and competition. These firms did not have substantial operations within the EC. They were primarily exporters to the Common Market. This decision's reliance upon a "place of implementation" effects test is similar to that used under the Sherman Act.

THE EFFECTS TEST IN UNITED STATES AND EUROPEAN LAW

It may be a substantial jump to predict that Articles 81 and 82 bear upon a business transaction done in the United States or another non-EC country which merely inures to the competitive disadvantage of a company located within the Common Market. Yet in one of the *Dyestuffs* cases as early as 1969 the Commission took the position that:

the rules of competition of the Treaty are therefore applicable to all restrictions on competition that produce within the Common Market effects to which Article 81, paragraph 1, applies. There is therefore no need to examine whether the enterprises that originated such restraints of competition have their head office within or outside of the Community. *Commission v. I.C.I.*, 8 Common Mkt.L.Rep. 494 (1969).

Although the Court's disposition of the *Dyestuffs* cases did not endorse such reasoning, the Commission has reasserted its "effects test" in subsequent arguments. The Commission's approach merits close consideration if only because the initiation of an Article 81 or 82 inquiry can generate local overhead costs for those involved in European business transactions. That courts in the United States have also used an "effects test" in connection with the question of the extraterritoriality of U.S. antitrust laws increases the potential for uncertainty and costs in international transactions.

United States courts have long asserted the right to apply the Sherman Antitrust Act to foreign commerce intended to or affecting the United States market. In some cases, this approach has been tempered to allow consideration of the interests of comity and foreign countries in the outcome. Some limits on the extraterritorial reach of the Sherman Act are created by the act of state doctrine and the Foreign Sovereign Immunities Act. But in the main, United States antitrust law has been applied to foreigners and overseas activities with a zeal sometimes approaching religious fervor. This fervor has carried over into other areas, such as the failed attempt of the Reagan administration to apply U.S. export control laws to European enterprises involved in the construction of the Soviet natural gas pipeline from Siberia to Western Europe.

Amendments to the Sherman Act in 1984 stress the "direct, substantial and reasonably foreseeable" nature of effects on U.S. foreign commerce as a prerequisite to antitrust jurisdiction. Nevertheless, the potential for conflict in this field is enormous. For example, a multinational enterprise headquartered in the U.S. but doing business in England could be constrained by United States antitrust law from fixing prices, yet permitted by European competition law under Article 81(3) to do exactly that. Assuming that the price fixing in question has effects in both markets, what course of action is to be followed? There is no easy answer. When the MNE is located within a country other than one of the member states of the EU or the United States, but engages in activity having effects within those markets, the problem potential of extraterritoriality may be even more acute. Reconciling a conflict of antitrust laws applied extraterritorially by these two jurisdictions could become a flashpoint in international business.

EXTRATERRITORIAL ANTITRUST LAWS, BLOCKING STATUTES AND INTERNATIONAL SOLUTIONS

MNE operations that transcend a nation's borders have focused concern about the extent to which the applicability of a nation's laws must stop at its territorial borders. Absent a controlling and readily enforceable international law, it is at least a fair question to ask whether national laws are needed to regulate extraterritorial business enterprises.

Extraterritoriality is a matter of balance. The Executive, Legislative, and Judicial branches of government in the United States have reached out extraterritorially in the law of admiralty, antitrust, crime, labor, securities regulation, taxation, torts, trademarks and wildlife management. A balance drawn wrongly by one nation invites retaliatory action by others. In the case of antitrust judgments emanating from courts in the United States, most notably the "Uranium Cartel" treble damages litigation of the late 1970s, many nations consider that the balance has been wrongly drawn. Many nations have taken retaliatory action by enacting "blocking statutes." In addition, the Commonwealth nations have resolved general support for a position similar to that of the United Kingdom.

The United Kingdom blocking statute is the Protection of Trading Interests Act of 1980. This Act (without specifying United States antitrust law) makes it difficult to depose witnesses, obtain documents or enforce multiple liability judgments extraterritorially in the U.K. Violation of the 1980 Act may result in criminal penalties. Furthermore, under the "clawback" provision of the Act, parties with outstanding multiple liabilities in foreign jurisdictions (*e.g.*, U.S. treble damages defendants) may recoup the punitive element of such awards in Britain against assets of the successful plaintiff. The British Act invites other nations to adopt clawback provisions by offering clawback reciprocity. United States attorneys confronted with a blocking statute need to understand that multiple liability judgments combined with contingency fee arrangements are virtually unknown elsewhere.

The extensive array of pre-trial discovery mechanisms allowed in U.S. civil litigation rarely, if ever, have a counterpart in foreign law. Discovery subpoenas originating in U.S. litigation are often "shocking" to many foreign defendants. And the U.S. Supreme Court has ruled that use of letters rogatory under the Hague Convention is not obligatory. *Société National Industrielle Aérospatiale v. U.S. District Court*, 482 U.S. 522 (1987). It is the blocking of discovery that potentially most threatens the extraterritorial application of United States laws, especially antitrust. Since U.S. courts may sanction parties who in bad faith fail to respond to discovery requests, foreign defendants requesting help from their home governments under blocking statutes are especially at risk. On the other hand, good faith efforts to modify or work around discovery blockades may favor foreign defendants. Such defendants are often caught in a "no win" situation. Either way they will be penalized.

Reasons advanced to support an extraterritorial application of United States antitrust laws are founded on the idea that some extraterritorial extension is necessary to prevent their circumvention by multinational corporations which have the business sagacity to ensure that anticompetitive transactions are consummated beyond the territorial borders of the United States. An extraterritorial extension of antitrust laws can help to protect the export opportunities of domestic firms. Extraterritorial application of the antitrust laws can also help to ensure that the American consumer receives the benefit of competing imports, which in turn may spur complacent domestic industries. The effect of foreign auto imports on the car manufacturers in the United States may be cited as an example. In an increasingly internationalized world, extraterritorial antitrust may merely reflect economic reality.

On the other hand, the British argue that extraterritoriality permits the U.S. to unjustifiably "mold the international economic and trading world to its own image." In particular, the U.S. "effects" doctrine creates legal uncertainty for international traders, and United States courts pay little attention to the competing policies (interests) of other concerned governments. As the House of Lords has stated: "It is axiomatic that in anti-trust matters the policy of one state may be to defend what it is the policy of another state to attack." *Rio Tinto Zinc Corp. v. Westinghouse Electric Corp.*, 2 W.L.R. 81 [1978].

The British also argue, not without some support, that customary international law does not permit extraterritorial application of national laws. In making this argument, the British have a convenient way of forgetting about the extraterritorial scope of Articles 81 and 82, which are now part of their law. Moreover, in a curious reversal of roles illustrating the extremes of the debate, the British government applied the Protection of Trading Interests Act to block the pursuit of treble damages in *United States* courts by the liquidator of Laker Airways against British Airways and other defendants. A House of Lords decision reversed this ban but retained government restrictions on discovery related to the case. *British Airways Board v. Laker Airways*, 3 W.L.R. 413 [1984].

Some evidence of international antitrust cooperation is contained in a 1967 recommendation of the OECD which provides for notification of antitrust actions, exchanges of information to the extent that the disclosure is domestically permissible, and where practical, coordination of antitrust enforcement. The OECD resolution served as a model for the 1972 "Antitrust Notification and Consultation Procedure" between Canada and the United States. Following the "Uranium Cartel" litigation, Australia and the United States reached an Agreement on Cooperation in Antitrust Matters (1982) to minimize jurisdictional conflicts. Australia has taken the position that United States courts are not a proper institution to balance interests of concerned countries within the context of private antitrust litigation.

The Agreement on Cooperation provides that when the Government of Australia is concerned with private antitrust proceedings pending in a United States court, the Government of Australia may request the Government of the United States to participate in the litigation. The United States must report to the court on the substance and outcome of consultations with Australia on the matter concerned. In this way, Australia's views and interests in the litigation and its potential outcome are made known to the court. The court is not required to defer to those views, or even to openly consider them. It merely receives the "report." Australia, in turn, has indicated a willingness to be more receptive to discovery requests in U.S. antitrust litigation and to consult before invoking its blocking statute.

Similar arrangements have been made between the U.S. and Canada. No such agreement has been reached with the United Kingdom, with whom the extraterritoriality issue remains contentious, a fact which has led some to wonder whether the United States ought to have its own blocking statute against extraterritorial European competition law. An antitrust cooperation agreement seems more appropriate and, indeed, late in 1991 the European Union (of which Britain is still a member) and the United States reached such an agreement. This accord commits the parties to notify each other of imminent enforcement action, to share relevant information and consult on potential policy changes. An innovative feature is the inclusion of "positive comity" principles, each side promising to take the other's interests into account when considering antitrust prosecutions. The agreement has had a significant effect on mergers of firms doing business in North America and Europe, and has led to several joint investigations of Microsoft's business practices.

CHAPTER TEN

NAFTA[1]

The United States has entered into three major free trade area agreements. The first was with Israel, enacted through the United States–Israel Free Trade Area Implementation Act of 1985. The Israeli–U.S. Agreement (IFTA) was fully implemented January 1, 1995. The second is with Canada, and this agreement was adopted through the United States–Canada Free Trade Area Agreement Implementation Act of 1988. The Canadian–U.S. Agreement (CFTA) was fully implemented by January 1, 1998. Lastly, the United States has negotiated along with Canada and Mexico a three-way North American Free Trade Area Agreement (NAFTA). The NAFTA took effect January 1, 1994 with full implementation in nearly all areas expected by the year 2003. NAFTA was incorporated into United States law by the North American Free Trade Agreement Implementation Act of 1993.

The evolutionary character of the free trade agreements of the United States is readily apparent. The first agreement in 1985 with Israel is noticeably narrower in scope and level of legal detail than the last in 1994 with Canada and Mexico on NAF-

1. For much more extensive coverage, see Folsom's NAFTA in a Nutshell.

TA. And the second with Canada in 1989 was nothing less than path breaking; the most sophisticated free trade agreement in the world. Yet, for full understanding, each agreement must be viewed in its own geopolitical and economic context.

CANADA—U.S. FREE TRADE

The United States and Canada have the largest bilateral trading relationship in the world. As early as 1854, the Elgin–Marcy Treaty concluded a free trade agreement covering agriculture, resource and other primary products between the U.S. and Canadian provinces. Termination of this treaty in 1866 led to adoption of protectionist national trade policy in Canada. Canada made repeated (1891, 1896, 1911) unsuccessful attempts to negotiate bilateral trade agreements of various kinds with the United States. In the post World War II era, Canada was an early participant in the GATT. The GATT proved successful in expanding U.S. and Canadian trade, but by the 1980s the pace of GATT had slowed and the significance of access to the U.S. market required attention.

Prior to the Canada–U.S. Free Trade Area Agreement (CFTA), about 70 percent of the trade between the two nations was already duty free. Tariffs on the remaining products averaged about 5 percent when entering the United States and about 10 percent when entering Canada. Annual trade between the two countries was valued at more than $200 billion U.S. dollars. This is more than three times U.S.–Japan trade. Roughly one-third of all Canada–U.S. trading concerns automotive goods, an industry still largely dominated by U.S. companies. Canada has continued to maintain a healthy trade surplus with the United States. Free trade between the United States and Canada is based upon reciprocity and can be terminated by either party with 6 months notice.

THE CFTA AGREEMENT IN OUTLINE

The Canada–United States Free Trade Agreement covered manufactured and agricultural goods. It was generally oriented around the principle of national treatment and the Article III GATT rule to that effect was specifically incorporated in Chapter 1. Although the parties affirmed their existing trade agreements (including the GATT), if there was an inconsistency between CFTA and most of these agreements, it was agreed that the CFTA will prevail. The Provinces of Canada and the States of the U.S. must accord most-favored-treatment to goods that qualify under the CFTA. At Canadian insistence, "cultural industries" were specially treated, subject to a right in the other party to take measures of equivalent commercial effect in response to actions that would otherwise be inconsistent with the CFTA. Essentially, there was free trade in these goods, but ownership of them may be reserved to nationals and preservation of their Canadian character secured. Cultural industries are defined to include the publication, sale, distribution or exhibition of books, magazines, newspapers, films, videos, music recordings, and radio, television and cable dissemination. This exemption continues under NAFTA.

The CFTA did not repeal or directly amend the longstanding U.S.–Canadian Automotive Agreement (1965) under which the large majority of trading in autos and original equipment auto parts is undertaken duty free. However, a tougher 50 percent CFTA content rule was established for autos entering the U.S. Canada agreed to phase out its embargo on used autos by 1994. Government procurement contracts for $25,000 or more were opened to firms from both countries, but their goods must have at least a 50 percent U.S.–Canadian content. The CFTA expanded upon the GATT Procurement Code by creating common rules of origin, mandating an effective bid challenge system and improving the transparency of the bid process. Canada has created a Procurement Review Board before whom bid challenges based upon the CFTA may be made. An analysis of the decisions of this Board suggests that it provides open and effective relief.

The CFTA tariff removals were phased in over ten years through 1998. The most sensitive tariff reductions occurred later in the decade and these included duties on plastics, rubber, wood products, most metals, precision instruments, textiles, alcoholic beverages, consumer appliances, and agricultural and fish products. There was a petitioning procedure which permits private parties on either side of the border to seek to accelerate duty free

entry in advance of 1999. This petitioning procedure was invoked to a significant degree, resulting
in increased duty free trade between the United
States and Canada. The CFTA terminated customs
user fees and duty drawback programs by 1994, and
duty waivers linked to performance requirements
by 1988 (excepting the Auto Agreement). All quotas
on imports and exports were removed unless allowed by the GATT or grandfathered by the CFTA.

The GATT Code on Technical Standards (1979)
was reaffirmed by mutual pledges not to use product standards (health, safety and environment) as
trade barriers. National treatment and mutual recognition of testing laboratories and certification
bodies was required, and general commitments to
harmonize federal standards as much as possible
were made. A mandatory 60–day notice and comment period on proposed standards' regulations operated at all levels of government. Canada challenged the 1991 upgrading of Puerto Rico's milk
standards to existing federal requirements as a violation of CFTA. The practical effect of this upgrading was to end Puerto Rican imports of long-life
milk from Canada.

On agriculture, the CFTA eventually eliminated
most bilateral tariffs and export subsidies, and selectively limited or removed quotas (including quotas on sugar, poultry, eggs and meat imports). The
Canadians agreed to terminate import licenses for
wheat, oats and barley whenever U.S. price supports for those commodities were equal or less than
those in Canada. Wine and distilled spirits (but not

beer) were generally opened to free and nondiscriminatory trade. Import and export restraints on energy products, including minimum export prices, were
prohibited. Petroleum, natural gas, coal, electricity,
uranium and nuclear fuels were covered. In short
supply conditions, export quotas must be applied so
as to proportionately share energy resources. There
was permission to export 50,000 barrels per day of
Alaskan oil to Canada, and a lengthy list of specific
regulatory changes by both sides.

Either nation could invoke escape clause proceedings if there was a surge of imports resulting in
injury to a domestic industry. Bilateral escape
clause proceedings were eliminated after 1998. A
"global" agreement altered traditional third party
escape clause criteria to allow relief against CFTA
goods only when these imports were substantial
(over 10 percent of total) and contributed importantly to serious domestic injury or the threat
thereof. Escape clause decisions were ultimately
referred to binding arbitration if consultation between the United States and Canada did not result
in a settlement.

The innovative rules of origin applicable under
the Canadian–U.S. Agreement were established in
Chapter 3. They differ from those found in United
States legislation adopting the GSP program, the
Caribbean Basin Initiative and the Israeli–U.S. Free
Trade Area Agreement. There were general and
product-specific rules of origin. Ordinarily, goods
must be either wholly-produced in the United
States or Canada or (if they contain materials or

components from other countries) must have undergone a transformation sufficient to result in a new designation under the Harmonized Tariff Classification System employed by both countries. This was treated as the equivalent of "substantial transformation."

In addition, regarding certain assembled products, at least 50 percent of the cost of manufacturing the goods must be attributable to U.S. or Canadian material or the direct cost of processing in the United States or Canada. Note that these rules focus on production costs. The costs of advertising, sales, profit and overhead were excluded for purposes of determining Canadian or U.S. origin. The 50 percent local content test also served as a residual rule of origin applicable whenever the required change in tariff classification was absent in certain cases (notably textiles). The Canadian–U.S. rules of origin are found in Section 202 of the United States–Canada Free Trade Area Agreement Implementation Act. Special U.S.–Canada Free Trade Agreement Certificates of Origin (U.S. Customs Form 353 or Revenue Canada Form B151) must be completed by exporters seeking duty free or reduced tariff entry. United States law required the retention of records, including these certificates, supporting CFTA preferential treatment for five years.

Apart from reductions in tariffs, one notable feature of the Canadian–U.S. Free Trade Area Agreement was its application to services and investment. Many provisions of the Agreement sought to liberalize trade in services and investment capital flows between the two nations. In Chapter 16, traditional Canadian controls over foreign investment were substantially reduced for United States investors. In 1973 Canada enacted a restrictive investment law, the Foreign Investment Review Act (FIRA), and created a Foreign Investment Review Agency to pass upon new investment and acquisitions in Canada. The law was not as restrictive as those in the developing nations, but it did require substantial review. Joint ventures were not mandated, although the review agency often extracted local content promises before it approved new investment. That practice was condemned by the GATT after a request for review was submitted by the United States. The GATT based its decision on Article III:4 national treatment requirements.

Canada replaced the FIRA with the Investment Canada Act in 1985. This Act continues the practice of reviewing proposed investment, but review is reserved for large investments. The Act is more investment encouraging and simplifies procedures. The CFTA changed the extensiveness of the restrictions that are placed on U.S. investment. Canada ended review of indirect acquisitions (U.S. firms buying U.S. firms with Canadian subsidiaries), but could still require divestiture of cultural subsidiaries to Canadian owners. For direct acquisitions, thresholds were increased, time for review shortened and procedures made easier. A general rule of national treatment in establishing, acquiring, selling and conducting businesses within CFTA was created. Transportation investments were notably excluded from this general rule. Most investment performance requirements were banned, and profits and earnings are freely transferable.

Not all services could be freely provided across the Canadian–U.S. border under the CFTA. A lengthy listing of covered services is found in Annex 1408 to Chapter 14 of the Agreement. These include agriculture and forestry, mining, construction, distribution, insurance, real estate, and various commercial and professional services. Engineering and accounting services were included but transportation, legal and most medical services were not. Covered services had to be accorded national treatment and a right of establishment, except as differences were required for prudential, fiduciary, health and safety and consumer protection reasons. State, provincial and local governments must grant most favored treatment to service providers. In addition, the U.S. and Canada agreed that their licensing and certification procedures not be applied on a discriminatory basis and be based upon assessments of competence.

A general "standstill" on trade restraints applicable to services was agreed. This had the effect of grandfathering most existing restraints or discrimination. Special rules permitting temporary entry for business persons in either country supported free movement in services. Individual rules for architecture, tourism, computer services and telecommunications network services were detailed in separate annexes to the CFTA. Professionals, investors, traders, business visitors and executives also benefitted from a newly created temporary entry CFTA visa agreement.

Financial services were covered in Chapter 17 of the CFTA. Each side made specific commitment to alter or apply its regulatory regimes for the benefit of the other's financial services' companies. For example, the U.S. promised not to apply less favorable treatment to Canadian banks than that in effect on Oct. 4, 1987 and to grant them the same treatment accorded U.S. banks if and when the Glass–Steagall Act is amended. The continuation of multi-state branches of Canadian banks was guaranteed. Canada, for its part, removed various statutory restraints on foreign ownership of financial institutions (including insurance and trust companies) and assets' controls over foreign bank subsidiaries. Applications for entry into the Canadian financial market were treated on the same basis as Canadian applications, and U.S. banks could underwrite and deal in Canadian debt securities. All of these commitments were continued under NAFTA. Financial services' disputes are subject to formal consultation between the U.S. Treasury Department and the Canadian Department of Finance.

DISPUTE SETTLEMENT UNDER CFTA

Disputes under CFTA were handled in one of two ways. Disputes of a general nature were taken up under the GATT (now WTO) or addressed under Chapter 18, first by consultation and then by a binding arbitration panel of five independent experts. Each side chose two experts and those experts chose a fifth. Panels were formed in 1989 on salmon and herring and in 1990 on lobsters. Other trade disputes of special note focused on the allegedly low level of Canada's "stumpage fees" for timber (treated as a subsidy by the U.S.), mutual recriminations about trade restraints in beer and a ruling of the U.S. Customs Service regarding the Canadian–U.S. content of Hondas manufactured in Canada. This ruling had the effect of disqualifying these automobiles from CFTA tariff treatment.

Special, unique dispute settlement rules applied to antidumping and countervailing duty tariffs under Chapter 19. Basically, both nations agree to allow a binational panel to solve disputes of this kind, the governing law changing according to which is the importing country. The panels were drawn from a roster of 50 Canadian and United States citizens, a majority of whom were lawyers. Any final determination at the national level could be appealed by private or governmental parties to this panel using pleadings similar to those used in judicial proceedings. This binational panel replaced traditional judicial review of antidumping and countervailing duty orders. The only appeal from a binational panel decision in countervailing duty and antidumping cases was to the so-called "Extraordinary Challenge Committee." This Committee was composed of ten judges or former judges from the United States and Canada. Three of these judges were chosen to hear extraordinary challenges. These could be raised only if the panel was guilty of gross misconduct, made errors in procedure, or exceeded its authority. Numerous antidumping or countervailing duty determinations had been reviewed under Chapter 19 by the end of 1994 and the arrival of NAFTA. Most of these panel decisions were unanimous.

The first Extraordinary Challenge Committee decision involved U.S. countervailing duties on Canadian exports of pork. These duties and the underlying subsidy law decisions by United States agencies were challenged before a binational panel. The panel's first decision found that the International Trade Commission's domestic injury determination was based upon questionable evidence. The panel remanded the matter to the ITC for reconsideration. Upon reconsideration, the ITC again found a threat of material injury to the U.S. domestic pork industry. A second binational panel decision held that the ITC had exceeded its own notice of remand proceedings. The second panel gave a number of specific evidentiary instructions to the ITC and again remanded the proceeding. In its second remand proceeding, the ITC found no threat of material injury expressly and only because of the binding nature of the Canadian–U.S. Free Trade Area Agreement. The ITC's second remand decision bitterly denounced the binational panel's second review decision. The ITC asserted that the panel's decision violated fundamental principles of the Agreement and contained egregious errors of U.S. law.

The USTR sought review by an Extraordinary Challenge Committee. The Committee ultimately ruled that the panel's decisions did not contain gross error. The Committee therefore declared itself jurisdictionally ineligible to hear the dispute. Specifically, there was no gross error even if some of the panel's rulings might not follow U.S. rules of evidence, but cautioned the panel not to rely on extra-record evidence. There were two additional extraordinary challenges to CFTA Chapter 19 panel decisions. Both were raised by the United States, and in both Canada prevailed. One challenge concerned Canadian live swine exports, and the other Canadian softwood lumber exports. In the latter case, a blistering dissent by a U.S. judge serving on the ECC asserted panelist conflicts of interest and egregious errors in applying U.S. law.

NORTH AMERICAN FREE TRADE

The economic integration of Canada and the United States is a certainty. The blueprint is already there. For most Canadians and Americans, revising the design to include Mexico required considerably more effort and discomfort. The discomfort came from years of observing protectionist Mexican trade policies, uncontrolled national debt, corruption, and the sense, somehow, that Mexico just did not "fit." In the end, these perspectives were overcome.

Mexico under Presidents de la Madrid, Salinas and Zedillo has been unobtrusively breaking down its trade barriers and reducing the role of government in its economy. More than half of the enterprises owned by the Mexican government a decade ago have been sold to private investors, and more are on the auction block. Tariffs have been slashed to a maximum of 20 percent and import licensing requirements widely removed. Export promotion, not import substitution, has become the highest priority. Like the U.S. and Canada, Mexico (since 1986) participates in the General Agreement on Tariffs and Trade (GATT) and World Trade Organization (WTO). This brings it into the mainstream of the world trading community on a wide range of fronts, including participation in nearly the full range of the Uruguay Round agreements.

Mexican debt, under the Brady Plan with its emphasis on loan forgiveness, hopefully promises to become a manageable problem, although the collapse of the peso in December of 1994 and Mexico's ensuing financial crisis casts doubt on this. One party rule has ended in several states, with signs of a more pluralistic democracy on the horizon. Admittedly, political and economic corruption still runs deep within Mexico, but the winds of change are blowing. Major prosecutions of leading police, union and business leaders are underway. Perhaps most significantly, the rapid privatization of the state-owned sector of the economy combined with increasing tolerance of international competition has reduced not only the need for government subsidies but also the opportunity for personal enrichment by public officials.

Presidents Bush and Salinas, and Prime Minister Mulroney, pushed hard in 1991 to open "fast track" negotiations for a free trade agreement. In 1992, these efforts reached fruition when a NAFTA agreement was signed by Canada, the United States and Mexico with a scheduled effective date of Jan. 1, 1994. President Bush submitted the agreement to Congress in December 1992. President Clinton supported NAFTA generally, but initiated negotiations upon taking office for supplemental agreements on the environment and labor. This delayed consideration of the NAFTA agreement in Congress until the Fall of 1993.

Ratification was considered under fast track procedures which essentially gave Congress 90 session days to either ratify or reject NAFTA without amendments. After a bruising national debate that fractured both Democrats and Republicans with each party doing its best to avoid Ross Perot's strident anti-NAFTA attacks, ratification was achieved in mid-November, just weeks before NAFTA's effective date. During this same period, Canada's Conservative Party suffered a devastating defeat at the polls. This defeat was partly a rejection by the Canadian people of the earlier ratification of NAFTA under Prime Minister Mulroney.

The United States is Mexico's largest trading partner, accounting for nearly 70 percent of all Mexican trade and more than 60 percent of its foreign direct investment. In contrast, trade with Mexico totaled only 7 percent of all U.S. international trade. Those facts help explain why Mexico is the major beneficiary of the NAFTA accord.

THE NAFTA AGREEMENT IN OUTLINE

Although each partner affirms its rights and obligations under the General Agreement on Tariffs and Trade (GATT), the NAFTA will generally take priority over other international agreements in the event of conflict. The NAFTA, for example, will prevail over the Multi–Fiber Arrangement on trade in textiles. Certain exceptions to this general rule of supremacy apply; the trade provisions of the international agreements on endangered species, ozone-depletion and hazardous wastes notably take precedence over the NAFTA (subject to a duty to minimize conflicts). Unlike the GATT, the NAFTA makes a general duty of national treatment binding on all states, provinces and local governments of the three countries.

TRADE IN GOODS

Prior to NAFTA, Mexican tariffs on U.S. goods averaged about 10 percent; U.S. tariffs on Mexican imports averaged about 5 percent. Under NAFTA, Mexican tariffs will be eliminated on all U.S. exports within ten years except for corn and beans which are subject to a fifteen-year transition. United States tariffs on peanuts, sugar and orange juice from Mexico will also last 15 years. Immediate Mexican tariff removals under the "A" list covered about half the industrial products exported from the United States. Further tariff eliminations will occur for the "B" list after 5 years and the "C" list when the treaty matures in ten years. Accelerated tariff reduction may occur by bilateral accord. The existing Canada–U.S. tariff reduction schedule remained in place.

NAFTA trade is subject to "rules of origin" that determine which goods qualify for its tariff preferences. These include goods wholly originating in the free trade area. A general waiver of the NAFTA rules of origin requirements is granted if their non-regional value consists of no more than 7 percent of the price or total cost of the goods. Goods containing non-regional materials are considered North American if those materials are sufficiently transformed so as to undergo a specific change in tariff classification. Some goods, like autos and light trucks, must also have a specified North American content. Ultimately, 62.50 percent of the value of such vehicles must be North American in origin. A 60 percent regional content rule will apply to other vehicles and auto parts. After 10 years, U.S. auto producers will no longer need to manufacture in Mexico in order to sell there.

Regional value may be calculated in most cases either by a "transaction value" or a "net cost" method. The former avoids costly accountings. The latter is based upon the total cost of the goods less royalties, sales promotion, packing and shipping, and allowable interest. Either will require manufacturers to trace the source of non-NAFTA components and maintain source records. The net cost method must be used for regional value calculations concerning automotive goods. Uniformity of tariff classification and origin decisions is promoted by NAFTA regulations, a common Certificate of Origin, and a trilateral working group.

Special rules of origin apply to free trade in textiles and apparel under NAFTA. For most products, a "yarn forward" rule applies. This means that the goods must be produced from yarn made in a NAFTA country. A similar "fiber forward" rule applies to cotton and man-made fiber yarns. Silk, linen and certain other fabrics in short supply within NAFTA are treated preferentially, as are yarns, fabrics and apparel covered by special tariff rate quotas. Safeguard import quotas and tariffs may be imposed during the transition period if a rise in textile and apparel trade causes serious damage. Other special rules of origin have been created for electronics. For example, if the circuit board (motherboard) is made in North America and transformed in the region so as to change a tariff classification, the resulting computer may be freely traded.

Import and export quotas, licenses and other restrictions are gradually being eliminated under NAFTA subject to limited rights to restrain trade, e.g. to protect human, animal or plant health, or to protect the environment. Customs user fees on internal NAFTA trade were eliminated in 1999 and existing tariff drawback refunds or waivers must be removed by January 1, 2001. These changes, it is thought, will discourage the creation of "export platforms" in one NAFTA country to serve markets in the other member states by insuring that non-NAFTA components and materials are tariffed. NAFTA will essentially phase out maquiladora tariff preferences over 7 years, notably disadvantaging producers who source heavily outside North America.

Export taxes and new waivers of customs duties are banned with few exceptions. Once goods are freely traded under NAFTA, they are subject to nondiscriminatory national treatment, including at the provincial and state levels of government. Goods sent to another NAFTA country for repair or alteration may return duty free.

Distinct rules govern energy and petrochemical products. Perhaps most notably, Mexico reserves to its state (as its Constitution provides) the oil, gas, refining, basic petrochemical, nuclear and electricity sectors. A limited range of new investment opportunities are created for non-basic petrochemicals, proprietary electricity facilities, co-generation and independent power production. As under the GATT, minimum or maximum import or export price controls are prohibited on energy products, but licensing systems may be used. Trade quotas or other restraints are permissible only in limited circumstances, e.g. short supply conditions, and a general duty of national treatment applies. Mexico, unlike Canada, has not committed itself to energy sharing during times of shortage.

A second set of distinct rules apply to agricultural trade. These are undertaken principally through separate bilateral agreements between the U.S. and Mexico and Canada and Mexico. The United States– Mexico agreement converts all nontariff trade barriers to tariffs or tariff rate quotas. These will be phased out over a maximum of 15 years. Roughly half of the bilateral trade in agriculture was made duty-free immediately. Under special rules, trade in sugar will be gradually liberalized with all restraints removed over 15 years. Safeguard tariff action may be undertaken during the first 10 years when designated "trigger" levels of agriculture imports are reached. All three countries have agreed to combat agricultural export subsidies, including consultation and what amounts to joint action against third-country subsidies affecting any one of their markets. Special rules of origin apply in the agricultural sector and standards on pesticide residues and inspections are being harmonized.

Another food-related issue is sanitary and phytosanitary measures against health, diseases, contaminants or additives (collectively known as SPS protection). Each country retains the right to establish its own SPS levels of protection provided they are based upon scientific principles and a risk assessment, apply only as needed and do not result in unfair discrimination or disguised restrictions on trade. Each NAFTA nation is committed to accepting the SPS measures of the others as equivalent to its own provided the exporting country demonstrates that its measures achieve the importing country's chosen level of protection. This is facilitated by procedural transparency rules requiring public notice of any SPS measure that may affect NAFTA trade. A committee on SPS measures strives to facilitate all of these principles and to resolve disputes.

Technical standards and certification procedures for products are classic nontariff trade barriers. The NAFTA reaffirms each country's commitment to the GATT Agreement on Technical Barriers to Trade (1979). In addition, each must provide national treatment and most favored nation treatment. As in the food products area, international standards will be used whenever possible, but each country may have more stringent requirements. Procedural transparency rules and a committee on standards are also created. One innovation of note allows companies and other interested parties to participate directly in the development of new standards anywhere within NAFTA. All three countries have agreed not to lower existing environmental, health and safety standards and to attempt to "upwardly harmonize" them. States, provinces and localities can adopt more stringent requirements in these fields provided they are scientifically justifiable, transparent and applied equally to local and imported goods. All health, safety and environmental regulations must be necessary, represent the least trade restrictive way of achieving these goals, and based on scientific principles and risk assessment. Loans from the newly created North Ameri-

can Development Bank will help finance the border
cleanup by Mexico and the U.S.

Escape clause rules and procedures are generally
applicable to United States–Mexico trade under the
NAFTA. These permit temporary trade relief
against import surges subject to a right of compensation in the exporting nation. During the 10–year
transition period, escape clause relief may be undertaken as a result of NAFTA tariff reductions only
once per product for a maximum in most cases of 3
years. The relief is the "snap-back" to pre-NAFTA
tariffs. After the transition period, escape clause
measures may only be undertaken by mutual consent. If a global escape clause proceeding is pursued
by one NAFTA partner, the others must be excluded unless their exports account for a substantial
share of the imports in question (top five suppliers)
and contribute importantly to the serious injury or
threat thereof (rate of growth of NAFTA imports
must not be appreciably lower than total imports).

There are a variety of other areas of law impacted
by the NAFTA accord. Government procurement,
apart from defense and national security needs,
generally follows nondiscriminatory principles on
the supply of goods and services (including construction services) to federal governments. The
threshold for the application of the NAFTA to such
procurement is $50,000 U.S. for goods and services,
and $6.5 million U.S. for construction services.
When state enterprises (e.g. PEMEX and CFE), not
agencies, are the buyers, thresholds of $250,000
U.S. and $8 million U.S. respectively apply. The use

of offsets or other requirements for local purchases or suppliers are prohibited. Independent bid challenge mechanisms must be created by each member state and transparency in the bidding process promoted by timely release of information. These provisions are particularly important because Mexico, unlike Canada, is not a signatory to the GATT Procurement Code. They do not apply to state and local procurement.

TRADE IN SERVICES

Cross-border trade in services is subject to national treatment, including no less favorable treatment than that most favorably given at federal, state or local levels. No member state may require that a service provider establish or maintain a residence, local office or branch in its country as a condition to cross-border provision of services. However, a general standstill on existing discriminatory or limiting laws affecting cross-border services has been adopted. Mutual recognition of professional licenses is encouraged (notably for legal consultants and engineers), but not made automatic. All citizenship or permanent residency requirements for professional licensing have been eliminated.

Additionally, a NAFTA country may deny the benefits of the rules on cross-border provision of services if their source is in reality a third country without substantial business activities within the free trade area. For transport services, these benefits may be denied if the services are provided with equipment that is not registered within a NAFTA nation. Most air, maritime, basic telecommunications and social services are not covered by these rules, nor are those that are subject to special treatment elsewhere in the NAFTA (e.g. procurement, financing and energy). Even so, the NAFTA considerably broadens the types of services covered by free trade principles: accounting, advertising, architecture, broadcasting, commercial education, construction, consulting, enhanced telecommunications, engineering, environmental science, health care, land transport, legal, publishing and tourism. Whereas the CFTA allowed free trade in services only for those sectors that were positively listed in the agreement, the NAFTA adopts a broader "negative listing" approach. All services sectors are subject to free trade principles unless the NAFTA specifies otherwise.

Unlike CFTA, the NAFTA creates a timetable for the removal of barriers to cross-border land transport services and the establishment of compatible technical, environmental and safety standards. This extends to bus, trucking, port and rail services. It should eliminate the historic need to switch trailers to Mexican transporters at the border. Cross-border truck deliveries in the border states were supposed to come on line late in 1995, but U.S. concerns about the standards of Mexican carriers and (one suspects) Teamsters Union influence have delayed this result. After 6 years, truckers are supposed to be able to move freely anywhere within NAFTA. Bus services should be totally free within 3 years, and 100 percent investment in Mexican truck and bus companies will be possible after 10 years. Investment in port services was be immediately open. However, national restraints upon domestic cargo carriage (cabotage) may be retained and the commitment to harmonize technical and safety laws is subject to a 6–year "endeavor."

Public telecommunications networks and services must be opened on reasonable and nondiscriminatory terms for firms and individuals who need the networks to conduct business, such as intracorporate communications or so-called enhanced telecommunications and information services. This means that cellular phone, data transmission, earth stations, fax, electronic mail, overlay networks and paging systems are open to Canadian and American investors, many of whom have entered the Mexican market. Each NAFTA country must ensure reasonable access and use of leased private lines, terminal equipment attachments, private circuit interconnects, switching, signaling and processing functions and user-choice of operating protocols.

Conditions on access and use may only be imposed to safeguard the public responsibilities of network operators or to protect technical network integrity. Rates for public telecommunications transport services should reflect economic costs and flat-rate pricing is required for leased circuits. However, cross-subsidization between public transport services is not prohibited, nor are monopoly providers of public networks or services. Such monopolies may not engage in anticompetitive conduct outside

their monopoly areas with adverse affects on NAF-
TA nationals. Various rights of access to information on public networks and services are established, and the NAFTA limits the types of technical
standards that can be imposed on the attachment of
equipment to public networks.

CROSS-BORDER INVESTMENT

Investment in the industrial and services sectors
of the NAFTA nations is promoted through rules
against nondiscriminatory and minimum standards
of treatment that even benefit non-NAFTA investors with substantial business operations in a NAF-
TA nation. For example, an Asian or European
subsidiary incorporated with substantial business
operations in Canada will be treated as a Canadian
investor for purposes of NAFTA. Investment, for
these purposes, is broadly defined to cover virtually
all forms of ownership and activity, including real
estate, stocks, bonds, contracts and technologies.
National and most favored treatment rights apply
at the federal, state and local levels of government,
and to state-owned enterprises (e.g. PEMEX, Canadian National Railway Corporation). Furthermore,
each country is to treat NAFTA investors in accordance with "international law," including fair and
equitable treatment and full protection and security. Performance requirements, e.g. specific export
levels, minimum domestic content, domestic source
preferences, trade balancing, technology transfer
and product mandates are disallowed in all areas

except government procurement, export promotion and foreign aid. Senior management positions may not be reserved by nationality, but NAFTA states may require that a majority of the board of directors or committees thereof be of a designated nationality or residence provided this does not impair the foreign investor's ability to exercise control.

A general right to convert and transfer local currency at prevailing market rates for earnings, sale proceeds, loan repayments and other investment transactions has been established. But this right does not prevent good faith and nondiscriminatory restraints upon monetary transfers arising out of bankruptcy, insolvency, securities dealings, crimes, satisfaction of judgments and currency reporting duties. Direct and indirect expropriations of investments by NAFTA investors are precluded except for public purposes and if done on a nondiscriminatory basis following due process of law. A right of compensation without delay at fair market value plus interest is created.

In the event of a dispute, a NAFTA investor may (and quite a few have) elect as between monetary (but not punitive) damages through binding arbitration in the home state of the investor under the ICSID Convention if both nations are parties, the Additional Facility Rules of the ICSID[2] if only one nation is a party to the Convention or the UNCITRAL arbitration rules. An arbitration tribunal for

2. International Center for Settlement of Investment Disputes (Washington, D.C.).

investment disputes will be established by the Secretary–General of ICSID if the parties are unable to
select a panel by choosing one arbitrator each and
having those arbitrators choose a third. However,
there are no time limits for the arbitration and
either side may appeal the award to the courts.
Alternatively, the investor may pursue judicial remedies in courts of the host state.

The NAFTA investment code does not apply to
Mexican constitutionally-reserved sectors (e.g. energy, railroads and boundary and coastal real estate)
nor Canada's cultural industries. It does, however,
remove Mexican foreign investment controls for
U.S. and Canadian investors below an initial $25
million U.S. threshold phased-up to $150 million
U.S. in ten years and open new Mexican mining
ventures to NAFTA investors after 5 years. Canadian review of direct U.S. investments in excess of
$150 million U.S. and indirect investments in excess
of $450 million (indexed for inflation from Jan. 1,
1993) will continue. Maritime, airline, broadcasting,
fishing, nuclear, basic telecommunications, and gov-
ernment-sponsored technology consortia are exempt
from the NAFTA investment rules. All of the NAF-
TA countries have agreed not to lower environmental standards to attract investment and permit (as
Mexico requires) environmental impact statements
for foreign investments. However, apart from consultations, there was no retaliatory remedy in this
area prior to the environmental side agreement
discussed below.

FINANCIAL SERVICES

Financial services provided by banking, insurance, securities and other firms are separately covered under the NAFTA. Trade in such services is generally subject to specific liberalization commitments and transition periods. Financial service providers, including non-NAFTA providers operating through subsidiaries in a NAFTA country, are entitled to establish themselves anywhere within NAFTA and service customers there (the right of "commercial presence"). Existing cross-border restraints on the provision of financial services are frozen and no new restraints may be imposed (subject to designated exceptions). Providers of financial services in each NAFTA nation will receive both national and most favored nation treatment. This includes equality of competitive opportunity, which is defined as avoidance of measures that disadvantage foreign providers relative to domestic providers. Various procedural transparency rules are established to facilitate the entry and equal opportunity of NAFTA providers of financial services. The host nation may legislate reasonable prudential requirements for such companies and, under limited circumstances, protect their balance of payments in ways which restrain financial providers.

The following are some of the more notable country-specific commitments on financial service are made in the NAFTA:

United States—A grace period allowed Mexican banks already operating a securities firm in the U.S. to continue to do so until July of 1997.

Canada—The exemption granted U.S. companies under the Canada–U.S. FTA to hold more than 25 percent of the shares of a federally regulated Canadian financial institution was extended to Mexican firms, as was the suspension of Canada's 12 percent asset ceiling rules. Multiple branches may be opened in Canada without Ministry of Finance approval.

Mexico—Banking, securities and insurance companies from the U.S. and Canada are able to enter the Mexican market through subsidiaries and joint ventures (but not branches) subject to market share limits during a transition period that ends in the year 2000 (insurance) or 2004 (banking and securities). Finance companies are able to establish separate subsidiaries in Mexico to provide consumer, commercial, mortgage lending or credit card services, subject to a 3 percent aggregate asset limitation (which does not apply to lending by affiliates of automotive companies). Existing U.S. and Canadian insurers may expand their ownership rights to 100 percent by 1996. No equity or market share requirements apply for warehousing and bonding, foreign exchange and mutual fund management enterprises.

INTELLECTUAL PROPERTY

The NAFTA mandates adequate and effective intellectual property rights in all countries, including national treatment and effective internal and external enforcement rights. Specific commitments are made for virtually all types of intellectual property, including patents, copyrights, trademarks, plant breeds, industrial designs, trade secrets, semiconductor chips (directly and in goods incorporating them) and geographical indicators.

For copyright, the NAFTA obligates protection for computer programs, databases, computer program and sound recording rentals, and a 50 year term of protection for sound recordings. For patents, the NAFTA mandates a minimum 20 years of coverage (from date of filing) of nearly all products and processes including pharmaceuticals and agricultural chemicals. It also requires removal of any special or discriminatory patent regimes or availability of rights. Compulsory licensing is limited. Service marks are treated equally with trademarks. Satellite signal poaching is illegal and trade secrets are generally protected (including from disclosure by governments). The NAFTA details member states' duties to provide damages, injunctive, antipiracy and general due process remedies in the intellectual property field. This has, for example, required major changes in Mexican law.

OTHER NAFTA PROVISIONS

The provisions on temporary entry visas for business persons found in the CFTA are extended under the NAFTA. These entry rights cover business persons, traders, investors, intra-company transferees and 63 designated professionals. Installers, after-sales repair and maintenance staff and managers performing services under a warranty or other service contract incidental to the sale of equipment or machinery are included, as are sales representatives, buyers, market researchers and financial service providers. White collar business persons only need proof of citizenship and documentation of business purpose to work in another NAFTA country for up to 5 years. However, an annual limit of 5,500 additional Mexican professionals may temporarily enter the United States during the first 10 years of the NAFTA. Apart from these provisions, no common market for the free movement of labor is undertaken.

The NAFTA embraces a competition policy principally aimed at state enterprises and governmentally sanctioned monopolies, mostly found in Mexico. State owned or controlled businesses, at all levels of government, are required to act consistently with the NAFTA when exercising regulatory, administrative or governmental authority (e.g. when granting licenses). Governmentally-owned and privately-owned state-designated monopolies are obliged to follow commercial considerations in their transactions and avoid discrimination against goods or services of other NAFTA nations. Furthermore, each country must ensure that such monopolies do not use their positions to engage in anticompetitive practices in non-monopoly markets. Since each NAFTA nation must adopt laws against anticompetitive business practices and cooperate in their enforcement, Mexico has revived its historically weak "antitrust" laws. A consultative Trade and

Competition Committee reviews competition policy issues under the NAFTA.

Other notable provisions in the NAFTA include a general duty of legal transparency, fairness and due process regarding all laws affecting traders and investors with independent administrative or judicial review of government action. Generalized exceptions to the agreement cover action to protect national security and national interests such as public morals, health, national treasures, natural resources, or to enforce laws against deceptive or anticompetitive practices, short of arbitrary discriminations or disguised restraints on trade. Balance of payments trade restraints are governed by the rules of the International Monetary Fund. Taxation issues are subject to bilateral double taxation treaties, including a new one between Mexico and the United States. The "cultural industry" reservations secured by the CFTA now cover Canada and Mexico, but are not extended to Mexican–U.S. trade. A right of compensatory retaliation through measures of equivalent commercial effect is granted when invocation of these reservations would have violated the Canada–U.S. FTA but for the cultural industries proviso.

The NAFTA is not forever. Any country may withdraw on 6 months notice. Other countries or groups of countries may be admitted to the NAFTA if Canada, Mexico and the United States agree and domestic ratification follows. In December of 1994, Chile was invited to become the next member of the

NAFTA. Negotiations have stalled for want of U.S. Congressional fast track negotiating authority.

DISPUTE SETTLEMENT
UNDER NAFTA

The institutional dispute settlement arrangements accompanying the NAFTA are minimal. A trilateral Trade Commission (with Secretariat) comprised of ministerial or cabinet-level officials meets at least annually to ensure effective joint management of the NAFTA is established. The various intergovernmental committees established for specific areas of coverage of the NAFTA (e.g. competition policy) to oversee much of the work of making the free trade area function. These committees operate on the basis of consensus, referring contentious issues to the Trade Commission.

Investment, dumping and subsidy, financial services, environmental-investment and standards disputes are subject to special dispute resolution procedures. A general NAFTA dispute settlement procedure is also established (Chapter 20). A right of consultation exists when one country's rights are thought to be affected. If consultations do not resolve the issue within 45 days, the complainant may convene a meeting of the Trade Commission. The Commission must seek to promptly settle the dispute and may use its good offices, mediation, conciliation or any other alternative means. Absent resolution, the complaining country or countries ordinarily commence proceedings under the

GATT/WTO or the NAFTA. Once selected, the chosen forum becomes exclusive. However, if the dispute concerns environmental, safety, health or conservation standards, or arises under specific environmental agreements, the responding nation may elect to have the dispute heard by a NAFTA panel.

Dispute settlement procedures under Chapter 20 involve nonbinding arbitration by five persons chosen in most cases from a trilaterally agreed roster of experts (not limited to NAFTA citizens), with a special roster established for disputes about financial services. A "reverse selection" process is used. The chair of the panel is first chosen by agreement or, failing agreement, by designation of one side selected by lot. The chair cannot be a citizen of the selecting side but must be a NAFTA national. Each side then selects two additional arbitrators who are citizens of the country or countries on the *other* side. The Commission has approved rules of procedure including the opportunity for written submissions, rebuttals and at least one oral hearing. Expert advice on environmental and scientific matters may be given by special procedures accessing science boards. Strict time limits are created so as to keep the panel on track to a prompt resolution. Within 90 days an initial confidential report must be circulated, followed by 14 days for comment by the parties and 16 days for the final panel report to the Commission.

Early NAFTA Chapter 20 arbitrations have concerned Canadian tariffication of agricultural quotas (upheld), U.S. escape clause relief from Mexican corn broom exports (rejected) and a Mexican challenge of the U.S. failure to implement cross-border trucking (pending). Once the Trade Commission receives a final arbitration panel report, the NAFTA requires the disputing nations to agree within 30 days on a resolution (normally by conforming to the panel's recommendations). If a mutually agreed resolution does not occur at this stage, the complaining country may retaliate by suspending the application of equivalent benefits under the NAFTA. Any NAFTA country may invoke the arbitration panel process if it perceives that this retaliation is excessive.

When NAFTA interpretational issues are disputed before domestic tribunals or courts, the Trade Commission (if it can agree) can submit an interpretation to that body. In the absence of agreement within the Commission, any NAFTA country may intervene and submit its views as to the proper interpretation or application of the NAFTA to the national court or tribunal.

The independent binational review panel mechanism established in the CFTA for dumping and subsidy duties is carried over into NAFTA, along with the extraordinary challenge procedure to deal with allegations about the integrity of the panel review process. Chapter 19 panels are substituted for traditional judicial review at the national level of administrative dumping and countervailing duty orders. Mexico has undertaken major improvements to its law in this area. The procedures and rules for such panels generally follow those found in the

CFTA. They are limited to issues of the consistency of the national decisions with domestic law, and once again have been numerous.

In addition, a special committee may be requested by any country believing that another's domestic law has prevented the establishment, final decision or implementation of the decision by such a panel. A special committee may also be invoked if the opportunity for independent judicial review on a dumping or subsidy determination has been denied (a concern focused especially on Mexico). This committee's findings, if affirmative, will result in member state consultations. Absent resolution, the complainant may suspend the panel system or benefits under the NAFTA agreement.

THE SIDE AGREEMENTS ON LABOR AND THE ENVIRONMENT

The NAFTA side agreements on labor (NALC) and the environment (NAEC) do not create additional substantive regional rules. Rather the side agreements basically create law enforcement mechanisms. The side agreements commit each country to creation of environmental and labor bodies that monitor compliance with the adequacy and the enforcement of *domestic* law. The Commission for Environmental Cooperation (CEC)(Montreal) and three National Administrative Offices (NAO) concerning labor matters are empowered to receive complaints. Negotiations to resolve complaints first ensue.

In the absence of a negotiated solution, the NAEC establishes five environmental dispute settlement mechanisms. *First*, the CEC Secretariat may report on almost any environmental matter. *Second*, the Secretariat may develop a factual record in trade-related law enforcement disputes. *Third*, the CEC Council can release that record to the public. *Fourth*, if there is a persistent pattern of failure to enforce environmental law, the Council will mediate and conciliate. *Fifth*, if such efforts fail, the Council can send the matter to arbitration and awards can be enforced by monetary penalties.

The NALC labor law enforcement system is a calibrated four-tier series of dispute resolution mechanisms. *First*, the NAOs may review and report on eleven designated labor law enforcement matters that correspond to the NALC Labor Principles. *Second*, ministerial consultations may follow when recommended by the NAO. *Third*, an Evaluation Committee of Experts can report on trade-related mutually recognized labor law enforcement patterns of practice concerning eight of the NALC Labor Principles (excluding strikes, union organizing and collective bargaining). *Fourth*, persistent patterns of failure to enforce occupational health and safety, child labor or minimum wage laws can be arbitrated and awards enforced by monetary penalties.

The NAEC and NALC law enforcement mechanisms have been used more frequently than many expected. Quite a few labor law enforcement complaints have focused on the organization of "independent" unions in Mexico. United States plant closings and treatment of immigrant workers have also been reviewed. Regarding the environment, a wide range of complaints have been filed asserting inadequate Canadian, Mexican and U.S. law enforcement. None of these environmental disputes have proceeded beyond development of a factual record.

COMPARISON WITH THE EUROPEAN UNION

Some of the most revealing aspects of the NAFTA agreement are found in what it does *not* provide. By comparison with the European Union, the NAFTA is politically, legislatively and judicially streamlined. There is no NAFTA Court of Justice, no NAFTA Parliament, nor a NAFTA Council of Ministers. The trilateral Trade Commission's powers pale in significance to those of the European Commission. Substantively, the most dramatic differences are the absence of any free movement rights for workers or the citizenry at large, the lack of a common external tariff and a common international trade policy, the complete omission of any single currency and economic convergence goals, and the right of member state withdrawal upon 6 months notice. Nor are there common NAFTA defense, foreign, internal affairs, regional development, research, technology transfer, education, taxation, company law, antitrust and social policies (to name only some of the areas in which the EU is quite active).

In short, when compared with European integration, the NAFTA is strikingly limited in its goals and techniques. This conclusion has a variety of implications for the future of North America. It suggests, on the one hand, that North America's limited trade and investment-oriented goals ought to be more obtainable than the grand panorama of European economic, social and political union undertaken in a treaty of unlimited duration. On the other hand, the European experience suggests that once commenced the process of integration in North America will gradually and inevitably advance to greater and greater degrees.

CHAPTER ELEVEN

REGIONAL ECONOMIC INTEGRATION

There is movement towards regional economic integration throughout the world, though not often of the consequence of that occurring in Europe and North America. Some of these developments are a competitive by-product of European and North American integration. Others simply reflect the desire (but not always the political will) to capture the economic gains and international negotiating strength that regionalization can bring. This is particularly true of attempts at integration in the developing world.

There is a continuum of sorts, a range of options to be considered when nations contemplate regional economic integration. In "free trade areas," tariffs, quotas, and other barriers to trade among participating states are reduced or removed while individual national trade barriers vis-à-vis third party states are retained. "Customs unions" not only remove trade barriers among participating states, but they also create common trade barriers for all participating states as regards third-party states. "Common markets" go further than customs unions by providing for the free movement of factors of production (capital, labor, enterprise, technology) among participating states.

"Economic communities" build on common markets by introducing some harmonization of basic national policies related to the economy of the community, e.g. transport, taxation, corporate behavior and structure, monetary matters, and regional growth. Finally, "economic unions" embrace a more or less complete harmonization of national policies related to the economy of the union, e.g. company laws, commercial treaties, social welfare, currencies, and government subsidies. The difference between an economic community and an economic union relates only to the number and importance of harmonized national policies.

DEVELOPING WORLD INTEGRATION

Numerous third world countries have formed regional economic groups. The formation of these groups is motivated principally by a desire for development and increased economic bargaining power. Several groups have been formed in Africa. In 1966 the central African countries of Cameroon, Central African Republic, Chad, Congo (Brazzaville) and Gabon formed the Economic and Customs Union of Central Africa (Union Douaniere et Économique de l'Afrique Centrale: UDEAC) to establish a common customs and tariff approach toward the rest of the world and to formulate a common foreign investment code. Implementation has proceeded very slowly. In 1967 Kenya, Tanzania and Uganda created the East African Community (EAC) in an attempt to harmonize customs and tariff practices among themselves and in relation to other countries. The practical effect of that Community has frequently been negated by political strife. In 1974 six French speaking West African nations formed the West African Economic Community (known by its French initials CEAO). This Community is a sub-group within and pacesetter for ECOWAS, the Economic Community of West African States.

ECOWAS was created in 1975 by Dahomey, Gambia, Ghana, Guinea, Guinea–Bissau, Ivory Coast, Liberia, Mali, Mauritania, Niger, Nigeria, Senegal, Sierra Leone, Togo and Upper Volta to coordinate economic development and cooperation. Some progress on liberalized industrial trade has been made and a Cooperation, Compensation and Development Fund established. In June of 1991, the Organization of African Unity (OAU) member states agreed to a Treaty Establishing the African Economic Community. This wide-ranging Treaty embraces 51 African nations, and includes a regional Court of Justice. In September of 1995, twelve southern African countries, with South Africa under Mandela participating for the first time, targeted free trade by the year 2000 under the Southern African Development Community.

Other regional groups have been established in Latin America and the Caribbean. Since 1973, the Caribbean countries of Barbados, Belize, Dominica, Jamaica, Trinidad–Tobago, Grenada, St. Kitts–Nevis–Anguilla, St. Lucia, and St. Vincent have participated in the Caribbean Community (CARICOM), an outgrowth of the earlier Caribbean Free Trade Association. In 1958 Costa Rica, El Salvador, Guatemala, Honduras and Nicaragua formed the Central American Common Market (CACM), another victim of political strife, but still functioning in a limited way. Numerous countries in Latin America were members of the Latin American Free Trade Association (LAFTA) (1961) which had small success in reducing tariffs and developing the region through cooperative industrial sector programs. These programs allocated industrial production among the participating states.

During the 1980s the pace of regionalization quickened. ECOWAS countries agreed upon formulative policies for the Community for the next ten years, especially regarding air transport, communications, agriculture, freedom of movement between Member States, currency convertibility, and a common currency. ECOWAS (now the West African Economic and Monetary Union, WAEMU)and CARICOM have agreed upon policies and programs for mutual promotion of inter-Community trade. The Grand Anse Declaration commits CARICOM to establishment of its own common market. The Comoros Islands, Djibouti, Ethiopia, Kenya, Malawi, Mauritius, Somalia, Uganda and Zambia have initiated a preferential trade arrangement tended by a permanent secretariat in Zambia. The Latin American Integration Association (LAIA) (1981), the eleven member successor to LAFTA, is continuing arrangements for intra-community tariff concessions.

They agreed to a 50 percent tariff cut on LAIA goods. Antigua, Dominica, Grenada, Montserrat, St. Kitts–Nevis, St. Lucia, St. Vincent and the Grenadines have formed the Organization of Eastern Caribbean States (OECS) in part "to establish common institutions which could serve to increase their bargaining power as regards third countries or groupings of countries". Some 37 nations signed the Association of Caribbean States agreement in 1994 with long-term economic integration goals.

Bahrain, Kuwait, Oman, Qatar, Saudi Arabia, and United Arab Emirates have formed the Gulf Cooperation Council (GCC) with objectives to establish freedom of movement, a regional armaments industry, common banking and financial systems, a unified currency policy, a customs union, a common foreign aid program, and a joint, international investment company, the Gulf Investment Corporation (capitalized in 1984 at two and one-half billion dollars). The Council has already implemented trade and investment rules concerning tariffs on regional and imported goods, government contracts, communications, transportation, real estate investment, and freedom of movement of professionals. Progress has been made on a Uniform Commercial Code and a Commission for Commercial Arbitration of the Gulf states. In 1987, the GCC entered into negotiations with the EU which resulted in a major 1990 trade and cooperation agreement.

Latin America has become a central focus in the 1990s of regional economic integration. Mexico not only has a free trade agreement with the United

States and Canada, it has also agreed to free trade with Colombia, Venezuela, Chile, Bolivia, Costa Rica and Nicaragua. It has even negotiated a free trade agreement with the European Union. Argentina, Brazil, Paraguay and Uruguay signed a treaty establishing the MERCOSUR (Southern Cone) common market in March of 1991 and Chile and Bolivia joined them as Associates in 1996. Panama has effectively joined the Central American Common Market, which is busy rejuvenating itself. All of this activity is broadly supported by the United States through the Enterprise for the Americas Initiative of President Bush and the Free Trade Area of the Americas initiative of President Clinton.

Some of the most interesting moves toward third world regional economic integration and rule-making relevant to the international business community were taken by the Andean Common Market (ANCOM) and the Association of Southeast Asian Nations (ASEAN). These two regional groups are analyzed below. Their problems, failures and successes are representative of third world attempts at legal and economic integration.

ANCOM has its start in the 1969 Cartagena Agreement and ASEAN its genesis in the 1967 Bangkok Declaration. ASEAN and ANCOM are regional country groupings with common trade rules in various states of growth, implementation and retrenchment—in ASEAN by way of internal tariff preferences, industrial development projects, "complementation schemes," and regional joint ventures—and in ANCOM by way of internal tariff reductions, common external tariffs, "sectoral development programs," and regional foreign investment and technology transfer law.

An important juncture in the integration process is the point in time at which member countries of a regional group accept a supranational mechanism for enforcing the regime's law irrespective of national feelings and domestic law within a member country. The 1957 Treaty of Rome provided for a supranational Court of Justice, which decided quickly upon a mandatory enforcement stance regarding national (Member State) compliance with regional law. In 1979, a Court of Justice was created within ANCOM. It is charged, in part, to enforce ANCOM law against noncompliant Member States. ASEAN does not have a comparable enforcement mechanism.

A vigorous administrator can also make regional law a reality. In Europe, the Commission frequently issues regulations and decisions which are binding within the territories of Member States. These rules are enforced through fines and penalties, and ultimately by the European Court of Justice and Court of First Instance. Violations are investigated and, if necessary, prosecuted by the Commission. In contrast, the ASEAN Secretary–General once remarked that ASEAN's Secretariat was "a postman collecting and distributing letters." The Junta of ANCOM does more, but its law enforcement powers are still developing and are only distantly comparable to those of the Commission. The surrender of national sovereignty to ANCOM and ASEAN institutions has been a painfully slow process.

THE ASSOCIATION OF SOUTHEAST ASIAN NATIONS [ASEAN]

ASEAN was formed in 1967 by Indonesia, Malaysia, the Philippines, Singapore and Thailand. Brunei joined in 1984, Vietnam in 1995. Laos and Myanmar(Burma) joined in 1997, and Kampuchea (Cambodia) would have done so but for a coup d'état. Rarely have such culturally, linguistically and geographically diverse nations attempted integration. The Bangkok Declaration establishing ASEAN as a cooperative association is a broadly worded document. Later proposals were made for a formal ASEAN treaty or convention, but were rejected as unnecessary. The Bangkok Declaration sets forth numerous regional, economic, cultural and social goals, including acceleration of economic growth, trade expansion and industrial collaboration.

The Bangkok Declaration establishes several mechanisms, but little supranational legal machinery, to implement its stated goals. An annual ASEAN Meeting of Foreign Ministers is scheduled on a rotational basis among the Member States. Special meetings are held "as required". The Declaration provides for a Standing Committee composed of the Foreign Minister of the State in which the next annual Ministerial Meeting is to be held, and includes the ambassadors of other ASEAN States accredited to that State. The Declaration provides for "Ad Hoc Committees and Permanent Committees of specialists and officials on specific subjects". Each Member State is charged to set up a National Secretariat to administer ASEAN affairs within that Member State and to work with the Ministerial Meeting and the Standing Committee.

There have been relatively few meetings of the ASEAN heads of government. This contrasts with the semiannual European "summits" that have kept that group moving forward along the path of integration. The third ASEAN summit was held in Manila in 1987. This summit produced an agreement for the promotion and protection of investments by ASEAN investors (national and most-favored-nation treatment rights are created), made revisions to the basic ASEAN joint venture agreement (*infra*), and continued the gradual extension of regional tariff and nontariff trade preferences. Goods already covered by the ASEAN tariff scheme were given a 50 percent margin of preference. New items received a 25 percent preferential margin. The nontariff preferences generally co-opt GATT rules, e.g. regarding technical standards and customs valuation. The fourth ASEAN summit in 1992 committed the parties to the creation of a free trade area within 15 years. Five years were cut from this schedule by agreement in 1994.

ASEAN TRADE RULES AND INDUSTRIAL PROJECTS

Between 1967 and 1976, few steps were taken to further the economic cooperation called for in the Declaration. As with most third world regional groups, ASEAN required a period in which its members got to know and trust each other. The annual Ministerial Meetings did facilitate, however, the formation of committees to study economic development projects and economic cooperation, to establish a working relationship with the EU, and to develop close ties with private sector industries within ASEAN Member States.

Early ASEAN economic cooperation focused upon showcase "industrial projects." A "Basic Agreement" and a set of general "Guidelines" govern their creation and operation. ASEAN industrial projects were modeled on the ANCOM "sectoral programs of industrial development" (SPIDs, *infra*). They are largely government owned industrial development projects. Several of these projects are now in place with the assistance of Japanese financing, notably the ammonia-urea plants in Indonesia and Malaysia. They are supported by certain monopoly production rights and tariff preferences. Foreign investors may participate in ASEAN industrial development projects through finance, supply, managerial, technical or limited equity relationships.

Since 1976 ASEAN cooperation has accelerated. Rather than focusing upon the creation of common, protective external tariffs, ASEAN has fostered freer trade by instituting preferential tariffs for goods originating in other Member States. Tariff reductions have been negotiated pursuant to the Agreement on ASEAN Preferential Trading Arrangements. (Manila, 1977). The "Manila Agreement" is aimed primarily at encouraging the establishment of preferential tariffs with respect to basic commodities, particularly rice and crude oil, products of ASEAN industrial projects, and products expanding intra-ASEAN trade. Some of the tariff preferences are negotiated on a bilateral basis; others are negotiated multilaterally by the ASEAN states.

By late 1982, tariff reductions had been agreed for approximately 9,000 products, and the scope of the preferences extended well beyond foodstuffs and textiles. Since then, the ASEAN preferential tariff arrangements have been extended to approximately 2,000 additional items each year. Across the board tariff cuts on items of lesser import value have also increased intra-ASEAN trade opportunities. Progress notwithstanding, these efforts stop short of the automatic tariff elimination schedules of the EU, and ANCOM. As ASEAN moves toward freer trade within the bloc, overhead costs for investors, practical sources of supply materials, and product marketing opportunities may undergo substantial change.

ASEAN has entered into negotiations with all of its major world trading partners, dealing with them as ASEAN rather than as individual states. For example, ASEAN negotiated a limited number of preferences for its products entering the EU, and annually negotiates with its biggest trading partners, Japan and the United States. These negotiations are a classic example of exercising bargaining strength through unity. Unlike the EU, where virtually all major trade relations are determined by the Union, ASEAN states also pursue individual commercial negotiations with trade partners. This less than completely united regional approach to trade relations is indicative of the gradual development of ASEAN supranationalism.

There is no ASEAN legislature and no ASEAN court. There is a voluntary ASEAN Law Association and an "emerging law" within ASEAN as evidenced by the various rules, agreements and guidelines supporting economic cooperation in the region. For example, ASEAN has established certain rules covering the "origin" of products subject to its tariff preferences. Under these rules, products not wholly produced or obtained within ASEAN cannot qualify for preferential tariff treatment unless they are processed so that the total value of the materials originating from nonASEAN countries or from an undetermined origin does not exceed 50 percent of the FOB value of the products. However, if the final process of manufacture is performed within ASEAN, the goods will qualify for ASEAN tariff preferences. The value of the nonoriginating materials is determined CIF at importation. In the case of goods entering another ASEAN nation from Indonesia (the least developed ASEAN nation prior to Vietnam), the nonASEAN component cannot exceed 40 percent. Reductions in these local content requirements were adopted in 1987. An investor producing goods in an ASEAN country might need to work with these rules so as to qualify for regional tariff reductions.

The "Framework Agreement on Enhancing ASEAN Economic Cooperation" (1993) as accelerated in 1994 envisions an ASEAN free trade area (AFTA) that will cover goods but not services or unprocessed agricultural products. The ASEAN countries also signed an agreement on Common Effective Preferential Tariffs (CEPT). Under this agreement, internal tariffs on manufactured products were reduced to 20 percent by 1998. To qualify, at least 40 percent of the content of the goods must originate within ASEAN. Vegetable oils, cement, chemicals, pharmaceuticals, fertilizer, plastics, rubber and leather products, pulp, textiles, ceramic and glass products, gems and jewelry, cooper cathodes, electronics and wooden furniture are included in this first round of tariff cuts. The goal is to have all tariffs on manufactured goods fall to no less than 5 percent by 2000. There are ongoing efforts to reduce the number of goods excluded from the CEPT.

ASEAN COMPLEMENTATION SCHEMES AND JOINT VENTURES

ASEAN has encouraged development in the private business sector by urging the formation of numerous regional "Federations" or "Clubs" in various areas of industry and commerce. Sponsored by the ASEAN Chambers of Commerce and Industry, the Clubs are ASEAN-wide and have been formed to assist with "Complementation Schemes." Complementation involves the reduction, as needed, of trade barriers between Member States so that entire manufacturing processes, such as automobile assembly, make maximal use of ASEAN products. Moreover, each participating country produces a component which can be traded within ASEAN as parts for assembly into a more finished manufacture. Each Club, such as the ASEAN Federation of Cement Manufacturers, plays an initiating role in proposing tariff reductions for products which are of concern to that industry. Formation of the Clubs, while not envisioned in principal ASEAN Agreements, has been encouraged at the Ministerial Meetings. Club recommendations are approved tentatively by the Committee on Industry, Minerals and Energy of the ASEAN Governments. Recommendations are forwarded from that Committee to the Economic Ministers and Foreign Ministers for final approval.

General Guidelines and a Basic Agreement for ASEAN industrial complementation schemes were completed in 1980 and 1981. The Guidelines have been approved by the Economic Ministers of ASEAN and include "exclusivity" provisions guaranteeing (with limited exceptions) that no similar public or private projects to manufacture a product covered by a complementation scheme will be approved by any Member State of ASEAN. The Guidelines also provide that complemented products will be given priority in other ASEAN countries having foreign exchange controls. Additional Guidelines deal with the percentage of equity ownership by non-ASEAN nationals, tax incentives, remittances, repatriation of profits and expropriation. In 1983, the ASEAN Foreign Ministers approved an ASEAN auto parts complementation scheme involving local content requirements, exclusivity rights and tariff preferences. Many foreign investors or licensors are potential beneficiaries of this scheme (e.g., a Ford Motor Co. subsidiary has an auto body plant in the Philippines). Despite its origins in the private sector, the success of ASEAN automotive complementation is problematic. The desire to produce "national cars" not "ASEAN cars" is strong and supported by local subsidies. Malaysia, for example, now produces the Proton Saga in cooperation with Mitsubishi Motors.

Since 1982, ASEAN has focused on creating rules for ASEAN Industrial Joint Ventures which involve participation by only two ASEAN Member States, permit foreign equity participation up to forty nine percent, contain limited monopoly rights and grant extensive tariff preferences. A set of general Guidelines and a Basic Agreement on ASEAN joint ventures have been promulgated. ASEAN joint ventures may be proposed through the private sector initiative of industry clubs, few of which seem to have taken up the opportunity as yet. A 1987 revision of the Basic Agreement on joint ventures permits exclusivity privileges and protection against unfair trade practices. ASEAN joint ventures are a unique contribution to regional development and represent an investment alternative holding out the possibility of significant economies of scale. Eight new joint ventures were approved in 1991, including enamel and heavy equipment production by Indonesia and Malaysia, aluminum hydroxide by Indonesia and Thailand and four food products' joint ventures with the Nestlé Co. In general, the ASEAN trade and investment programs have been hard to implement because of tariff exemptions and nontariff trade barriers.

ASEAN complementation schemes and joint ventures present potential antitrust law problems for U.S. participants insofar as American foreign commerce is affected. For example, if Ford Motor Co.'s participation in the automotive complementation scheme reduces U.S. export or import opportunities, the scheme could fall within the extraterritorial reach of the Sherman Act. If so, United States prosecutors and plaintiffs will surely claim that ASEAN "clubs" amount to government sponsored cartels. There may also be U.S. customs law problems when and if complemented "ASEAN cars" are exported to the American market. Such cars could, for example, be subject to countervailing tariff duties if it is determined that ASEAN has subsidized their production and the U.S. auto industry is threatened with injury. These potential legal problems may deter involvement in ASEAN joint ventures and complementation schemes by U.S. firms and their business affiliates within the region.

THE ANDEAN COMMON MARKET (ANCOM)

ANCOM ("The Cartegena Agreement") was founded by Bolivia, Chile, Colombia, Ecuador, and Peru in 1969 primarily to counter the economic power of Argentina, Brazil and Mexico and to reduce dependency upon foreign capital. A major boost came in 1973 with the addition of Venezuela, but some dynamics of the regional grouping are illustrated by Chile's withdrawal in 1977, Bolivia's withdrawal in 1981 and resumption of membership barely four months later, and Peru's economic (but not political) withdrawal in 1991 and return in 1996. Late in 1994 the ANCOM and MERCOSUR groups commenced free trade negotiations.

Two ANCOM organs were established in 1969 by the Cartagena Agreement: the Commission and the Junta. Ancillary institutions include meetings of the national foreign and economic ministers, the Andean Development Bank, and the Andean Reserve Fund. In 1979, the Member States added an Andean Court of Justice and an Andean Parliament.

The Commission is composed of one plenipotentiary representative from each Member State; the representatives have not been of cabinet rank. The Commission is the "supreme organ" of ANCOM and is empowered to formulate regional policies, coordinate Member States' development plans, appoint Junta members, approve, veto and amend Junta legislative proposals, and supervise compliance with or propose reforms of the Cartagena Agreement. The Commission issues "Decisions", the most noted of which has been Decision No. 24 of 1970 (repealed in 1987) relating to foreign investment and technology transfers. In practice, the AN-COM Commission has not been an activist on behalf of regional integration like the European Commission. It mostly reacts to proposals put forth by the Junta.

The Junta is the administrative organ of AN-COM. Its three members may be from any ANCOM state. The members of the Junta are charged to act in the interests of ANCOM as a whole and are not to be influenced by national interests. The Cartagena Agreement empowers the Junta to supervise the implementation of Commission decisions, issue "Resolutions," and to prepare proposals which accelerate compliance with the Cartagena Agreement. The Junta has become more than a technical body and has assumed a leading role within ANCOM.

ANCOM Member States adopted a Treaty Concerning the Court of Justice of the Cartagena Agreement in 1979. Ratification of this treaty was completed in 1983. The Treaty was drafted with the aid of several judges from the European Court of Justice. It represents an attempt at establishing a mechanism for resolving regional disputes and securing a uniform interpretation of regional law.

The Treaty Preamble acknowledges that some of the difficulties of ANCOM regional economic integration were caused by the "complexities of its juridical structure." Such complexities included a decision by the Colombian Supreme Court that Commission Decision No. 24 on foreign investment was adopted unconstitutionally, as a matter of Colombian law. Although this problem was quickly remedied by executive action, the need for a regional court was underscored.

The Court, with one justice from each ANCOM nation, is to decide "the nullification of Decisions of the Commission and Resolutions of the Junta adopted in violation of the norms which comprise the juridical structure of the Cartagena Agreement, including *ultra vires* acts, when these are impugned by any member country, by the Commission, by the Junta, or by natural or juridical persons." Such persons may bring nullification actions before the Court when applicable Decisions or Resolutions cause them harm. It is specifically provided that Andean Court rulings do not require homologation or exequatur to be enforceable in the courts of Member States.

The Junta may seek compliance by Member States with the Cartagena Agreement through actions before the Court. In such cases, the Court may allow other members to restrict or suspend Agreement advantages benefitting the noncomplying country. Disputes involving ANCOM law ("the norms which comprise the juridical structure of the Cartagena Agreement") before national courts *may* be referred to the Andean Court of Justice for interpretation, which *must* be followed. Significantly, courts of last resort do not have to make such references. Article 234 of the Treaty of Rome establishes such a requirement and this has given the European Court of Justice effective control over national tribunals involved with regional legal issues.

The process of the selection of ANDEAN Court judges was completed in the mid–1980s. The Court sits in Quito, Ecuador. It has rendered a small number of opinions on ANCOM law relating to tariffs, measures of equivalent effect to tariffs and various Decisions of the Commission, including No. 24 on investment. All of these opinions were given at the request of national courts. Other national courts undoubtedly rendered their own interpretations of ANCOM law. The Court's ability to push the integration of ANCOM forward is limited, especially by its lack of power to ultimately decide all questions of ANCOM law. This power, which has been instrumental to European integration through Court of Justice rulings, would be a welcome reform.

Another 1979 Treaty established the Andean Parliament located in Lima, Peru. It is the "common deliberative body of the subregional integration process." Direct election of representatives is anticipated, but not yet implemented. Perspective on the difficulties of implementing direct elections within regional groups can be had by recalling that it took the Europeans nearly twenty years to achieve this goal for its Parliament. The Parliament's mandate includes: assisting integration; fostering freedom, social justice and democracy; monitoring human rights in accordance with valid international instruments; promoting people participation in Andean integration; stimulating the development of Andean consciousness; promoting the region and its norms; fostering the integration of Latin America as a whole; and contributing to international peace and justice.

To these ends, the Parliament is given limited powers to: evaluate the Andean integration process, maintain cooperative relations with national parliaments, and propose measures which establish closer relations among the national parliaments. The Andean Parliament's powers may be exercised only through the issuance of recommendations. Its powers do not compare with the budgetary controls and tangible ability to influence law-making of the European Parliament. But the European Parliament did not begin to seriously acquire these powers until at least twenty years after its formation. This suggests that it is too early to pass judgment on the nascent ANDEAN Parliament.

ANCOM TRADE RULES AND INDUSTRIAL DEVELOP-MENT PROGRAMS

ANCOM development has been marked by some trade liberalization, a common external tariff, Sectoral Programs of Industrial Development, contro-

versial regulation of foreign investment and technology transfers within the region, and a major
retrenchment in 1987 under the "Quito Protocol."
Most importantly this Protocol abandons the multilateral foundations of the Cartagena Agreement on
economic integration in favor of bilateral trade,
licensing and investment arrangements.

Reduction of tariff and non-tariff barriers facilitated a small amount of intra-ANCOM trade. The
elimination of tariff barriers was a delicate process
under the Cartagena Agreement, as amended by a
Lima Protocol. Certain product lists, proposed by
the Junta and approved by the Commission, contain
agreed, reduced tariffs. Two lists gave preferences
to Bolivia and Ecuador: the first included goods not
produced in the region but reserved for possible
production in Bolivia or Ecuador, and the second
contained items for which Bolivia and Ecuador had
duty-free access to Colombia, Peru and Venezuela.
Items not included on these product lists came
within the ANCOM progressive or automatic tariff
cutting program under which all tariffs were to be
reduced gradually until eliminated totally. Colombia, Peru and Venezuela were to have achieved such
elimination by 1983; Ecuador and Bolivia by 1988.
Both of these deadlines were extended as the drive
to regionalize lost momentum in the face of mount-
ing international debt problems and political dis-
trust within the group. In 1987, the Quito Protocol
acknowledged that the ANCOM customs union was
a dream that had not materialized.

The Cartagena Agreement provides for the development of a Common External Tariff (CET) for imports from nonANCOM nations. Development of a CET was to involve two steps. The first step began in 1970 when the Commission established minimum common external tariffs for certain broad classes of goods, thus necessitating tariff increases by certain Member States. The second step set CET levels expressed in terms of a minimum and maximum; tariffs within the agreed levels are deemed acceptable. Discussions about CET levels took place during 1970–1979 with implementation scheduled for Colombia, Peru, and Venezuela in 1983, and for Bolivia and Ecuador by 1989. Implementation was again postponed. In November of 1990, the Andean Group made new commitments for a free trade zone and a common external tariff that were largely realized in 1995.

Sectoral Programs of Industrial Development (SPID) were designed to deal with a factor which ANCOM Member States considered critical and long range—the development of heavy industry as the heart of Andean economic development. None of the Andean States currently has the capital or a market size to support such industry. SPID were based upon a belief that ANCOM, as a whole, has economies of scale adequate for heavy industry and for efficient use of ANCOM resources. The SPID idea was a joint plan to expand existing industries and to create new industries by distributing them among different Member States. The Members received what was essentially a production monopoly, supported (at least in theory) by external tariff protection and internal free trade. Under the Cartagena Agreement, the Commission is authorized to approve SPIDs proposed by the Junta after giving attention to a program's financing and time frame. Petrochemical, metalworking and automotive SPIDs were approved. In operation, they generally did not meet expectations. ANCOM nations continue to prefer imports, and SPID products did not consistently pass duty free across borders. The Quito Protocol scrapped the SPID programs.

DECISION NO. 24

An early Commission Decision (No. 24 of 1970, as supplemented and amended frequently by later Decisions) constituted the ANCOM Foreign Investment and Transfer of Technology Code until the Quito Protocol. The Foreign Investment Code (the "Code") was a regulatory mechanism apart from and in addition to national rules of each Member State. Primarily, however, such national rules were thought to complement provisions of the Code. The Code was a major reason for the formation of ANCOM as a subgroup within the Latin American Free Trade Association (LAFTA). It represented a reaction against dependency upon foreign capital for investment and technological development. Decision No. 24 illustrates a regulatory system which (with many variations) is found in virtually all major Latin American nations. In 1987, ANCOM replaced Decision No. 24 with Decision No. 220, which allows each nation to adopt its own foreign investment and technology transfer rules. This repeal has influenced other Latin American laws of this kind. In 1991, Decision No. 220 was replaced by Decision No. 291, an even more liberal foreign investment regime.

Decision Nos. 220 and 291 not only repeal Decision No. 24, but affirmatively support foreign investment incentives. This is a remarkable and symbolic reversal of perspective. These decisions provide that foreign investors may purchase stock owned by nationals, remit earnings without restriction, and freely transfer royalties and technology fees to home country parent corporations.

Decision No. 24 reflected the ANCOM states' desire to promote economic development through a controlled use of foreign investment and technology. New foreign investment was excluded from certain economic sectors. Existing, foreign-owned enterprises within ANCOM were theoretically required to change ("fade-out") equity participation by foreigners from a majority to a minority control position. New foreign investments were subject to similar rules before being allowed to locate within ANCOM. The use of industrial property rights was regulated, and capital repatriation and profit remittances controlled. All of this clearly discouraged direct foreign investment and technology transfers to ANCOM nations.

All ANDEAN nations adopted Decision No. 24 as part of their internal law, but Venezuela and Peru traditionally took a strict approach, while Colombia, Ecuador and Bolivia enforced it more selectively. Decision No. 24 was the major reason why Chile withdrew from ANCOM in 1977 in order to pursue less regulatory policies with foreign investors and licensors. In 1983, Ecuador and Colombia enacted foreign investment regulations which clearly violated the norms of Decision No. 24. In 1986, Venezuela adopted Decree No. 1200, a thorough repudiation of the ANDEAN position on foreign investment. By 1987, the Quito Protocol repeal of Decision No. 24 was merely a recognition of reality.

ANDEAN MULTINATIONALS AND INTELLECTUAL PROPERTY

In 1991, Decision No. 292 was adopted. This decision follows Decision 244 and seeks to promote the creation by ANCOM parties of regional or bilateral multinational enterprises. Foreign investment in such AMEs is restricted to 40 percent holdings. Few AMEs have been created, but the opening of the ANCOM market may generate more interest in these "local" alternatives to foreign MNEs.

In 1993, the ANCOM nations approved Decisions 344, 345 and 351. These decisions grant greater patent, trademark and copyright protection throught the region. Among other things, they extended patents to 20 years, eased compulsory license rules, and enhanced protection of well-known trademarks. The availability of patents for computer programs, pharmaceuticals and biotechnology was increased. These ANCOM decisions have, nevertheless, been criticized for inadequate focus on piracy and infringement problems.

EAST ASIAN INTEGRATION

East Asia, ranging from Japan in the North to Indonesia in the South, enjoyed truly remarkable economic growth during the 1980s. United States and other foreign investors participated in this growth largely on a country-by-country basis. All signs were that this growth, especially in China, would continue through the 1990s. When the Asian financial crisis hit in 1997–98, the region took it on the chin economically.

East Asia, unlike Europe, has not developed a formal Common Market with uniform trade, licensing and investment rules. Only recently has the APEC (Asia–Pacific Economic Cooperation) group even begun to address this idea. The APEC group is comprised of 18 Asia–Pacific nations including the United States. Late in 1994 the APEC nations targeted free trade and investment for industrial countries by 2010 and developing countries by 2020. Nine industries have been targeted for initial trade liberalization efforts.

With the European Union and the North American Free Trade Area maturing rapidly, one provocative question is the future of Japan. It is not in the interests of any nation that Japan should feel economically isolated or threatened. Yet it is hard to imagine incorporating Japan into the NAFTA, though some have suggested this. To some degree, what appears to be happening is that regional cooperation in East Asia is growing along lines that follow Japanese investment and economic aid decisions. Indeed, it has been reported that Japan's Ministry of International Trade and Industry (MITI) has detailed economic plans for the development of the economies of Thailand, Malaysia, Indonesia and the Philippines (all ASEAN members). Some fear a return to "co-prosperity" and Japanese dominance.

European and North American investors are being sought as a counterweight to Japanese influence in the region. The role of China in all of this is not clear. China and Japan are clearly rivals for economic leadership of the region. China could quietly, more by osmosis than anything else, join the East Asian economic sphere. Hong Kong's return in 1997 moves in this direction. China could, on the other hand, withdraw economically into itself as it has done in the past. For now, it is cultivating trade and investment relations with Singapore, South Korea, Taiwan, ASEAN and, to a lesser extent, Japan. Some commentators foresee, as a practical matter, the emergence of a powerful Southern China coastal economic zone embracing Hong Kong, Taiwan, Guangdong and Fujian.

CHAPTER TWELVE

MOVEMENT OF PEOPLE ACROSS NATIONAL BORDERS

The movement of people across national borders is often an underplanned aspect of international trade and investment. There is no settled legal framework for dealing with such movement notwithstanding a fairly stable but diverse background of passport laws, immigration laws, and over seventy years of labor standards-setting by the International Labor Organization. However, there is a clear trend toward greater legal control of the personnel aspect of an international business. Here are some examples.

Several United States trade laws require the President to determine the existence of "internationally recognized workers rights" before granting tariff and other benefits to a particular country. Such rights are defined by statute to include: a right of association; a right of organization and collective bargaining; a right to be free of forced or compulsory labor; minimum employment ages for children; and acceptable working conditions. The NAFTA agreement is supplemented by a special North American Agreement on Labor Cooperation.

European Union law has adopted the principle of equal pay for equal work ("comparable worth"), and a general rule of equal treatment of men and women in employment relations. The People's Republic of China requires equal pay for foreign and Chinese managers of joint ventures located in the PRC. This has usually caused the joint venture wages of foreign executives to be lowered to Chinese standards, the executives also receiving other income from their parent employers who complain that they are thus forced to subsidize the joint venture.

DISCRIMINATORY EMPLOYMENT PRACTICES

Some U.S. treaties dealing with the employer-employee relationship are wide in scope. For example, Article VIII(1) of the Japan–United States 1953 Treaty of Friendship, Navigation and Commerce (FCN) provides: "Nationals and companies of either Party shall be permitted to engage, within the territories of the other Party, accountants and other technical experts, executive personnel, attorneys, agents and other specialists of their choice. Moreover, such nationals and companies shall be permitted to engage accountants and other technical experts regardless of the extent to which they may have qualified for the practice of a profession within the territories of such other Party...."

This provision, which is repeated similarly in most United States FCN treaties, was held by the

U.S. Supreme Court not to exempt Japanese subsidiaries doing business in America from examination of allegedly discriminatory employment practices favoring Japanese nationals. *Sumitomo Shoji America, Inc. v. Avagliano*, 457 U.S. 176 (1982). These examinations took place under Title VII of the 1964 Civil Rights Act. Subsequent Federal Court of Appeals decisions involving clashes between Title VII and FCN treaties have concerned Greece, Korea and (again) Japan. Title VII has generally although not absolutely prevailed. See especially *Fortino v. Quasar*, 950 F.2d 389 (7th Cir. 1991).

Unlike most United States labor legislation, Title VII has been held on several occasions to apply extraterritorially to the foreign operations of U.S. employers. Such an approach can result in cultural and legal clashes, as when female or Jewish employees are located in predominantly Muslim countries. The Fifth Circuit, for example, upheld an award of backpay to two Jewish doctors excluded from Baylor College of Medicine surgical teams staffing a Saudi Arabian hospital. *Abrams v. The Baylor College of Medicine*, 805 F.2d 528 (5th Cir.1986). In a different case involving termination of a naturalized U.S. citizen, the issue reached the U.S. Supreme Court in 1991 on appeal from an en banc 9 to 5 decision of the Fifth Circuit against applying Title VII extraterritorially to ARAMCO in Saudi Arabia. The Supreme Court agreed, citing the "well-established presumption" against the extraterritoriality of statutes. *EEOC v. Arabian American Oil Co.*, 499 U.S. 244 (1991).

The Civil Rights Act of 1991, rejecting the Supreme Court decision in ARAMCO, extends the coverage of Title VII of the Civil Rights Act of 1964 and the Americans with Disabilities Act (ADA) to U.S. citizens employed in foreign countries by companies "controlled" by U.S. employers. However, such firms may engage in discrimination when the failure to do so would violate the law of the host country (the "foreign compulsion defense"). By special amendment in 1984, the Age Discrimination in Employment Act of 1967 also applies extraterritorially.

INTERNATIONAL LABOR ORGANIZATION STANDARDS

Many labor related treaties have origins in the work of the International Labor Organization (ILO), created as an outgrowth of Part XIII of the 1919 Treaty of Versailles and presently a Specialized Agency of the United Nations. The ILO is headquartered at Geneva and has a membership of more than 120 countries. It has drafted multilateral treaties (Conventions) dealing with over 150 different aspects of employment. The United States has been party to very few ILO Conventions. France, on the other hand, has been party to many of the Conventions.

Additionally, the ILO Conference has helped to create international labor standards for member countries by the adoption of official Recommenda-

tions dealing with employment. ILO Conventions
and Recommendations are submitted to each member state for ratification or for enactment into law.
The corpus of ILO Conventions and Recommendations, as a set of employment standards, is sometimes referred to as the International Labor Code.

The ILO in 1982 passed a Convention on Termination of Employment which differs sharply from
the "firing at will" practice commonly used in the
United States. This Convention promises to have a
significant impact on MNE employee relations in
countries other than the United States. U.S. firms
operating in Europe will undoubtedly encounter
employee, agent and distributor termination rights
unlike anything found in United States law. Under
the Convention, employers must give dischargeable
workers notice and hearing before an impartial
tribunal (e.g., a court) except in cases of criminal
misconduct. The employers must carry the burden
of proof about reasons for the discharge, and cannot
terminate an employee because of race, sex, ethnic
origin, affiliation with a union, or for protesting
allegedly illegal MNE conduct. Workers are entitled
to advice and counsel from unions, coverage for
extended illness, access to certain business information, and prior consultation before certain MNE
business judgments are made.

Law dealing with severance from employment
may also reflect cultural sensitivities. In the United
States, private contracts often create "golden para-
chutes" to accompany the exit of top management,
while dismissed workers are lucky to obtain a few

weeks' severance pay. Other countries are more actively involved in regulating employment terminations. The Supreme Court of Thailand, for example, has ruled favorably on the Labor Protection Act, which obligates an employer to pay an employee of three years seniority severance pay in an amount equal to at least six months salary. The more common practice is to award severance compensation in an amount which reflects the length of employment, the relative position in the employer's enterprise and the circumstances of the discharge. For example, in 1972 an Italian company managerial employee, long associated with the enterprise, had to be paid nearly $1 million. In that same year a wrongfully discharged Belgian clerical employee had to be paid severance compensation equivalent to nearly $20,000.

INTERNATIONAL LABOR AGREEMENTS

Ideological and cultural differences have inhibited the international labor movement. Multinational labor contract negotiations are extremely rare. Practically speaking, international labor organizations do not remotely compare in power and scope to MNEs. Multinational enterprises have played one bargaining unit against another in their international labor relations, sometimes raising output elsewhere to compensate for strikes. Some MNE deliberately establish "twin plants" in different countries to minimize the labor disruptions.

Even under optimal circumstances, it is difficult for an international labor bargaining unit to guarantee MNE management that workers in all countries can or will honor specific contours of an agreement. For example, workers in some countries prefer labor settlements on a locality and plant basis. Workers at various skill levels may have markedly different approaches to dealing with an international employer. Furthermore, different national laws make it burdensome to negotiate international labor agreements concerning:

(a) the right to demand wage and other information from an employer;

(b) prohibitions on the "export of jobs" (as illustrated by a contract clause such as,

"The Company shall not transfer or relocate any of its operations covered by this agreement to a foreign country, nor shall it establish any plant or facility in any country to perform any of the operations customarily performed by employees covered by this contract.");

(c) consumer product picketing (which urges consumers, at retail locations, not to buy products or use services originating from outside the country);

(d) pressures on local government to restrict alien workers (often by way of denying needed work permits), or to restrict imports of parts (often by way of import license restrictions) which may adversely affect local jobs;

(e) secondary product boycotts (whereby local labor refuses to work with component imports which have come from a foreign country where there is labor difficulty);

(f) sympathy strikes against parent or subsidiary enterprises to show solidarity with worker grievances in another country;

(g) refusals to work overtime when the need arises because of a strike at a similar production facility in another country; and

(h) worker insistence upon common expiration dates for labor contracts.

EMPLOYMENT OF LOCAL PERSONNEL

The movement of employees across national borders raises legal considerations which are linked with the balance that a country draws between job opportunities for alien (expatriate) and local personnel. In some countries, foreigners are allowed work permits only until sufficient numbers of local workers are adequately trained. For example, it is not uncommon for host governments in newly industrializing countries to require, as a condition of entry for expatriate employees, that the investor undertake to educate local personnel to replace expatriates. In return for such human resource development, such countries may offer special tax exemptions or other benefits. The training of local personnel is often a requirement for investment permits. In Indonesia, for example, the Fluor Corporation was required to offer classroom, laboratory, and construction training for local labor. Ghana, Kenya and Nigeria have had policies requiring training of indigenous labor. In Saudi Arabia, MNEs from the United States have established training centers in Yanbu and Jubail to train up to 1,000 persons at a time in essential technical skills.

In other countries, the position of foreign workers may be less clearly defined. An oversupply of foreign workers has caused Germany and Singapore to offer monetary incentives to those willing to return to their home nations. In 1983, Nigeria summarily expelled tens of thousands of foreign workers. The uncertain position of the United States toward "illegal alien" workers from Mexico has involved years of negotiations between the two countries, leading to the Immigration Reform and Control Act of 1986.

This Act allows aliens who have been in the United States since 1982 to obtain permanent residency status and, ultimately, citizenship. It establishes, for the first time, sanctions against employers who knowingly hire illegal aliens. The Act also creates a new "unfair immigration-related employment practice." It is now illegal to discriminate in employment because of the national origin or citizenship status of authorized aliens. But the many illegal aliens who came to the United States after 1982 face deportation, a chilling prospect to Ireland, Mexico and many economically struggling Central American countries.

The decision whether to move an expatriate into a host country or whether to draw someone from the local labor supply is largely non-legal. Investors using expatriates point out that intra-enterprise communication, reporting and control are facilitated by having expatriates (preferably from the investor's home country) in managerial positions in the host country. Expatriates often have a better grasp of the enterprise's history and technology. Investors drawing an employee from the local labor supply point out that such people are often favored by the host country government, usually do not require complicated compensation schemes, and are more knowledgeable about local conditions. The extent to which expatriate labor does not duplicate local labor and the extent to which expatriate labor skills are needed in connection with a country's planned economic development color host country attitudes toward expatriates. Rules relating to passports, visas, and work permits often reflect such attitudes.

PASSPORTS

There was an era when travel without passports was the rule. In modern times, virtually all countries require that foreigners possess a valid passport. There is nothing in customary international law to preclude a nation from issuing a passport to any person, although countries usually issue passports only to their "nationals." A passport may be revoked. In the United States, successive passport control acts dating from 1856 have made passports the only means by which an American can lawfully leave the country or return to it, absent a Presidentially granted exception. The U.S. Supreme Court has repeatedly held that the freedom to travel abroad with a United States passport is subordinate to national security and foreign policy considerations. Thus, travel by U.S. passport holders to "enemy" countries (Cuba, Iraq, Iran) has been periodically denied. The Court has made it plain that the *freedom* to travel outside the United States must be distinguished from the *right* to travel within the United States.

It is possible that a person may possess a passport from two or more countries (dual nationals), although any valid passport may suffice for meeting immigration requirements of a particular country. Other persons are "stateless," those to whom no nation will issue a passport.

VISAS

Visas are used by virtually all countries in the world as a means of regulating the movement of noncitizens across their borders. In its discretion, a country may issue a visa to permit an alien to enter its territory for varying purposes and varying periods of time. For example, almost all countries require aliens to obtain a form of "visitor's visa" prior to entry. In many countries this is a formality; but others, such as North Korea and Iraq, have made it difficult for Westerners to obtain permission to enter as visitors. Visa qualifications differ greatly from country to country but the need for a visa is almost universally applied.

Countries differ in the extent to which one visa may be valid for multiple re-entries, the extent to which aliens may be required periodically to re-register with appropriate authorities or to obtain an identification card, and the extent to which an alien may remain in the country once the circumstances of admission have expired or changed. Violation of visa laws is often a criminal offense and nationality laws may be applied extraterritorially. The kind of visa held by an alien may determine the extent to which he or she may be compensated by an employer while in a host country.

Government work permit requirements are common both in industrial and developing countries, particularly where there are large numbers of low-skilled workers. The denial of a work permit and alteration of the requirements for holding a permit have been used as a means for expelling or rejecting aliens from a country. For example, certain Singapore regulations with which an employer must comply before work permits will be issued to expatriate labor are:

(a) Foreign workers must be paid at the same rate and receive the same benefits as local employees;

(b) Adequate dormitories or hostels must be provided;

(c) Workers must be supervised properly, especially after working hours;

(d) A security deposit must be tendered to the controller of Immigration;

(e) Foreign workers are required to contribute to the Central Provident Fund (pension and social benefits), must be between 16 and 50 years of age, cannot change jobs, and must not marry a Singaporean; and

(f) The workers must be examined medically and repatriated immediately if unhealthy or pregnant.

In contrast, nationals of European Union member states are permitted to seek employment anywhere within the region without the need for a work visa and thus may compete directly in local job markets. People who are "dual nationals" can use their European citizenship to take advantage of European Union employment opportunities. Many persons of Irish, Italian and Spanish heritage are finding it useful to obtain citizenship in the countries of their forebears under "laws of return." Multinational firms even search their personnel files to locate staff who qualify. Another variation on this theme can be found in the movement of people provision of the North American Free Trade Agreement entered into between Canada, the United States and Mexico. The NAFTA permits business visitors, investors, intracompany transferees and certain professionals temporary entry into each country to engage in a task that is limited in scope and duration. Thousands of Canadian professionals have headed south under these rules. The NAFTA provision is a middle ground between the rigid guidelines of Sing-

apore and the open border policy found in the
European Union.

U.S. IMMIGRATION LAWS

Aliens entering the United States must obtain
either an immigrant visa or a nonimmigrant visa.
The Immigration and Nationality Act distinguishes
between those aliens coming to the United States
permanently ("immigrants") and those coming
temporarily ("nonimmigrants"). In most cases it is
easier to obtain a temporary visa than it is a permanent visa (i.e., a green card) because it is understood that once the visa expires the alien will be
leaving the country. However, some aliens will find
it difficult to obtain even a nonimmigrant visa because of a belief held by the U.S. Immigration
Service that aliens from certain countries (e.g. Mexico, Philippines) will not leave the United States
when their visas expire.

To be eligible for a nonimmigrant visa aliens
must establish that they have an unabandoned foreign residence and that they do not intend to permanently reside in the United States. Nonimmigrant visas are available to: visitors for business or
pleasure ("B" visas); investors ("E" visas); students
("F" visas and "M" visas); professionals ("H–1B"
visas); non-professionals ("H–2" visas); trainees
("H–3" visas and "J" visas); fiancees ("K" visas);
intra-company transferees ("L" visas); athletes and
entertainers ("O" visas and "P" visas); participants
in cultural exchange programs ("Q" visas); religious

workers ("R" visas); and, NAFTA professionals ("TN" visas). The common thread among visas is the fact that they are given for a temporary period of time to perform a specific task. Once the duration has expired or the task has been either concluded or abandoned then the visa becomes invalid and the alien must either leave the country or obtain another visa.

An alien seeking permanent resident status may have numerous options including refugee or asylum claims, legalization statutes or diversity immigration. However, the majority of potential immigrants will eventually look to either family or employment based immigrant visa options. An alien may obtain a family based immigrant visa through a U.S. citizen spouse, child, parent or sibling; or through a permanent resident spouse or parent. The length of time it takes to obtain a family based immigrant visa varies greatly depending upon which family member is filing the petition.

Employment based immigrant visas are available to aliens coming to the United States to permanently engage in employment within the United States. There are five "Preference Categories" of immigrant visas:

(1) Priority Workers: aliens of extraordinary ability, outstanding professors and researchers, and, certain multinational executives or managers.

(2) Professionals With Advanced Degrees and Aliens of Exceptional Ability in the sciences, arts or business.

(3) Skilled Workers, Professionals and Other Workers.

(4) Special Immigrants.

(5) Immigrant Investors: the million dollar green card.

These categories offer numerous options to immigrants seeking permanent residence in the United States. Similar to the family based category, a "Petitioner" is required to apply for an employment based immigrant visa; however, in this case the Petitioner is the employer not a family member.

Generally, an alien applying for an employment based immigrant visa must receive labor certification. Labor certification is issued by the United States Department of Labor ("DOL") once it has been established that there is an unavailability of qualified United States workers to fill the position the alien desires to occupy. In certain professions (e.g., nurses, physical therapists, aliens of exceptional ability in science or arts), the DOL has pre-certified all applications because the government has determined that there are not sufficient United States workers who are able, willing, qualified and available for these occupations. In most other cases, with the notable exception of the First Preference Category, aliens must receive labor certification prior to receiving an employment based immigrant visa.

As a result of the 1986 Immigration Reform and Control Act ("IRCA"), whether an alien can be employed in the United States now hinges upon employer verification of the alien's eligibility to work in the country. A failure to do so could result in severe sanctions being placed on the employer, backpay to affected U.S. workers and a bar to future employment of aliens. The net effect is that employers should now be sure to familiarize themselves with the IRCA provisions and verify that the alien being employed is eligible to work in the United States.

EXPATRIATE COMPENSATION PLANNING

Compensation planning for an expatriate encompasses not only wages, allowances, and taxation, but also all aggregate costs of moving the expatriate from a present location to the host country and thereafter possibly to a place outside the host country. Legal questions may arise in connection with:

1. *Salary, wages and other forms of monetary compensation (e.g., education, home leave, housing, relocation, transportation allowances).* These amounts may be taxable in the host country, in the country of the expatriate's nationality, and other countries where the expatriate is considered a resident for purposes of taxation. In one or more such countries, the amounts of money earned while "abroad" may be excluded from taxation, or the tax on such compensation may be forgiven to the extent that a tax has been levied by another jurisdiction (foreign tax credit). The risk of being subjected to double taxation may be controlled by an applicable

treaty, such as the United Kingdom–United States Tax Convention. The U.S. has entered into approximately 45 such "double taxation treaties."

All of an expatriate's income, including those parts arising from sources in another country, may be subject to unitary taxation by one or more countries. This again can lead to multiple taxation of the same income. On the other hand, if a country (such as Brazil) taxes an expatriate's income only upon receipt or when legally available, both the employer and the expatriate employee may wish to explore the desirability of structuring a part of the compensation as future income. The expatriate's *ad hoc* financial needs within the host country may be met by loans drawn from the investor's financial resources within the host country.

2. *Movement of money, or of things having money value, into and outside of the host country.* Foreign exchange controls in many countries sharply limit the amount of money which may be taken from those countries. For example, for 40 years until late 1979 citizens of the United Kingdom were subject to strict currency controls. At one point, Ghana did not permit any money to be sent outside the country. Things other than money, but having monetary value, may be subject to an import duty if brought into the host country. For example, imported automobiles are frequently subject to such a tax, especially in a country like Brazil, which manufactures its own automobiles. A country may prohibit certain items, such as electric appliances, from being brought into the country in an expatriate's

luggage. One who fails to declare travelers' checks being brought into a country may not be able to convert them into local currency. Limitations about what money, or other things having money value, can be taken by an expatriate leaving the host country may affect what an expatriate is advised to bring into the host country. For example, it may be difficult to remove money from a country if the money has not been declared at time of entry.

3. *Place of payment and currency denomination.* Brazilian law has prohibited an employee from sending money abroad to contribute to a stock option plan, but has permitted payment from funds which the employee has abroad already. Similar kinds of circumstances in other countries make it advisable to consider whether an expatriate is compensated best by being paid within the host country. The place of payment, in conjunction with comparative rates of inflation and exchange rates between the currency of the place of payment and place where the expatriate wishes to use the money, also serve to substantially determine an expatriate's effective compensation. Should the expatriate have a wage dispute and wish to use legal means to recover wages, a tribunal may be inclined to hear the dispute and to apply its own law if it is seated at the place where payment should have been made.

THE INTERNATIONAL EMPLOYMENT AGREEMENT

Uncertainty multiplied by the number of (and perhaps unknown) countries which may ultimately

have an interest in international employment relationships typically causes them to be covered by a
formal written contract or by letter of understanding. Sometimes there is no choice in this matter.
For example, Article 12 of the Labor Regulations in
the People's Republic of China provides that "The
employment of foreign workers and staff members
and their dismissal, resignation, pay, welfare and
social insurances and other matters concerned
should all be stipulated in the employment contracts."

Most international employment contracts will attempt to include carefully drawn provisions concerning:

(a) The choice of forum to hear any disputes
and the choice of law which the parties wish the
forum to apply;

(b) The specification of duties to be performed
(including an honoring of local customs and
promises to act in an orderly way);

(c) The length and terms of employment (including specification of which country's holidays
apply);

(d) Severance provisions (including whether
the employee may be terminated at will, as well
as amounts to be paid at severance);

(e) The definition of compensation (including
transportation and moving expenses to and from
the overseas location, pensions, medical coverage,

home leave benefits, family benefits, deferred compensation and special travel allowances);

(f) How and where the compensation is to be paid, in what currency (including exchange rate), and which deductions and taxes will apply and who will pay for them;

(g) The kind of housing at the overseas location and local transportation (including who pays both);

(h) What constitutes inability to work (culture shock?), limitations on liability for injury or death, and the duty to insure; and

(i) The safeguarding of trade secrets and confidential information (including who is authorized to release what to local authorities), and covenants not to compete.

INDEX

References are to Pages

443